Essentials of WPPSI™-III Assessment

Essentials of Psychological Assessment Series

Series Editors, Alan S. Kaufman and Nadeen L. Kaufman

Essentials of WAIS®-III Assessment
by Alan S. Kaufman and Elizabeth O. Lichtenberger

Essentials of CAS Assessment
by Jack A. Naglieri

Essentials of Forensic Psychological Assessment
by Marc J. Ackerman

Essentials of Bayley Scales of Infant Development-II Assessment
by Maureen M. Black and Kathleen Matula

Essentials of Myers-Briggs Type Indicator® Assessment
by Naomi Quenk

Essentials of WISC-III® and WPPSI-R® Assessment
by Alan S. Kaufman and Elizabeth O. Lichtenberger

Essentials of Rorschach® Assessment
by Tara Rose, Nancy Kaser-Boyd, and Michael P. Maloney

Essentials of Career Interest Assessment
by Jeffrey P. Prince and Lisa J. Heiser

Essentials of Cross-Battery Assessment
by Dawn P. Flanagan and Samuel O. Ortiz

Essentials of Cognitive Assessment with KAIT and Other Kaufman Measures
by Elizabeth O. Lichtenberger, Debra Broadbooks, and Alan S. Kaufman

Essentials of Nonverbal Assessment
by Steve McCallum, Bruce Bracken, and John Wasserman

Essentials of MMPI-2™ Assessment
by David S. Nichols

Essentials of NEPSY® Assessment
by Sally L. Kemp, Ursula Kirk, and Marit Korkman

Essentials of Individual Achievement Assessment
by Douglas K. Smith

Essentials of TAT and Other Storytelling Techniques Assessment
by Hedwig Teglasi

Essentials of WJ III® Tests of Achievement Assessment
by Nancy Mather, Barbara J. Wendling, and Richard W. Woodcock

Essentials of WJ III® Cognitive Abilities Assessment
by Fredrick A. Schrank, Dawn P. Flanagan, Richard W. Woodcock, and Jennifer T. Mascolo

Essentials of WMS®-III Assessment
by Elizabeth O. Lichtenberger, Alan S. Kaufman, and Zona Lai

Essentials of MMPI-A™ Assessment
by Robert P. Archer and Radhika Krishnamurthy

Essentials of Neuropsychological Assessment
by Nancy Hebben and William Millberg

Essentials of Behavioral Assessment
by Michael C. Ramsay, Cecil R. Reynolds, and R.W. Kamphaus

Essentials of Millon™ Inventories Assessment, Second Edition
by Stephen N. Strack

Essentials of PAI® Assessment
by Leslie C. Morey

Essentials of 16 PF® Assessment
by Heather E. P. Cattell and James M. Schuerger

Essentials of WPPSI™-III Assessment
by Elizabeth O. Lichtenberger and Alan S. Kaufman

Essentials

of WPPSI™-III Assessment

Elizabeth O. Lichtenberger

Alan S. Kaufman

John Wiley & Sons, Inc.

Library of Congress Cataloging-in-Publication Data:

Lichtenberger, Elizabeth O.
    Essentials of WPPSI-III assessment / Elizabeth O. Lichtenberger and Alan S. Kaufman.
      p. cm. — (Essentials of psychological assessment series)
    Includes bibliographical references and index.
    ISBN 0-471-28895-0 (pbk.)
    1. Wechsler Preschool and Primary Scale of Intelligence. I. Kaufman, Alan S., 1944- II. Title. III. Series.

    BF432.5.W424L53 2003
    155.42'3393—dc21

                                                   2003053482

Printed in the United States of America

10 9 8 7 6 5 4 3

CONTENTS

SERIES PREFACE

I n the *Essentials of Psychological Assessment* series, we have attempted to provide the reader with books that will deliver key practical information in the most efficient and accessible style. The series features instruments in a variety of domains, such as cognition, personality, education, and neuropsychology. For the experienced clinician, books in the series will offer a concise yet thorough way to master utilization of the continuously evolving supply of new and revised instruments, as well as a convenient method for keeping up-to-date on the tried-and-true measures. The novice will find here a prioritized assembly of all the information and techniques that must be at one's fingertips to begin the complicated process of individual psychological diagnosis.

Wherever feasible, visual shortcuts to highlight key points are utilized alongside systematic, step-by-step guidelines. Chapters are focused and succinct. Topics are targeted for an easy understanding of the essentials of administration, scoring, interpretation, and clinical application. Theory and research are continually woven into the fabric of each book but always to enhance clinical inference, never to sidetrack or overwhelm. We have long been advocates of what has been called intelligent testing — the notion that a profile of test scores is meaningless unless it is brought to life by the clinical observations and astute detective work of knowledgeable examiners. Test profiles must be used to make a difference in the child's or adult's life, or why bother to test? We want this series to help our readers become the best intelligent testers they can be.

In *Essentials of WPPSI™-III Assessment*, the authors have attempted to provide readers with succinct, straightforward methods for competent clinical interpretation and application of the third edition of Wechsler's test for children ages 2 years, 6 months to 7 years, 3 months. This book helps ease the transition of examiners who have been longtime WPPSI-R users, and provides a solid foundation for new examiners who are learning their first or second Wechsler test. This latest version of the WPPSI reflects the blend of its rich 35-year tradition with innovations that include brand-new subtests and composite scores. So, too, this book integrates the research and clinical history of the test's ancestors (Wechsler Bellevue II, WISC, WPPSI, and WPPSI-R) with sets of guidelines that enable the examiner to give and then systematically interpret and apply this thoroughly revised and restandardized instrument.

Alan S. Kaufman, Ph.D., and Nadeen L. Kaufman, Ed.D., Series Editors
Yale University School of Medicine

One

Despite the plethora of IQ tests available for psychologists to use today, the Wechsler instruments remain the most widely used measures of intelligence for children, adolescents, and adults. Much has been written on these measures over the years, from clinical use of the scales to esoteric statistical procedures for interpreting the profiles that they yield. Our goal for this book is to provide an easy reference source for those who use the Wechsler Preschool and Primary Scale of Intelligence–Third Edition (WPPSI-III; The Psychological Corporation, 2002). This book was developed for those who test children within the 2-1/2 to 7-year age range and wish to learn the essentials of the WPPSI-III in a direct, no-nonsense, systematic manner. The main topics covered include administration, scoring, interpretation, and clinical use of the instrument. Important points are highlighted throughout the book by Rapid Reference boxes, Caution boxes, and Don't Forget boxes. Each chapter contains questions that are intended to help you consolidate what you have read. After reading this book, you will have, at your fingertips, in-depth information that will help you to become a competent WPPSI-III examiner and clinician.

HISTORY AND DEVELOPMENT

Although interest in testing intelligence developed in the latter half of the 19th century, the assessment of preschool-age children is a relative newcomer in the history of testing (Kelley & Surbeck, 2000). In the early 1900s, the majority of tests were developed for school-age children, leaving a hole in the area of preschool measures.

Shortly after the end of the 19th century, Alfred Binet and his colleagues developed tasks to measure the intelligence of children within the Paris public schools (Binet & Simon, 1905). Binet's tasks were primarily language oriented, emphasizing judgment, memory, comprehension, and reasoning. In the 1908 revision of his scale, Binet included age levels ranging from 3 to 13 years; and in its next revision in 1911, the Binet-Simon scale was extended to age 15 and included five ungraded adult tests (Kaufman, 1990a). Kuhlmann (1912, 1914) published two versions of the Binet scales, the second of which extended test items downward to assess intelligence beginning at 2 months of age. Although the versions of intelligence tests published by Kuhlmann (1914), Yerkes and Foster (1923), and Burt (1921) increased attention to assessment of preschoolers, these early tests were methodologically lacking (Stott & Ball, 1965).

Gesell (1925) subsequently undertook a seminal study in child development. Children were examined at 10 age levels — birth, 4, 6, 9, 12, 18, 24, 36, 48, and 60 months. Although precise methodology was not used, the study yielded "developmental schedules" across four areas: motor development, language development, adaptive behavior, and personal-social behavior. The developmental profiles derived from Gesell's work were subsequently used in the development of tests for infants and preschoolers.

Key assessment instruments for measurement of infant and preschool development were published in the first half of the 20th century. Most notable were the Merrill-Palmer Scale of Mental Tests (Stutsman, 1931), the Minnesota Preschool Scale (Goodenough, 1926; Goodenough, Maurer, & Van Wagenen, 1940), the California First Year Mental scale (Bayley, 1933), and the Iowa Test for Young Children (Fillmore, 1936). These early infant and preschool tests focused more on mental and physical growth than on intelligence.

The 1940s saw many new tests published for infant and preschool assessment, most notably the Cattell Infant Intelligence Scale (Cattell, 1940), the Northwest Infant Intelligence Scale (Gilliland, 1948), the Leiter International Performance Scale (Leiter, 1948), and the Full Range Picture Vocabulary Test (Ammons & Ammond, 1948). Although these tests made unique contributions to the field of preschool assessment (e.g., the Leiter was a non-language, allegedly culture-free test and the Full Range Picture Vocabulary tests had high reliability and validity), the Stanford-Binet continued to be the most widely used test of mental ability (Goodenough, 1949).

The Stanford-Binet, however, had some major competition after David Wechsler's tests entered the playing field in the mid-1930s. Wechsler's approach combined his strong clinical skills and statistical training with his extensive experience in testing, gained initially as a World War I examiner. Wechsler weighted verbal and nonverbal abilities equally, an innovative idea at that time. Wechsler's goal was to create a battery that would yield dynamic clinical information from his chosen set of tasks. This focus went well beyond the earlier use of tests simply as psychometric tools. Wechsler's first test for children, the Wechsler Intelligence Scale for Children (WISC; Wechsler, 1949), was a downward extension of Form II of the Wechsler Bellevue (Wechsler, 1946) and covered the age range of 5–15 years. Years later, the WISC became one of the most frequently used tests in the measurement of preschool functioning (Stott & Ball, 1965), although it was not able to be used with children below age 5. The practice of using tests designed for school-aged children in assessing preschoolers was criticized because of the level of difficulty for young children; nonetheless, the downward extension of tests designed for school-aged children was common practice prior to the development of tests specifically geared for children under age 5 (Kelley & Surbeck, 2000).

The primary focus of the testing movement prior to the 1960s was the assessment of children in school and of adults entering the military (Parker, 1981). However, in the 1960s, the U.S. federal government began to play a role in education, and this involvement spurred growth in the testing of preschool children. The development of government programs such as Head Start focused attention on the need for effective program evaluation and the adequacy of preschool assessment instruments (Kelley & Surbeck, 1991). In 1967 the Wechsler Preschool and Primary Scale of Intelligence (WPPSI) was developed to meet the growing need of how to evaluate programs such as Head Start. The WPPSI was basically developed as a downward extension of many of the WISC subtests, but it provided simpler items and an appropriately aged standardization sample. Unfortunately, the WPPSI accommodated the narrow 4- to 6 1/2-year age range, failing to meet the needs of program evaluations because most of the new programs were for ages 3 to 5 years.

Shortly after the WPPSI, the McCarthy Scales of Children's Abilities (MSCA; McCarthy, 1972) was published. The McCarthy was based on normative data gathered on 1,032 children ages 2 1/2 through 8 1/2 years. The unique features of the McCarthy made it valuable for the assessment of children with learning problems or other exceptionalities. The McCarthy yielded not only a general measure of intellectual functioning but also a profile of abilities including verbal ability, nonverbal reasoning, number aptitude, short-term memory, and motor coordination.

Public Law 94-142, the Education for All Handicapped Children Act of 1975, played an important role in the continued development of cognitive assessment instruments. This law and its followers (Individuals with Disabilities Education Act [IDEA], IDEA of 1991, and IDEA Amendments in 1997) included provisions requiring that an individualized education program (IEP) be developed and maintained for each disabled child (Kelley & Surbeck, 2000). A key feature of the development of the IEP is the evaluation and diagnosis of each child's level of functioning. Thus, these laws directly affected the continued development of standardized tests such as the WPPSI. The WPPSI has had two revisions — one in 1989 and its most recent in 2002. The Don't Forget box on page 5 shows the history of Wechsler's scales.

THEORETICAL FOUNDATION

Historically, the concept of intelligence has been difficult to define, and even today it remains elusive (Flanagan, Genshaft, & Harrison, 1997). Wechsler's (1944) conception of intelligence as "the capacity to act purposefully, to think rationally, and to deal effectively with his [or her] environment" (p. 3) provided the foundation of all Wechsler tests, including the current editions. Practical and clinical perspectives were the cornerstone of Wechsler's tests rather than theory per se (except, perhaps, for Spearman's *g* or general intelligence theory). However, test developers at The Psychological Corporation created some of the newest WPPSI-III subtests to update the test's theoretical foundations. The origin of each of the WPPSI-III subtests is shown in Rapid Reference 1.1.

Like the WISC-III and WAIS-III, the third edition of the WPPSI contains subtests that were designed to tap more specific theoretically-based abilities, such as processing speed and fluid reasoning. Fluid reasoning is a specific cognitive ability that has been emphasized by several theorists (Carroll, 1997; Cattell, 1941, 1963; Cattell & Horn, 1978; Horn & Noll, 1997). Fluid reasoning tasks involve the process of "manipulating abstractions, rules, generalization, and logical relationships" (Carroll, 1993, p. 583). Three new subtests

DON'T FORGET

History of Wechsler Intelligence Scales

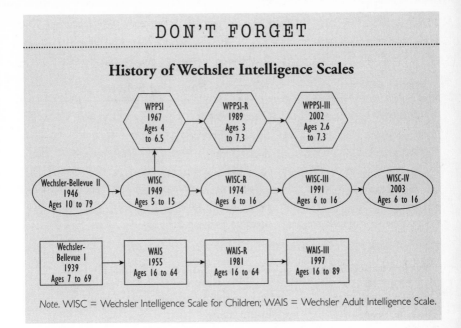

Note. WISC = Wechsler Intelligence Scale for Children; WAIS = Wechsler Adult Intelligence Scale.

were added to the WPPSI-III to enhance the measurement of fluid reasoning: Matrix Reasoning, Word Reasoning, and Picture Concepts. Carroll (1993) and other theorists (e.g., Horn & Noll, 1997) also identified processing speed as an important domain of cognitive functioning. Thus, two new subtests measuring processing speed were added to the WPPSI-III battery, namely Symbol Search and Coding.

Although the newest version of the WPPSI has increased its emphasis on the importance of theoretical foundations, originally Wechsler believed that IQ tests offered a way to peer into an individual's personality. Since the development of the Wechsler scales, extensive theoretical speculations have been made about the nature and meaning of these tests and their scores (Kaufman, 1990a, 1994b), but originally the tests were developed without regard to theory. The Wechsler tests are strongly supported as measures of general intelligence (g; e.g., Kaufman, 1994b), but — as we show throughout this book — much more can be gleaned from the Wechsler scales than simply an understanding of a child's level of g.

Wechsler made a major contribution to the fields of cognitive and clinical assessment with his inclusion of both Verbal and Performance Scales on his

≡Rapid Reference 1.1

Origin of WPPSI-III Subtests

Verbal Subtest	Historical Source of Subtest
Vocabulary	Stanford-Binet
Similarities	Stanford-Binet
Information	Army Alpha
Comprehension	Stanford-Binet, Army Alpha
Word Reasoning	Kaplan's Word Context Test (Werner & Kaplan, 1950)
Receptive Vocabulary	Stanford-Binet
Picture Naming	Stanford-Binet

Performance Subtest	Historical Source of Subtest
Picture Completion	Army Beta, Army Performance Scale Examination
Coding	Army Beta, Army Performance Scale Examination
Block Design	Kohs (1923)
Matrix Reasoning	Raven's Progressive Matrices (1938)
Symbol Search	Shiffrin & Schneider (1977) and S. Sternberg (1966)
Object Assembly	Army Performance Scale Examination
Picture Concepts	Novel task developed by Psychological Corporation

tests. The dual-scaled tests went against the conventional wisdom of his time. In the 1930s and 1940s, it didn't make sense to most examiners to waste their time administering a lengthy nonverbal subtest when a quick verbal subtest could glean just as much data. However, now it is obvious to clinicians and researchers alike that Verbal and Performance both have critical value for understanding brain functioning and theoretical distinctions between fluid and crystallized intelligence. In addition, because Wechsler stressed the clinical value of intelligence tests, this innovative approach provided a new layer to the psychometric, statistical emphasis of testing that accompanied the use and interpretation of earlier tests such as the Stanford-Binet. Finally, Wechsler's inclusion of a multiscore subtest profile (as well as three IQs instead of one) met the needs of the emerging field of learning disabilities assessment in the 1960s to such an extent that Wechsler's scales replaced the Stanford-Binet as king of IQ during that decade. It has maintained that niche ever since.

PURPOSES OF ASSESSING PRESCHOOLERS AND SCHOOL-AGE CHILDREN

Children are assessed for a variety of reasons; thus, the WPPSI-III may be applied in many different situations. Typically, children are referred by a teacher for a psychological evaluation to determine whether they are eligible for an educationally related disability and special education or other special services. Some of the most common reasons that a child is referred for an assessment include diagnosing for developmental delay, learning disabilities, mental retardation, behavioral problems, neuropsychological impairments, or giftedness. Often, the end goal of a child's assessment is to create effective interventions. The number of children ages 3 to 5 years in the United States who were served in federally supported programs for persons with disabilities (including specific learning disabilities, mental retardation, developmental delay, and other disabilities) numbered nearly 600,000 in 1999–2000 (U.S. Department of Education, 2001). The settings in which these assessments take place are varied and include psychologists' private practices, schools, clinics, hospitals, and research programs.

As mentioned earlier, the Wechsler scales remain by far the most popular test for children (Daniel, 1997). In a survey of school psychologists who assess children to identify mental retardation, the Wechsler scales were the most frequently used tests for deriving IQs (Woodrich & Barry, 1991). Even in assessing children with bilingual and limited-English students, the WISC-R and WISC-III were reported to be the most frequently used measures (Ochoa, Powell, & Robles-Pina, 1996). School psychologists rated the Wechsler scales as most useful and as actually used the most (Giordano, Schwiebert, & Brotherton, 1997), and in another survey of school psychologists, the WISC-III was reportedly used 10 times per month, whereas the next most frequently used test (of 11 listed) was used only twice (Wilson & Reschly,

1996). Because of the Wechsler scales' popularity throughout the years, the WPPSI and WPPSI-R have remained strong forces in the assessment of preschool-aged children, and the WPPSI-III is sure to follow suit.

DESCRIPTION OF WPPSI-III

The WPPSI-III is a measure of cognitive functioning of children from ages 2 years, 6 months (2-6) to 7 years, 3 months (7-3). Its age range is divided into two age bands (2-6 to 3-11 and 4-0 to 7-3), each with its own battery of subtests. Like its predecessors, the WPPSI-III offers a Verbal IQ (V-IQ), Performance IQ (P-IQ), and Full Scale IQ (FS-IQ). However, departing from the previous versions of the WPPSI, the WPPSI-III adds a General Language Composite (GLC) and — for the older age band — a Processing Speed Quotient (PSQ) to the three familiar IQs. Like the IQs, the GLC and PSQ are standard scores with a mean of 100 and standard deviation of 15. Mainly motor responses are required on the Performance scale (pointing, placing, or drawing), and spoken responses are usually required on the Verbal scale.

For each age band, WPPSI-III subtests are categorized as core, supplemental, or optional. Core subtests are those that comprise the V-IQ, P-IQ, and FS-IQ. The composition of the scales for each age group is presented in Figures 1.1 and 1.2. In the younger age bracket, two core subtests comprise the V-IQ and two comprise the P-IQ. The four subtests of the V-IQ and P-IQ together yield the FS-IQ for children ages 2–6 to 3–11. In the older age bracket, three subtests comprise the V-IQ and three comprise the P-IQ. In addition to the six subtests of the V-IQ and P-IQ, an additional core subtest (Coding) is added in the calculation of the FS-IQ for those aged 4–0 to 7–3. For both age groups, the GLC comprises two subtests: Receptive Vocabulary and Picture Naming (a supplemental subtest for children under age 4 and an optional one for those age 4 and above). Only the older age bracket has a fourth standard score, the PSQ, which is composed of Coding and Symbol Search (a supplemental subtest). Because GLC and PSQ require the administration of noncore subtests, these two global scores are supplements, not core standard scores. Consistent with the metric used for all Wechsler subtests, each WPPSI-III subtest yields a scaled score with a mean of 10 and a standard deviation of 3. Rapid Reference 1.2 lists and describes each WPPSI-III subtest.

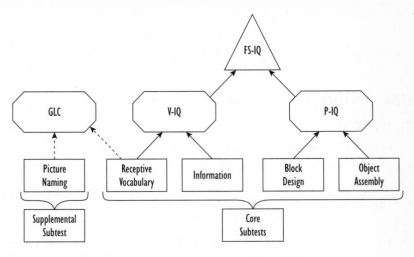

Figure 1.1 WPPSI-III building blocks for Ages 2-6 to 3-11.

Note. FS-IQ = Full Scale IQ; V-IQ = Verbal IQ; P-IQ = Performance IQ; GLC = General Language Composite. Picture Naming can be substituted for a core Verbal subtest if necessary.

CHANGES FROM WPPSI-R TO WPPSI-III

With their revision of the WPPSI-R, the professionals at The Psychological Corporation intended to improve the psychometric properties, strengthen the test's theoretical foundations, enhance its clinical utility, increase the age appropriateness, and enhance the user friendliness of the test. We believe that they achieved their goals. Rapid Reference 1.3 lists the five WPPSI-III revision goals and how those goals were met.

Significant changes in the composition of the scales were made when the WPPSI-R was transformed into the WPPSI-III. Most notably, five WPPSI-R subtests were dropped (Arithmetic, Animal Pegs, Geometric Design, Mazes, and Sentences), and seven new subtests were added: Receptive Vocabulary, Picture Naming, Word Reasoning, Matrix Reasoning, Picture Concepts, Coding, and Symbol Search. The Psychological Corporation (2002) stated that the five deleted subtests were removed in part because the total number of subtests was too great with the additional seven new tasks. The deleted subtests were all influenced by factors other than intellectual capability, including neurological and motor development, as well as familiarity with numbers and abstract concepts. The eliminated subtests were also those that tapped memory capabilities of young children. The creators of the WPPSI-III recognize

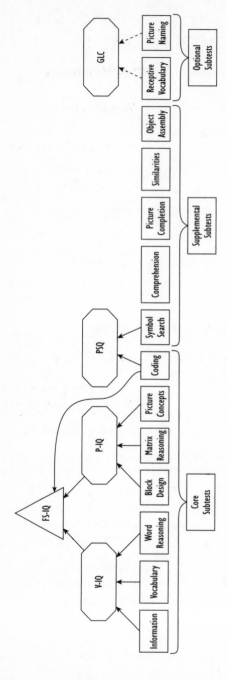

Figure 1.2 WPPSI-III building blocks for Ages 4-0 to 7-3.

Note. FS-IQ = Full Scale IQ; V-IQ = Verbal IQ; P-IQ = Performance IQ; PSQ = Processing Speed Quotient; GLC = General Language Composite. Either supplemental Verbal subtest may be substituted for one core Verbal subtest. Supplemental Performance subtests may be substituted for one core Performance subtest.

≡Rapid Reference 1.2

Description of WPPSI-III Subtests

Performance Subtests

Retained from WPPSI-R

Object Assembly. Child is required to fit puzzle pieces together to form a meaningful whole.

Block Design. Child reproduces patterns made from 1- or 2-colored blocks.

Picture Completion. Child identifies what is missing from pictures of common objects.

Newly Developed for WPPSI-III

Matrix Reasoning. The child looks at an incomplete matrix and selects the missing section from four or five response options.

Picture Concepts. Child is presented with two or three rows of pictures and chooses one picture from each row to form a group with a common organizational concept.

Symbol Search. Child indicates, by marking a box, whether a target symbol appears in a series of symbols.

Coding. Using a key, the child draws symbols that are paired with simple geometric shapes.

Verbal Subtests

Retained from WPPSI-R

Information. Child must either point to a picture or verbally answer brief oral questions about commonplace objects and events.

Comprehension. Child verbally responds to questions about consequences of events.

Vocabulary. Child names pictured items and provides verbal definitions of words.

Similarities. Child completes a sentence that contains a verbal analogy.

Newly Developed for WPPSI-III

Picture Naming. The child names pictures that are displayed singularly in the stimulus booklet.

Receptive Vocabulary. The child looks at a group of four pictures and points to the one that the examiner describes aloud.

Word Reasoning. The child is read an increasingly specific series of one to three clues and identifies the common object or concept being described.

Note. Subtests that were retained from the WPPSI-R have new items and contain changes in administration and scoring.

≡ Rapid Reference 1.3

Revision Goals of the WPPSI-III

1. Improve Psychometric Properties

- Updated norms with well-stratified standardization sample based on 2000 US Census data
- Improved evidence of reliability and validity (see Rapid Reference 1.4)
- Extended floors and ceilings on subtests retained from WPPSI-R
- Reexamined bias
- Reduced item overlap with WISC-III

2. Strengthen Theoretical Foundations

- Composite scores are factor-based
- Incorporated measures of processing Speed
- Enhanced measure of fluid intelligence (added Matrix Reasoning, Picture Concepts, and Word Reasoning)

3. Enhance Clinical Utility

- Extended bottom of age range from 2 years, 11 months to 2 years, 6 months
- Added more clinical studies on mental retardation, giftedness, developmental delay, at-risk, language disorder, ADHD, and reading delay
- Added validity studies with other measures including, WISC-III, Bayley, DAS, CMS, and WIAT-II

4. Increase Age-appropriateness

- Determined core subtests according to age
- Reduced emphasis on speed of responding
- Reduced emphasis on verbal expression
- Simplified instructions
- Included teaching or practice for a subtests
- Made scoring criteria more developmentally appropriate
- Redraw all artwork and changed Block Design blocks

5. Enhance User Friendliness

- Decreased core testing time
- Simplified administration and scoring procedures
- Modified layout of stimulus booklet
- Eliminated object assembly shield
- Organized manuals and record form in a practical manner

the importance of memory for young children (The Psychological Corporation, 2002, p. 23) and suggest that examiners administer a comprehensive test of memory if it is warranted.

With the extra subtests in the WPPSI-III came the two additional composite scores, the GLC and PSQ. These new composites follow well from the factorial and theoretical structure of the scale. Rapid Reference 1.4 shows the relationships between old WPPSI-R and current WPPSI-III scales and subtests. Correlations were strongest between the WPPSI-R and WPPSI-III Information (.80) and Vocabulary (.77) subtests, each of which endured only minor changes. Four items were added to Vocabulary and 16 were retained, and on Information, six new picture items were added along with nine verbal items (19 verbal items were retained). The weakest relationships were for Object Assembly (.53) and Similarities (.57), both of which were modified substantially. Object Assembly retained only two WPPSI-R items and added 12 new ones; administration and scoring procedures were also changed.

≡Rapid Reference 1.4

Correlations Between WPPSI-III and the WPPSI-R Subtests of the Same Name and IQ Scales of the Same Name

Subtest or IQ Scale	Corrected r
Information	.80
Vocabulary	.77
Comprehension	.68
Picture Completion	.66
Block Design	.57
Similarities	.57
Object Assembly	.53
Verbal IQ	.86
Performance IQ	.70
Full Scale IQ	.85

Note. All values are corrected using Fisher's z transformation. Ns varied across individual subtests and ranged from 129 to 176. Coefficients are from WPPSI-III Technical and Interpretive Manual (Table 5.7).

Similarities was modified by removing two of the three WPPSI-R item types and adding 16 new items (eight old items were retained).

STANDARDIZATION AND PSYCHOMETRIC PROPERTIES OF WPPSI-III

Standardization

The WPPSI-III was standardized on a sample of 1,700 children who were chosen to match closely the 2000 U.S. Census data on the variables of age, gender, geographic region, ethnicity, and parental education. The standardization sample was divided into nine age groups, each composed of 200 children, except for the 7-0 to 7-3 age group that was composed of 100 children. The sample was split equally between boys and girls.

Reliability

The reliability and validity information is presented in the *WPPSI-III Technical and Interpretive Manual* (The Psychological Corporation, 2002) and is summarized in Rapid Reference 1.5. The average internal consistency coefficients are .95 for V-IQ, .93 for P-IQ, .89 for PSQ, .93 for GLC, and .96 for FS-IQ. Internal consistency values for individual subtests across all ages ranged from 0.75 for Block Design (for the 4-0 to 4-5 age group) to .96 on Similarities (for ages 4-6 to 4-11 and 5-6 to 5-11). The median internal consistency value for the individual subtests was 0.88.

The WPPSI-III is a fairly stable instrument with average test-retest coefficients of 0.91, 0.86, and 0.92 for the V-, P-, and FS-IQ, respectively (see Rapid Reference 1.5 for a reliability summary that includes internal consistency and stability values). The stability values of the PSQ (.86) and GLC (.91) were consistent with the coefficients for the IQs with the P-IQ and PSQ emerging as the least stable of all the composite scores. The largest practice effects (i.e., score increases from first testing to second) for the combined age bands were 5–6 points for P-IQ and PSQ. The average practice effects for all ages for V-IQ and GLC were just under 3 points (see Rapid Reference 1.6).

═Rapid Reference 1.5

Average WPPSI-R and WPPSI-III Reliability Coefficients

WPPSI-R/WPPSI-III Scale or Subtest	WPPSI-R		WPPSI-III	
	Split-half reliability	Test-retest reliability	Split-half reliability	Test-retest reliability
Verbal IQ	.95	.90	.95	.91
Performance IQ	.92	.88	.93	.86
Full Scale IQ	.96	.91	.96	.92
Processing Speed Quotient	—	—	.89	.90
General Language Composite	—	—	.93	.91
Verbal				
Information	.84	.81	.88	.86
Similarities	.86	.70	.95	.90
Arithmetic	.80	.71	—	—
Vocabulary	.84	.75	.89	.84
Comprehension	.83	.78	.88	.81
Picture Naming	—	—	.88	.88
Receptive Vocabulary	—	—	.88	.83
Word Reasoning	—	—	.91	.82
Sentences	.82	.79	—	—
Performance				
Picture Completion	.85	.82	.90	.85
Coding	—	—	—	.84
Matrix Reasoning	—	—	.90	.81
Block Design	.85	.80	.84	.76
Object Assembly	.63	.59	.85	.74
Symbol Search	—	—	—	.83
Picture Concepts	—	—	.91	.75
Mazes	.77	.52	—	—
Geometric Design	.79	.67	—	—
Animal Pegs[a]	—	.66	—	—

[a]For Animal Pegs, Coding, and Symbol Search, and for the Processing Speed Quotient, only test-retest coefficients are reported because of the timed nature of the subtests.

The youngest age band (2-6 to 3-11) had smaller practice effects than the older two bands (4-0 to 5-5 and 5-6 to 7-3). Like P-IQ, the individual Performance subtests generally had larger gains in scaled scores on retesting than did the Verbal subtests. Rapid Reference 1.7 shows the subtests that have relatively large gains from test to retest (large gains are defined as those at least 0.9 scaled score points, which equals 0.3 of a standard deviation).

Validity

Construct validity of the WPPSI-III is supported by the factor-analytic studies described in the *Technical and Interpretive Manual.* For the 2-6 to 3-11 age group, the WPPSI-III is a two-factor test, Verbal and Performance. For ages 4-0 to 7-3, a third factor emerges, Processing Speed. When only the core subtests were analyzed, the WPPSI-III subtests each loaded on its predicted factor, with the exception of Picture Concepts. At every age level except 6-0 to 7-3, Picture Concepts loaded on its intended factor — Performance — but in the oldest age range, Picture Concepts was more decisively a Verbal than Performance subtest.

≡ Rapid Reference 1.6

Practice Effects for the WPPSI-III Global Scales

Scale	Ages 2.6-3.11 (N = 41)	Ages 4.0-5.5 (N = 34)	Ages 5.6-7.3 (N = 82)	All Ages (N = 157)
V-IQ	+1.6	+5.0	+2.4	+2.8
P-IQ	+4.2	+4.8	+5.7	+5.0
FS-IQ	+3.4	+6.4	+5.5	+5.2
GLC	+3.0	+5.2	+1.5	+2.7
PSQ	—	+6.0	+6.3	+6.2

Note. Data are from *WPPSI-III Technical and Interpretive Manual* (Table 4.4). Intervals ranged from 14 to 50 days with a mean of 26 days.

≡Rapid Reference 1.7

Practice Effects for the Separate WPPSI-III Scaled Scores: Subtests With Relatively Large Gains From Test to Retest

Ages 2.6-3.11 (N = 41)	Ages 4.0-5.5 (N = 34)	Ages 5.6-7.3 (N = 82)
Block Design (+0.9)	Picture Completion(+1.5)	Picture Completion(+1.4)
	Matrix Reasoning (+1.1)	Matrix Reasoning (+1.3)
	Coding (+1.1)	Coding (+1.1)
	Symbol Search (+1.1)	Symbol Search (+1.0)
	Object Assembly (+1.1)	Similarities (+0.9)
	Word Reasoning (+1.0)	
	Receptive Vocab. (+1.0)	
	Information (+0.9)	
	Picture Naming (+0.9)	

Note. Relatively large gains are defined as at least 0.3 SD (a gain of at least 0.9 scaled-score points from test to retest). Data are from WPPSI-III Technical and Interpretive Manual (Table 4.4). Intervals ranged from 14 to 50 days with a mean of 26 days.

When factor analyses included WPPSI-III supplemental as well as core subtests, the results were not as consistent with predictions. Picture Concepts was, again, a maverick subtest. As shown in Table 1.1, it loaded equally on both Processing Speed and Verbal at ages 4-0 to 4-11, it loaded primarily on Performance at ages 5-0 to 5-11, and it was primarily a Verbal subtest at ages 6-0 to 7-3.

Table 1.1 Factor Loadings for Picture Concepts Derived from Exploratory Analysis With Core and Supplemental WPPSI-III Subtests

Age	Verbal	Performance	Processing Speed
4-0 to 4-11	.33	.07	.34
5-0 to 5-11	.15	.46	.15
6-0 to 7-3	.51	.10	.06

Note. Loadings > .30 are in italics. Coefficients are from WPPSI-III Technical and Interpretive Manual (Table 5.4).

Table 1.2 Subtests With Four Highest and Four Lowest Correlations with Picture Concepts

Subtest	r
Highest	
Word Reasoning	.51
Similarities	.51
Information	.49
Matrix Reasoning	.48
Lowest	
Picture Naming	.42
Block Design	.41
Object Assembly	.39
Coding	.32

Note. Coefficients are from *WPPSI-III Technical and Interpretive Manual* (Table 5.1).

Table 1.3 Factor Loadings for Matrix Reasoning Derived From Exploratory Analysis With Core and Supplemental WPPSI-III Subtests

Age	Verbal	Performance	Processing Speed
4-0 to 4-11	.16	.19	*.39*
5-0 to 5-11	.12	*.36*	*.30*
6-0 to 7-3	.26	*.59*	-.09

Note. Loadings > .30 are in italics. Coefficients are from *WPPSI-III Technical and Interpretive Manual* (Table 5.4).

Like Picture Concepts, Matrix Reasoning also loaded on multiple factors in the exploratory factor analyses (see Table 1.3). At ages 4-0 to 4-11, Matrix Reasoning loaded only on Processing Speed, and it loaded about equally on Processing Speed and Performance at ages 5-0 to 5-11. At 6-0 to 7-3, it loaded only on the Performance factor. Therefore, the age trends suggest that

Table 1.4 Matrix Reasoning's Correlations With Processing Speed Subtests Across Six Separate Age Groups

	Correlations With Matrix Reasoning						
	Ages 4-0 to 4-5	Ages 4-6 to 4-11	Ages 5-0 to 5-5	Ages 5-6 to 5-11	Ages 6-0 to 6-11	Ages 7-0 to 7-3	Median
Symbol Search	.44	.52	.52	.48	.50	.50	.50
Coding	.41	.44	.55	.40	.22	.12	.41

Note. Coefficients are from *WPPSI-III Technical and Interpretive Manual* (Tables A.4, A.5, A.6, A.7, A.8, and A.9).

as children progress from age 4 to 7 years, Matrix Reasoning becomes increasingly a function of Performance ability. Possible explanations of the age trends for Picture Concepts and Matrix Reasoning appear in chapter 4.

In addition to factor analyses, validity of the WPPSI-III is further supported by correlations with the following instruments (The Psychological Corporation, 2002): Bayley Scales of Infant Development–II (BSID-II; Bayley, 1993), WPPSI-R (Wechsler, 1989), WISC-III (Wechsler, 1991), and Differential Abilities Scale (DAS; Elliott, 1990). Each of the global scales of these four instruments correlated strongly with the WPPSI-III FS-IQ. Correlations ranged from .80 to .89 (see Rapid Reference 1.8). Rapid Reference 1.9 also shows that the WPPSI-III Verbal Scale correlated substantially higher with the verbal scales of the WPPSI-R, WISC-III, and DAS than it did with the nonverbal scales of each instrument. These patterns of correlations support the convergent and discriminant validity of the WPPSI-III. Chapter 5 presents a more detailed review of validity issues, and chapter 6 touches on the validity of the WPPSI-III in special populations.

To evaluate the relationship of the WPPSI-III scores to the key criterion of academic achievement (The Psychological Corporation, 2002), 208 children were administered both the WPPSI-III and the Wechsler Individual Achievement Test–Second Edition (WIAT-II; The Psychological Corporation, 2001).

≡Rapid Reference 1.8

Correlations of WPPSI-III Full Scale IQ With Other Global Measures

	WPPSI-III FS-IQ
Bayley Scales of Infant Development–II (BSID-II) (N = 84)	
Mental Score	.80
WPPSI-R (N = 176)	
Full Scale IQ	.85
WISC-III (N = 94)	
Full Scale IQ	.89
Differential Ability Scales (DAS) (N = 153)	
General Conceptual Ability (GCA) Standard Score	.87

Note. All values are corrected for the variability of the standardization sample. Coefficients are from WPPSI-III Technical and Interpretive Manual (Tables 5.7, 5.9, 5.11, and 5.13).

The strongest correlation was between the WPPSI-III FS-IQ and WIAT-II Total Achievement (.78) and the weakest was between the PSQ and Reading (.31). The coefficients between WPPSI-III and WIAT-II global scores are presented in Rapid Reference 1.10. As shown, V-IQ correlated strongly with Total Achievement (.77), and the P-IQ correlated substantially with the Mathematics Composite (.60). The validity of new WPPSI-III Verbal subtests was also supported with correlations to WIAT-II composites (see Rapid Reference 1.11). Picture Naming (.71) and Word Reasoning (.70) were among the best correlates of Total Achievement. New Performance subtests were not as strongly correlated with Achievement: Matrix Reasoning and Picture Concepts both correlated .35 with Total Achievement. However, as shown in Rapid Reference 1.11, the old subtests tended to be both the best and worst correlates of achievement on the WIAT-II. Information and Similarities were the highest correlates of Mathematics, Oral Language, and Total Achievement. Picture Completion, Object Assembly, and Coding were the lowest correlates of Reading and Total Achievement. Overall, the WPPSI-III–WIAT-II relationships replicate prior research and support the validity of the WPPSI-III.

≡Rapid Reference 1.9

Convergent and Discriminant Validity of the WPPSI-III Verbal-Performance IQ Discrepancy: Correlations of WPPSI-III V-IQ and P-IQ with Other Measures of Verbal and Nonverbal Ability

	WPPSI-III V-IQ	WPPSI-III P-IQ
WPPSI-R (N = 176)		
V-IQ	**.86**	.59
P-IQ	.60	**.70**
WISC-III (N = 96)		
V-IQ	**.82**	.67
P-IQ	.60	**.79**
DAS (N = 112)		
Verbal	**.78**	.54
Nonverbal Reasoning	.56	**.76**

Note. Coefficients in bold denote convergent validity of WPPSI-III Verbal and Performance IQs. All values are corrected for the variability of the standardization sample. Most values are from WPPSI-III Technical and Interpretive Manual (Tables 5.7, 5.9, and 5.13). The remaining values were kindly provided by J. J. Zhu (personal communication, October 23, 2002).

≡*Rapid Reference 1.10*

WPPSI-III IQs and the Processing Speed Index: Correlations With WIAT-II Achievement Composites

WIAT-II Composite	N	Verbal IQ	Performance IQ	Full Scale IQ	Processing Speed Index
Reading	58	.60	.44	.66	.31
Math	133	.56	.60	.77	.55
Written Language	58	.59	.36	.62	.41
Oral Language	201	.72	.44	.67	.39
Total	56	.77	.55	.78	.36

Note. All values are corrected for the variability of the standardization sample. Coefficients are from *WPPSI-III Technical and Interpretive Manual* (Table 5.14).

COMPREHENSIVE REFERENCES ON THE TEST

The *WPPSI-III Technical and Interpretive Manual* (The Psychological Corporation, 2002) provides detailed information about the development of the test; descriptions of the subtests and scales; and information about the test's standardization, reliability, and validity. We have found no other comprehensive references on the WPPSI-III. There are, however, several comprehensive treatments of its predecessor, the WPPSI-R. Chapter 11 of Sattler's (2001) *Assessment of Children: Cognitive Applications (4th edition)* presents an overview of what the test measures and an approach to interpretation. Gyurke's (1991) chapter on the WPPSI-R describes the subtests and scales, summarizes psychometric information, and provides steps for interpreting the test. Kaufman and Lichtenberger's (2000) *Essentials of WISC-III and WPPSI-R Assessment* provides the same type of treatment of WPPSI-R administration, scoring, interpretation, and applications that is detailed in the present book for the WPPSI-III. Rapid Reference 1.12 provides basic information on the WPPSI-III and its publisher.

≡Rapid Reference 1.11

WPPSI-III Subtests: The Highest and Lowest Correlates of WIAT-II Achievement Composites

Correlations of WPPSI-III Scaled Scores with WIAT-II Achievement Composite Standard Scores

Reading (N = 58)	Written Math (N = 133)	Oral Language (N = 58)	Language (N = 201)	Total (N = 56)
Highest	**Highest**	**Highest**	**Highest**	**Highest**
I (60)	I (54)	WR (57)	I (67)	I (72)
PN (60)	S (54)	C (57)	S (63)	WR (71)
RV (59)	RV (51)	RV (54)	WR (62)	S (70)
	BD (51)			PN (70)
Lowest	**Lowest**	**Lowest**	**Lowest**	**Lowest**
Cd (24)	OA (37)	PC (31)	OA (26)	PC (32)
PC (29)	MR (36)	MR (22)	MR (24)	OA (26)
OA (16)	WR (35)	OA (16)	Cd (19)	Cd (25)

Note. Decimal points are omitted. All values are corrected for the variability of the standardization sample. Within each column, coefficients are listed from high to low. So, for example, the best predictor of WIAT-II Reading is Information and the worst is Object Assembly. Coefficients are from *WPPSI-III Technical and Interpretive Manual* (Table 5.14).

Note. I = Information; V = Vocabulary; WR = Word Reasoning; C = Comprehension; S = Similarities; RV = Receptive Vocabulary; PN = Picture Naming; BD = Block Design; MR = Matrix Reasoning; PCon = Picture Concepts; SS = Symbol Search; Cd = Coding; PC = Picture Completion; OA = Object Assembly.

≡ *Rapid Reference 1.12*

Basic Information About the Wechsler Preschool and Primary Scale of Intelligence–Third Edition

Author   The Psychological Corporation

Publication date   2002

What the test measures   Verbal, nonverbal, and general intelligence, processing speed, and general language abilities

Age range   2 years, 6 months to 7 years, 3 months

Administration time   Ages 2 years, 6 months to 3 years, 11 months: 30–45 min

                               Ages 4 years to 7 years, 3 months: 60 min

Qualification of examiners Graduate- or professional-level training in psychological assessment

Publisher   The Psychological Corporation
                               555 Academic Court
                               San Antonio, TX 78204-2498
                               800-211-8378
                               http://www.PsychCorp.com

Price (from 2003 catalog) **WPPSI™–III Kit**

                               Includes all necessary stimulus and manipulative materials, Examiner Manual, Technical Manual, 25 Record Forms for ages 2-6 to 7-3, 25 Record Forms for ages 2-6 to 3-11, and 25 Response Booklets

                               $725.00 (in box) or $775 (in attaché or soft-sided case)

                               WPPSI™–III Scoring Assistant®
                               CD-ROM Windows®
                               $165.00

                               WPPSI™–III Writer™
                               CD-ROM Windows®
                               $350.00

TEST YOURSELF

1. **Prior to the development of the Wechsler scales, the Stanford-Binet was the most widely used test of mental ability for preschoolers.** True or False?

2. **Prior to the development of the WPPSI, which Wechsler test was commonly administered to preschoolers?**

   (a) WAIS

   (b) Wechsler Bellevue-II

   (c) WISC

   (d) WIAT

3. **What law played an important role in the continued development of cognitive assessment instruments for children?**

4. **Preschool assessment measures such as the WPPSI-III were developed as upward extensions of infant tests of intelligence.** True or False?

5. **The WPPSI-III P-IQ significantly correlated with which achievement measure?**

   (a) WIAT-II Listening Comprehension

   (b) WIAT-II Oral Language

   (c) WIAT-II Mathematics

   (d) WIAT-II Reading

6. **Given the results of the factor analyses of the WPPSI-III, you should not be surprised if a 6-year-old's score on Picture Concepts (a Performance subtest) is more similar to scores on Verbal subtests than to scores on other Performance subtests.** True or False?

7. **The two new composites added to the WPPSI-III are**

   (a) Processing Speed Quotient and General Language Composite.

   (b) Freedom from Distractibility and Processing Speed Quotient.

   (c) General Memory Index and General Language Composite.

   (d) General Language Composite and Working Memory Index.

Answers: 1. True; 2. c; 3. Public Law 94-142, Education for All Handicapped Children Act of 1975; 4. False; 5. c; 6. True; 7. a.

Two

HOW TO ADMINISTER THE WPPSI-III

When administering norm-referenced tests such as the WPPSI-III, both standardized and nonstandardized procedures must be used together to uncover a child's true abilities and disabilities. Because an individual child's WPPSI-III scores are compared to those of a norm group, following standardized procedures under a set of standard conditions is critical for accuracy. Fair comparisons between examinees and members of the normative group are only possible when standardized procedures are followed. However, to provide an integrated and full picture of children, use both nonstandardized procedures such as interviews, behavioral observations, and informal assessments together with standardized tests. Simply taking a snapshot of children's abilities through time-limited samples of performance, as is done during administration of the WPPSI-III, does not provide adequate information about children for the purposes of making diagnoses and recommendations.

APPROPRIATE TESTING CONDITIONS

Testing Environment

Consider the following issues about the testing environment, regardless of whether you are assessing a young preschool child or a school-age child. Have a testing environment that is relatively bland and free of distractions (both visual and auditory) for a child of any age. Ideally, test in a room without too many toys or windows that might be distracting. However, also try to create a setting that is not too formal or adult-like (you don't want the children to feel as though they are in a medical examining room). Ensure that the setting is comfortable for both you and the child. When testing a school-age child, in most cases, have only the examiner and the child in the examination room. However, when testing a very young child (age 2 1/2 to 4) or when evaluating a child who is anxious about separating from a parent or caregiver, allow the parent to accompany you into the testing room, at least for a period of time. Parental presence in such cases helps establish rapport.

A table is necessary for all testing situations. If possible, have an appropriately sized table and chairs (similar to those you may see in a preschool classroom). If such a table and chairs are not available, then at a minimum use a booster chair or highchair (with safety restraints) to raise the child to a comfortable level, even with the table. In some cases, when testing a highly energetic young preschool child, you can benefit from moving the testing materials onto the floor (if that seems to be the location at which the child will best attend to you). With highly energetic or easily distractible children, try to fluctuate between highly structured testing activities at a table and more informal activities that can be done on the floor. In all cases, use a clipboard because it provides a smooth writing surface and it can be easily transported to the floor if necessary.

Testing Materials

While the testing is taking place, sit either opposite the child or at a 90° angle from the child (kitty-corner) in order to most easily view the test-taking behaviors and manipulate the test materials (see Figure 2.1). Position the *Administration and Scoring Manual* on the table in a manner that shields the record form from the child's view. This positioning allows the examiner to easily read the necessary directions but prevents the child from being distracted by what the examiner is writing on the record form. Place only the testing materials that are immediately being used in the sight-line of the child. Young children are especially prone to distraction by excess stimuli materials if

> # DON'T FORGET
>
> Keys for preparing to administer the test:
> - Quiet, distraction-free room
> - Table and chairs of appropriate size for the child
> - Smooth writing surface
>
> Extra needed materials not in the kit:
> - Two no. 2 pencils without erasers
> - Stopwatch
> - Clipboard
> - Extra paper and writing utensils (just in case)

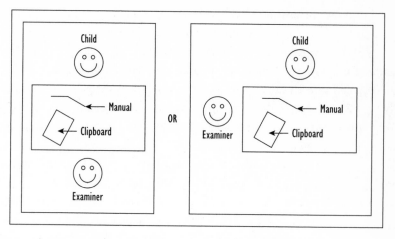

Figure 2.1 Alternative seating arrangements for testing.

such materials are in view. Keep other testing materials on the floor or on a chair beside you so that they are readily available.

The WPPSI-III kit contains multiple pieces, so double-check that all pieces are present and accounted for prior to beginning the testing. A young child is not likely to remain attentive while you are searching for a missing piece from an Object Assembly puzzle. A few necessary materials are not contained within the testing kit: a stopwatch, clipboard, two No. 2 graphite pencils without erasers, and extra paper for taking notes.

RAPPORT WITH EXAMINEE

Establishing Rapport

When you are working with preschoolers or school-age children, building rapport is crucial to obtaining valid testing results. Juggling the maintenance of rapport with adherence to standardized procedures challenges even experienced examiners. Upon initially interacting with the child, allow the child enough time to become accustomed to you and the testing situation before jumping into the evaluation. The manner in which a parent or caregiver has introduced his or her child to the testing situation can have rippling effects throughout the evaluation. Encourage parents to explain to their children ahead of time what they may expect during the evaluation. For example, let the child know the examiner will be showing him or her some puzzles and blocks and will be asking some questions. We advise parents not to use the word *test* when introducing the situation to their child. The word *test* has a negative connotation to many children and can elicit a fear reaction. However, if a child directly asks, "Am I going to do a test?" then do not to lie, but rather explain to the child, "Most of the things you are going to be doing are not like the tests you take at school. In fact, lots of kids think that these special activities are pretty fun."

Prior to bringing the child to the examination room, gather information from the parents about how their child typically separates from them. If parents indicate that their child is usually shy or is upset upon separation from them, then ask the parents to accompany their child into the testing room until the child is comfortable with the examiner and examination situation. Be flexible in structuring the assessment sessions depending on the child's needs. Some children may need their parents to accompany them into the beginning of each of the testing sessions, whereas others need only a brief 5 minutes with their parents in the testing room during only the first evaluation session.

To ease into the testing situation, allow the child to remain standing until he or she is comfortable or is less threatened by the testing situation. Do not speak too loudly or too formally because your voice and intonation may

---

DON'T FORGET

Keys to Establishing Positive Examiner-Child Rapport

Effectively introduce child to the testing activities.

• Do not use the word *test.*

• Explain that many activities will be done: puzzles, blocks, drawing, and answering questions.

Allow the child ample time to adjust to the testing situation.

• If you are testing a very young child, allow a parent to accompany the child to the testing room.

Achieve a balance between professional (formal) and friendly (informal) demeanor.

Allow child to stand if necessary, until he or she is comfortable.

CAUTION

Appropriate Feedback and Encouragement

- Praise frequently, but don't be repetitive; too much praise diminishes the reinforcement value.
- Encouragement and feedback may be verbal or nonverbal.
  - Smile
  - Pat on the hand
  - *"Good job; you sure are working hard"* etc.
- Praise and encourage the child's level of effort.
- Be careful *not* to reveal whether a particular response is right or wrong.
- Give encouragement throughout items, not just when the child is struggling.

startle a young child. However, do not use baby talk or talk down to younger children. Try to adjust your vocabulary to a level that is appropriate to the child's age level. Achieve a balance between formality and informality — between being professional and friendly — in testing a child of any age.

Maintaining Rapport

Grabbing the attention of a child is not as difficult as keeping the attention and motivation of a child. Delicately balance maintaining rapport and adhering to standardized procedures. Provide frequent praise for a child's efforts in order to maintain children's motivation and attention. Vigilantly watch for signs that the child's attention is waning or that his or her frustration, fatigue, or lack of motivation is growing. Look for verbal (e.g., "How much longer?" or "These are too hard.") or nonverbal (e.g., increased fidgeting, sighing, grimacing) signs. These cues are signals to increase praise and encouragement or perhaps to take a break.

Deliver encouragement and praise in many different ways (an understanding smile, a pat on the hand, "we've got a lot more fun things to do," "you're working so hard," "wow, you're a hard worker"). However, don't praise again and again because mindless praise will lose its reinforcing effects. Also exercise caution so that children aren't given feedback about whether their responses are correct. In other words, give encouragement throughout items, not just when a child is struggling or giving incorrect responses.

Some children require more than verbal and nonverbal praise to maintain motivation. Develop a reward system with such children. For example, reach an agreement that the child can play with certain toys after a required number of tasks are completed. Use a small snack as a reward on occasion, but always discuss this strategy with parents ahead of time (some parents disapprove of certain types of foods, don't want dinner spoiled, or may have a child with food allergies).

Maintaining the motivational level of children requires consistent effort on the examiner's part. Remove materials skillfully and present the next task quickly to create smooth and rapid transitions between subtests. Continue small talk while recording behavioral observations between subtests because it helps maintain a child's attention. Keep eye contact with children to facilitate rapport. Hence, familiarize yourself with the standardized instructions so that you don't have to bury your head in the manual to meticulously read them word for word.

DON'T FORGET

Keys to Maintaining Rapport

- Provide frequent praise and encouragement.
- Set up a reward system if necessary.
- Give frequent breaks if necessary.
- Reschedule testing if child is too tired, anxious, or uncooperative.
- Give eye contact; don't bury your head in the manual.
- Make smooth transitions *between* subtests. Move rapidly and use some small talk.
- Avoid small talk *during* a subtest.
- Familiarize yourself ahead of time with test directions and test materials.
  - Use precise wording of questions and directions.
  - Only the mildest of paraphrasing is acceptable occasionally.
- Be subtle, not distracting, when using a stopwatch.
- Use abbreviations when writing down child's responses.

Children occasionally refuse to cooperate altogether, are easily fatigued, or are sometimes too nervous to continue. In such situations, give several breaks throughout the testing or reschedule the testing for another day. Be aware that many children are skilled in testing the limits of examiners and may try to distract you from the task at hand. Be alert to such behavior to help keep the testing flowing. When children indicate that they do not want to go on with a subtest (perhaps a challenging subtest), provide encouragement such as "Just try your best" or "Give it your best shot." To prevent undue frustration during timed subtests, allow children a few extra seconds past the time limit to work if they are actively involved in the task. Although any response given after the time limit has expired is *not* counted toward the score, allowing the few extra seconds may lessen discouragement.

TESTING INDIVIDUALS WITH SPECIAL NEEDS

Children with special needs require certain modifications during an evaluation in order to obtain an accurate assessment. For example, children with impairments in speech, language, hearing, or vision or children with mental retardation, neurological deficits, physical handicaps, or behavioral disorders may require modifications in the assessment. Obtain thorough information from caregivers prior to beginning the assessment to determine whether children have special needs. Children's caregivers may be able to provide suggestions about the best way for children to respond stimuli (e.g., verbally or nonverbally) and may give clues as to what special accommodations are made in other structured settings, such as school.

Children with impairments — especially those with multiple handicaps — will challenge you to find what the children's best means of expression are while minimizing the impact of their handicapping conditions. Depending on the child's particular special needs and the level of the problem's severity, use various strategies during assessment procedures. Be prepared to be flexible, and heighten your awareness of factors such as fatigue, which may arise more quickly when you are testing children with special needs. The bottom line is that you should not penalize children because of the effects of sensory or motor deficits.

Modifications to standardized procedures to accommodate children with special needs influence test scores and may invalidate use of the norms. Use

CAUTION

Modifying Standardized Procedure

- Modifications to the standardized procedure to accommodate children's limitations may invalidate the scores on the test.
- Clinical judgment is key in determining what quantitative and qualitative data are interpretable from the test administration.
  - Making adaptations in the time limits allowed on speeded subtests will invalidate the use of the norms.
  - Translating the test into another language may also cause problems in interpreting the scores.

clinical judgment to determine whether the modifications made or the level of the child's impairment invalidates scores on all or part of the test. Keeping these cautions in mind, consider the following modifications to the WPPSI-III:

- Administer only the Verbal scale subtests to a child with visual impairment.
- Administer the test in American Sign Language (if you are specially trained) or allow the child to lip-read if they are deaf or hard-of-hearing.
- Extend or eliminate the time limits for children who have motor difficulties or neurological impairments.
- Allow a nonverbal (nodding or pointing) or a written response for a child who has severe expressive difficulties.
- Provide translation for a child for whom English is a second language.
- Extend the testing over more than one session for any child with special needs.

The aforementioned suggestions are clearly not an exhaustive list and are not rigid rules. To successfully evaluate children with special needs, consider administering supplemental instruments or another instrument altogether to obtain an accurate estimate of the children's abilities. Determine which types of modifications are best with careful consideration coupled with astute observation of children you are assessing.

ADMINISTRATION CONSIDERATIONS

Special Considerations for 6- and 7-Year-Olds

Either the WPPSI-III or the WISC-IV (Wechsler, 2003) may be adminis-tered to children who are ages 6–7 years, 3 months. Decide which is the most appropriate for any particular child on a case-by-case basis. To choose the instrument, consider the following: the reliability of each subtest, the floor of each subtest, the ceiling of each subtest, and the recency of the test's norms. Keeping these considerations in mind, we make the recommendations outlined in Table 2.1 when assessing children who fall in this overlapping age range.

Six- to 7-year-old children with Below Average cognitive ability will be at risk of not being capable of achieving above the level of the floor on the WISC-IV and will be able to better demonstrate what they are capable of answering on the WPPSI-III. However, if a child in this age range is esti-mated to be functioning in the Above Average range, he or she may not be able to achieve a ceiling on the WPPSI-III but will be able to be properly assessed with the more difficult items on the WISC-IV. For those children who are functioning in the Average range of cognitive ability, the WPPSI-III is, of course, preferred over the outdated WISC-III because the norms are more recent. Flynn (1987) has demonstrated that norms in the United States become outdated by about 3 points per decade. Thus, newer norms are gen-erally preferable to older norms. However, if you have both the WPPSI-III and WISC-IV available, either test will adequately assess 6- to 7-year-old children functioning in the Average range of cognitive ability.

The overlap in tests at ages 6 and 7 is beneficial in cases of retesting. If a child who was recently tested on the WPPSI-III needs to be reassessed, then

Table 2.1 Deciding on the WPPSI-III Versus the WISC-IV for Children Ages 6-0 to 7-3

Estimated Ability Level of Child	Wechsler Test to Administer
Below Average	WPPSI- III
Average	WPPSI-III or WISC-IV
Above Average	WISC-IV

the child may be retested on the WISC-IV if he or she is in the 6- to 7-year, 3-month-old age range. The reverse is also true for a child who has recently been evaluated with the WISC-IV. The WPPSI-III may be administered rather than reusing the WISC-IV and increasing the risk of practice effects.

STARTING AND DISCONTINUING SUBTESTS

The administration rules of the WPPSI-III are listed in the *Administration and Scoring Manual* and on the record form. In this section, we highlight for you the general rules.

All children ages 2-6 to 3-11 begin each subtests at Item 1. However, for children ages 4-0 to 7-3, some subtests start at predetermined items according to children's ages, whereas other subtests require that all children begin at Item 1. Rapid Reference 2.1 details which subtests have age-based starting points and which require all children to start at Item 1. The subtests with the age-based starting points allow examiners to shorten the testing times for most children but also allow easier items to be administered to those children who cannot answer items correctly at the designated starting point.

Specific reverse rules are employed that enable examiners to go back to easier items if the first items cause difficulty for the child. To administer items in reverse sequence, you require a child to return to earlier items in reverse order until a perfect score is obtained on two consecutive items. For example, if a 5-year-old child begins the WPPSI-III Matrix Reasoning subtest at Item 4 (after first completing the sample items), as suggested by the record form, but misses either Items 4 or 5, then administer the child Item 3, Item 2, Item 1, and so on, until two consecutive correct responses are given. Sample items are not part of the reversal procedure. Unlike the WISC-III and WAIS-III there is not another method for returning to easier items if the initial item(s) is missed on the WPPSI-III (the normal sequence is used on some WISC-III and WAIS-III subtests). The WPPSI-III *Administration and Scoring Manual* provides examples of reverse-sequence administration procedures (Figures 2.3, 2.4, and 2.5 on pp. 28–30 of Wechsler, 2002).

Uncertainty about how to score a response — and therefore, whether a subtest should be discontinued — will arise. Most often scoring questions appear during subtests with some subjectivity in scoring, such as Vocabulary,

≡Rapid Reference 2.1

Starting Points of WPPSI-III Subtests for Ages 4-0 to 7-3

Subtest	Age-Based Starting Point	Start Point at Item 1
Block Design	✓	
Information	✓	
Matrix Reasoning	✓	
Vocabulary	✓	
Picture Concepts	✓	
Symbol Search		✓
Word Reasoning	✓	
Coding		✓
Comprehension	✓	
Picture Completion	✓	
Similarities		✓
Receptive Vocabulary	✓	
Object Assembly	✓	
Picture Naming	✓	

Note. If a child misses either the first or second item on subtests with age-based starting points, then administer items in reverse sequence (e.g., 4, 3, 2...) until two consecutive items are answered correctly. Begin all subtests at Item 1 for children aged 2-6 to 3-11.

Similarities, and Comprehension. If you cannot quickly determine whether a response is correct, continue administering further items until you are certain that the discontinue rule has been met. This procedure is the safest because the scores can always be reviewed later and items that are passed after the discontinue criterion has been met (indeed, must be) excluded from the child's raw score on the subtest. However, the information obtained on the items that were accidentally administered beyond the discontinue criterion may provide valuable *clinical* information. If you do not follow the procedure described previously and later notice that items should have been administered beyond where the subtest was ended, the test may be unscorable.

CAUTION

....

Common General Errors in Administration

- Forgetting that if the child gets the second item administered incorrect, you may have to apply the reverse rule (even though the child got the first item administered correct).
- Forgetting that when applying the reverse rule, you administer until *two* consecutive perfect scores are obtained, *including* previously administered items.
- Neglecting to administer enough items to meet the discontinue rule.

RECORDING RESPONSES

The manner in which responses are recorded during administration of the WPPSI-III is very important. Be careful to write down responses for all items administered or attempted. This recording is especially important for the Vocabulary, Similarities, Information, and Comprehension subtests that tend to elicit a good amount of verbiage from children. However, even when children give only brief verbal responses, such as during Word Reasoning, Picture Naming, or Picture Completion, record these responses as well. Some examiners are tempted to write only children's scores rather than their exact responses, but this practice is discouraged. If only a 0 or 1 is recorded on the record form, then irretrievable clinical information may be lost. When all responses are written, this record affords the examiner an opportunity to note useful patterns in responding and subtle clinical information. Thus, attempt to capture most of what is said verbatim. Extremely verbose children challenge you to carefully record what is said. Use abbreviations to make the process of recording information easier and to balance the maintenance of rapport with the gathering of essential information (Rapid Reference 2.2 shows a list of commonly used abbreviations).

In addition to recording what a child says, also record your own statements that have influenced how children respond. For example, if you probed to clarify an answer by saying, "Tell me more about that," always record the letter *Q* in parentheses on the record form directly after the response that you queried to indicate that you prompted the child. To interpret a child's performance, integrate the fact that many of a child's responses

≡ Rapid Reference 2.2

Abbreviations for Recording Responses

@........	At
B........	Both
DK......	Don't know
EO......	Everyone
F........	Fail (child responded incorrectly)
INC.....	Incomplete (response not completed within the time limit)
LL.......	Looks like
NR......	No response
OT......	Overtime
P........	Prompt
PC......	Points correctly
PPL.....	People
PX......	Points incorrectly
Q........	Question or query
R........	Are
Shd.....	Should
SO......	Someone
ST.......	Something
↓........	Decrease
↑........	Increase
U........	You
w/.......	With
w/o.....	Without
Wld.....	Would

were elicited by querying (or that the child produced them spontaneously). Beyond noting the level of prompting typically required for a child, examine whether children typically improve the quality of their response after being queried. Some children do not add anything to their first response, "I don't know," whereas other children elaborate after a query but may not improve their score.

TIMING

Use precision in the administration of timed subtests. You will use your stopwatch for about half of the WPPSI-III subtests. Five of the seven Performance subtests require a stopwatch during administration. Use the stopwatch unobtrusively so that children are not distracted by it. If possible, use a stopwatch that does not make beeping sounds. If children ask whether they are being timed, respond with something like, "Yes, but you don't need to worry about that." The WPPSI-III record form provides a reminder in the form of a clock icon at the top of each subtest that requires a stopwatch.

As you are giving the directions to the timed subtests, have your stopwatch out and ready for use. This level of preparation is especially important when it comes to testing children who are impulsive. Children who are a bit impulsive may jump into the testing earlier than when you would anticipate, and you must be ready to time them immediately. Although beginning the timing can be tricky, knowing when to stop timing holds even more complications. Even if a child asks for clarification or repetition of an item, continue timing an item after it has begun. Although the directions explicitly ask children to tell you when they are finished on many of the timed subtests, often children do not clearly indicate that they are done. In such cases, if a child appears to have completed working on an item, ask, "Are you done?" and immediately record the time. On the other hand, if you stop timing children because you think they are finished, and then they continue working, restart the stopwatch and count the entire time work was in progress. In such cases in which the stopwatch was restarted, estimate the number of seconds that the stopwatch was off and add that to the total completion time.

Most WPPSI-III subtests have time limits regardless of whether the actual completion time is recorded or not. In fact, all but two of the untimed subtests suggest a recommended allowable time limit for each item. Specifically, for Information, Matrix Reasoning, Vocabulary, Picture Concepts, Receptive Vocabulary, and Picture Naming, the *Administration and Scoring Manual* states to "score 0 points for incorrect responses or no response within approximately 30 seconds." However, the "approximately 30 seconds" has more to do with how to administer the subtests than how to score it. The so-called time limit is intended to tell you that after about 30 seconds, you should go on to the next item. However, if you stay on the same item and the child gives the correct response while the item continues to be exposed, then you

≡Rapid Reference 2.3

Time Limits on WPPSI-III Subtests

Subtest	Time Limit	Time Recorded
Block Design	30–90s per item	Yes
Information	30s per item	No
Matrix Reasoning	30s per item	No
Vocabulary	30s per item	No
Picture Concepts	30s per item	No
Symbol Search	120s total	Yes
Word Reasoning	5s per clue	No
Coding	120s total	Yes
Comprehension	None	No
Picture Completion	20s per item	No
Similarities	None	No
Receptive Vocabulary	30s per item	No
Object Assembly	90s per item	Yes
Picture Naming	30s per item	No

should give the child credit regardless of how many seconds have elapsed. There is no justification for penalizing a child for responding late to items that have no specific time limit. Similarly, Picture Completion has a 20-second limit in which the child is allowed to respond to an item, and Word Reasoning has a 5-second limit in which the child is allowed to respond to each clue. Rapid Reference 2.3 lists which subtests are timed, which have time limits, and which have no time restrictions.

QUERYING

The judgment of examiners often comes into play during subtests that allow a wide variety of responses, such as many of the Verbal subtests. If children's responses are too vague or ambiguous to score, use judgment to decide whether to query or prompt for clarification. The administration manual of the WPPSI-III lists responses to Vocabulary, Similarities, and Comprehension items that should be queried. However, the responses in the manual are only illustrative, leaving you to decide whether to query other responses that are not presented in the *Administration and Scoring Manual*'s scoring system. The key to deciding whether to query a response is its level of ambiguity or incompleteness. Use a child's nonverbal cues, such as the tone of voice or facial expression, to help determine whether to query.

The manner in which children are queried may strongly affect how they respond. Therefore, query with neutral, nonleading questions, as suggested in the manual. Good queries are those such as "Tell me more about that" or "Explain what you mean." Avoid providing hints or clues to the answer and attempt to use the queries listed in the *Administration and Scoring Manual*. Be careful not to ask, "Can you tell me more?" because a possible answer to that question is "no." When a query is made, note it in the record form with the letter *Q* in parentheses, as mentioned earlier. Do not query spontaneously produced responses that are completely incorrect.

REPEATING ITEMS

Occasionally children you are testing may not completely hear or understand the instructions or questions that are read. In some cases, the children may ask you to repeat questions, and in some instances you may need to use your judgment to know that you should take it upon yourself to repeat what you have just said. For all but one WPPSI-III subtest, you may repeat instructions whenever it is requested or when the child does not respond. The Word Reasoning subtest is the one subtest that limits repetition. Word Reasoning rules state that you may repeat each clue one time only. Provide the repetition after the child requests it or after the child has a 5-second delay in responding.

If a child provides answers to difficult items but only gives "I don't know" responses to earlier, easier items, then readminister the earlier items (if in your judgment, the child likely knows the correct response). However, you may not readminister timed items. Factors such as anxiety or insecurity can interfere with a child's initial response on easier items, leading to quick, "I don't know" responses. Therefore, if a child correctly responds to a readministered early item, give the child credit for that correct response.

SUBTEST-BY-SUBTEST RULES OF ADMINISTRATION

The specific rules for administering each of the WPPSI-III subtests are presented in the *Administration and Scoring Manual* (and the record form also highlights the starting and discontinue rules). In this section, we present some important reminders for competent administration of each of the subtests. This section will be especially useful to new users of the tests, but may also be a good guide for refreshing your memory if you have already learned the details of test administration. We list the Verbal subtests and then the Performance subtests. Along with carefully following standardized procedures during administration, astutely observe children's behavior. Obtain detailed behavioral observations during testing to gain insight into how to interpret a particular subtest and how to link patterns of behavior across multiple subtests to provide additional interpretive information. Because of the importance of behavioral observations, for each subtest we also list key behaviors for which you may want to watch.

Verbal Subtests

Information

For Items 1–6 of Information, Stimulus Book 1 is needed for administration, but for the last Information items, only the *Administration and Scoring Manual* with the questions and the record form are needed for administration. On the first 6 items of Information, urge the child to point to the correct answer in the stimulus booklet. If the child does not respond to the first item correctly (either verbally or by pointing) then demonstrate the correct answer by pointing to the correct picture. Do not give help on any of the other Information items. Each question may be repeated as often as necessary if a child does not understand it or was not paying attention. Throughout the subtest, be aware of specific queries required for certain responses (i.e., on Information items 11, 12, 16, 18, 22, 25, 28, 29, 31, 32, and 34). Querying a child's response with neutral prompts is also perfectly acceptable. Rapid Reference 2.4 lists possible behaviors to note during administration of Information.

≡*Rapid Reference 2.4*

Behaviors to Note on Information

• Note any observable pattern in a subject's responses. Patterns of responding that include missing early, easier items and having successes on harder items may suggest anxiety, poor motivation, or retrieval difficulties.

• Observe whether items on which errors are made are those that are especially related to child's cultural background, such as a question about geography of a specific location. Such observations should be incorporated in interpretation.

• Note whether children provide unnecessarily long responses. If such long responses filled with excessive detail are given, it may be indicative of obsessiveness or a desire to impress the examiner.

• Note whether the content of failed items is consistently due to lack of knowledge in a certain area (e.g., numerical information, history, or geography).

• Inhibited children or children with speech difficulty may be more inclined to respond by gesturing or pointing (beyond the first 6 items that instruct examinees to point).

Vocabulary

Administration of the Vocabulary test requires Stimulus Book 1 in addition to the *Administration and Scoring Manual* and the record form. The first 6 items of Vocabulary are pictures that the child has to name. On the first picture item, if the child does not produce the correct response, then give the child the correct answer before moving on to the next item. There are four general types of responses to the Vocabulary picture items that require particular queries, which we review in the Don't Forget box on page 45.

The remaining Vocabulary items (6–25) are words read aloud to the child, which the child is then asked to define. Pronounce all words carefully and correctly because you want to ensure that a child's errors are not due to your unclear pronunciation. If the child does not provide a 1-point response on either Item 6 or Item 7, then provide the correct response and move on to the next item. Items may be repeated as often as necessary.

Children sometimes respond by defining a homonym of a word. If this occurs, then ask one of the following acceptable clarifying questions: "What do you mean?" or "Tell me more about it." Do not give credit for definitions of such homonyms. Children sometimes also respond with a regionalism or slang response not found in dictionaries. If you are unsure about the acceptability of a response involving a colloquialism, ask the child for another meaning. Children never receive credit for simply pointing to an object, so if a child responds nonverbally, encourage the child to give a verbal response: "Tell me in words what a _____ is." Occasionally children mishear the word that you asked them to define (e.g., defines *concise* instead of *precise*), in such a case, say, "Listen carefully, what does _____ mean?" However, you should never spell the word you are asking the child to define. As with other Verbal subtests, if a child's response if unclear, vague, or ambiguous, or you feel that it is a 0.5 or 1.5-point response, use a neutral query to prompt a better response. Rapid Reference 2.5 lists possible behaviors to note during administration of Vocabulary.

DON'T FORGET

Responses to Vocabulary Picture Items Requiring Queries

Response Type	Definition	Query for Clarification
Marginal	Response is appropriate but not 100% correct (e.g., responding *timer* to the clock).	"Yes, but what *else* is it called?"
Generalized	Response is correct but not specific enough (e.g., responding *vehicle* to the car).	"Yes, but what kind of (*Insert child's response*) is it?"
Functional	Response describes the function of an item (e.g., responding *it takes you from place to place* to the car).	"Yes, but what is it called?"
Hand gesture	Child appropriately gestures or pantomimes for an item (e.g., pretending to drive a car in response to the car item).	"Yes, but what is it called?"

═Rapid Reference 2.5

Behaviors to Note on Vocabulary

- Note whether children have difficulties pronouncing words or whether they seem uncertain about how to express that they think. Some children supplement what they say with gesturing; some may rely on nonverbal communication more than on verbal expression.
- Make note of *I don't know* responses because such responses may be indicative of children with word retrieval problems who struggle with this test. Word fluency can affect an individual's performance as much as his or her word knowledge can.
- Hearing difficulties may be apparent on this test. The Vocabulary words are not presented in a meaningful context. Note behaviors such as leaning forward during administration to hear better. Other clues to watch are indications of auditory discrimination problems (defining *confine* rather than *confide*).
- Note children who are overly verbose in their responses. They may be attempting to compensate for insecurity about their ability, or they may be obsessive, or may be inefficient in their verbal expression.

Word Reasoning

Administration of Word Reasoning requires only the *Administration and Scoring Manual* and the record form. All children administered this subtest begin with Samples A and B. Children ages 4–5 then commence with Item 1, and children ages 6–7 commence with Item 6. Because this test is orally presented, be careful in your pronunciation and make sure that the child is attending to you before you begin each item. Unlike most other verbal subtests, Word Reasoning allows each clue to be repeated only once. The first 9 items include only one clue; Items 10–23 include two clues each; Items 24–28 include three clues each. Because children do not know that some items have one clue and others have multiple clues, clearly indicate when a new item is being administered by saying, "Let's try another one."

The administration procedures for Items 10–28 (with multiple clues) require you to restate the preceding clues as more clues are added. If a child responds correctly after the first clue, then you simply circle the *Y* and move on to the next item. However, if a child responds incorrectly to the first or second clue, then present the next clue (or item). Only allow 5 seconds for the child to respond; then move on to either the next clue or next item, as appropriate. Rapid Reference 2.6 lists specific behaviors to note during Word Reasoning.

Comprehension

Only the *Administration and Scoring Manual* and the record form are needed to administer the Comprehension subtest. Children ages 4–5 begin with Item 1 and children ages 6–7 begin with Item 4. Read questions at a pace that children will easily follow. If you need to repeat a question, reread it verbatim, without abbreviation. As in other Verbal subtests (except Word Reasoning), items may be repeated as often as necessary. On the first 2 items, if a child does not give a 1-point response, then illustrate with a 1-point answer; this is done in order to teach the child the type of response you will be looking for during the task. In addition, the final item has a specific prompt that you should say if a child says they "vote at school." In addition to prompting this specified item, query responses that are unclear or ambiguous with a neutral probe. The *Administration and Scoring Manual* lists some responses that must be queried (i.e., those followed by a red *Q* in parentheses), but you may query any response that is unclear or vague. Rapid Reference 2.7 lists possible behaviors to note during administration of Comprehension.

≡Rapid Reference 2.6

Behaviors to Note on Word Reasoning

- Note whether children are more often responding correctly after the first clue or whether they need the second and third clues before getting it right.
- Some children may attend only to the first clue (or the final clue) and disregard the others. This pattern of responding may indicate inattention or may even be indicative of a child who is easily overwhelmed by verbal stimuli.
- Some children process auditory information slowly. Note whether children consistently have no response after the 5-second limit or whether they ask for an item to be repeated.

≡Rapid Reference 2.7

Behaviors to Note on Comprehension

- Observe whether unusually long verbal responses are an attempt to cover up for not actually knowing the correct response or whether the child is giving such responses because he or she tends to be obsessive about details.
- Because Comprehension requires a good amount of verbal expression, word-finding difficulties, articulation problems, and circumstantial or tangential speech may be apparent during this subtest.
- Some of the Comprehension questions have rather long verbal stimuli. Note whether inattention is affecting a child's responses to such items. For example, only part of the question may be answered.
- Note whether defensiveness is occurring in responses to some Comprehension items. For example, when asked about dog tags, if the child's response doesn't really answer the question and is something like *Dogs don't need tags on their collars,* this may be defensive responding.
- Note whether children require consistent querying to clarify their response or whether they spontaneously provide clear enough information in their answers.
- Observe children's responses carefully to determine whether poor verbal ability is the cause of a low score or whether it is more due to poor social judgment.
- Note how subjects respond to queries. Some may be threatened or frustrated with the constant interruption, and others may seem quite comfortable with the extra structure. Some children, when asked for clarification, simply restate their initial response rather than clarifying.

Similarities

The Similarities subtest requires only the *Administration and Scoring Manual* and the record form for administration. All children administered Similarities begin with Item 1. For all items, the child is asked to tell how two words are alike. The first 2 Similarities items are teaching items, so give corrective feedback if the child provides an incorrect response, as exemplified in the *Administration and Scoring Manual.* This teaching is provided to guide children to the level of response for which the test is asking. However, help on items beyond those listed in the manual is prohibited. Neutral queries may be given throughout the subtest to clarify vague or ambiguous responses.

Sample responses in the *Administration and Scoring Manual* that are followed by a red *Q* must be queried. Rapid Reference 2.8 lists possible behaviors to note during administration of Similarities.

Receptive Vocabulary

The materials needed to administer the Receptive Vocabulary subtest are the *Administration and Scoring Manual,* Stimulus Book 1, and the record form. There are three separate age-based starting points for this subtest: Item 1 for ages 2–3 (or children suspected of intellectual deficiency), Item 6 for ages 4–5, and Item 16 for ages 6–7. The child is asked to point to which pictured item represents the word that is said. Record the child's response by circling the number of the picture pointed to or DK (don't know) on the record form. If the child adds extra verbiage to his or her response, then record that on the record form as well.

On the first item only, provide the correct answer if the child responds incorrectly. Repeat items as often as necessary through about the subtest, but only repeat items verbatim; do not modify wording in your repetition. Rapid Reference 2.9 suggests behaviors to note during the administration of Receptive Vocabulary.

≡Rapid Reference 2.8

Behaviors to Note on Similarities

- Observe whether the child benefits from feedback on items that provide an example by the examiner (if feedback was given). Children who learn from the example given by the examiner may have flexibility, whereas those who cannot may be more rigid or concrete.
- Observe whether the quality of response decreases as the items become more difficult.
- Length of verbal responses give important behavioral clues. Overly elaborate responses may suggest obsessiveness.
- Quick responses or abstract responses to easy items may indicate overlearned associations rather than high-level abstract reasoning.
- How a child handles frustration may be apparent on this test. For example, the child may respond by saying, "They are not alike," indicating defensiveness or avoidance. Other children may give up when faced with frustration by repeatedly responding, "I don't know."

≡Rapid Reference 2.9

Behaviors to Note on Receptive Vocabulary

- Note whether children tend to respond repeatedly by pointing to the same location on each page. Such responding may indicate lack of motivation or lack of understanding the task.
- Note whether children respond impulsively or whether they carefully and methodically examine each choice before responding.
- Note whether children provide any verbal explanation for a wrong choice; that is, there may be some logic that they used to arrive at their response.
- Some children will guess when they are uncertain, whereas others do not want to attempt items for fear of making a mistake. Note whether children show a particular style in responding when they are uncertain.

Picture Naming

The materials needed to administer the Picture Naming subtest are the *Administration and Scoring Manual,* Stimulus Book 2, and the record form. As in Receptive Vocabulary, there are three separate age-based starting points for this subtest: Item 1 for ages 2–3 (or children suspected of intellectual deficiency), Item 7 for ages 4–5, and Item 11 for ages 6–7. On Item 1 only, provide the correct response if the child responds incorrectly or does not respond at all.

During this subtest, children name pictures that are displayed in the stimulus book. Do not penalize children for articulation problems (e.g., pronouncing *star* as *tar* or *teeth* as *teef.* If it is apparent that a child knows the correct name of the object but mispronounces it, give the child credit.

Query responses that are unclear or that are followed by a red *Q.* Four particular types of responses require query (the same response situations as in the picture items of the Vocabulary subtest listed in the Don't Forget box on page 45). In addition, Item 9 requires an additional special query if a child responds "toothpaste" to the picture of the toothbrush. Be sure to record all of a child's response verbatim. Also note behaviors observed during assessment of Picture Naming (see Rapid Reference 2.10).

Performance Subtests

Block Design

The stimuli materials for Block Design include red and white blocks (some single colored and others bicolored), a stopwatch, the *Administration and*

Scoring Manual, and the record form. Children ages 2–3 (and children suspected of intellectual deficiency) begin with Item 1, and children ages 4–7 begin with Item 6. Timing is important and must be done and recorded vigilantly. Timing begins after you read the last word of instructions and ends when children say or gesture that they are done (if you are unsure, simply ask whether the child has finished working).

Some Block Design items are presented as a block model (Items 1–12) and others are presented as a picture (Items 14–20). Look at the record form to see how many blocks are needed for each item, and remove all unnecessary blocks from the child's view after each item is administered. When setting up the last 10 items, which use bicolor blocks, only one block should have a red-and-white side facing up. However, before the bicolor blocks are used for the final 10 items, administer the bicolor-block sample item to introduce the child to the new type of blocks.

Two trials are permitted on the first 6 items. If the child completes the design correctly within the time limit, move on to the next item; otherwise, demonstrate a second time how to complete the design and give the child a second trial. Beginning with Item 13, a picture of a block design is presented

≡Rapid Reference 2.10

Behaviors to Note on Picture Naming

- Note any articulation and pronunciation problems that a child may have. Although mispronunciations are not penalized on this subtest, they can give insight into difficulties a child may have in his or her day-to-day communications.

- Note whether children have a pattern of responding with generalized responses. If they consistently give a more global concept rather than the specific desired response, they may think that you are asking them to do something more complex than what the task demands.

- If a child consistently describes objects by describing the function rather than by saying what the objects are, the child may have word-finding difficulties. Such talking around an answer by including elaborate functional descriptions or other descriptions may mask such word-finding problems.

- Repeated hand gesturing may also be indicative of word-finding problems or general expressive language difficulties.

- Personalized responses such as *my mommy has one* or *my brother took mine* may indicate immaturity.

for the child to copy in addition to a three-dimensional model; then on Items 14–20, only the picture is shown. The record form clearly denotes the presentation method of each item.

Remember several general directions during administration of Block Design. Sit the child squarely at the table because orientation of the child to the design is very important. Place the model or stimulus book approximately 7 ft away from the child's edge of the table and slightly to the left of the child's midline if the child is right-handed and slightly to the right if the child is left-handed. When laying out the blocks for the child, place a variety of sides facing upward. When demonstrating the construction of a design, verbally mediate your process (e.g., "I put a red block here and a white one here").

Separate rules are used for Part A and Part B of Block Design regarding a child's rotated designs. On Part A (Items 1–10), children are not penalized for rotation of a design, but in Part B (Items 11–20) consider a rotation of 30° or more an error. On both Parts A and B, if a child rotates the design 30° or more, then correct the child — one time in Part A and once in Part B. If the child completely reverses the design, the child is not penalized in Part A, but consider reversals in Part B a failure. In both Parts A and B, children are not penalized for gaps or misalignments between blocks that are less than or equal to .25 in (larger gaps are penalized). Record children's responses, including rotations and misalignments, by sketching the final designs in the spaces provided on the record form. This pictorial record will allow analysis of any patterns of responding for interpretive purposes. Behaviors to note during Block Design are listed in Rapid Reference 2.11.

Matrix Reasoning

The materials needed to administer Matrix Reasoning include the *Administration and Scoring Manual,* Stimulus Book 1, and the record form. Begin administration of Matrix Reasoning with the three sample items for all children. Then proceed to Item 1 for children age 4, to Item 4 for children age 5, and to Item 6 for children ages 6–7. During this subtest, children look at an incomplete matrix and select the missing portion from four or five response options. Children must indicate their responses by pointing or by saying the number of the option. If any other verbalization is given as a response, ask the child to clarify ("Show me which one."). Responses are simple to record — just circle the appropriate number or DK. However, if a

≡Rapid Reference 2.11

Behaviors to Note on Block Design

- Observe problem-solving styles during children's manipulation of the blocks. Some use a trial-and-error approach, whereas others appear to haphazardly continue to complete the design, seemingly without learning from earlier errors.

- What level of planning is involved? Does the child systematically examine the problem and appear to carefully plan before moving any of the blocks or does the child appear impulsive?

- Observe whether the subject tends to pair up blocks and then integrates the smaller segments into the whole. On the designs requiring nine blocks, observe whether children work from the outside in or perhaps start in one corner and work their way around the design.

- Motor coordination and hand preference may be apparent during this task. Note whether individuals seem clumsy in their manipulation of the blocks, whether they have hands that are noticeably trembling, or whether they move very quickly and steadily.

- Look to see whether children refer back to the model while they are working. This could be indicative of visual memory ability, cautiousness, or other factors.

- Examine whether children tend to be obsessively concerned with details (such as lining up the blocks perfectly). Such behaviors may negatively affect the child's speed.

- Observe how well children persist, especially when the task becomes more difficult and they may face frustration. Note how well they tolerate frustration. Do they persist and keep on working even past the time limit or do they give up with time to spare?

- Look to see whether children lose the square shape for some designs, even if they have managed to recreate the overall pattern. This kind of response could be indicative of figure-ground problems.

- Note whether children are noticeably twisting their bodies to obtain a different perspective on the model or whether they are rotating their own designs. Such behaviors may be indicative of visual-perceptual difficulties.

- It is important also to note whether children fail to recognize that their designs look different from the models.

child responds with additional verbiage, be sure to record that on the record form as well. Rapid Reference 2.12 lists other behaviors to note during the administration of Matrix Reasoning.

≡Rapid Reference 2.12

Behaviors to Note on Matrix Reasoning

- Note whether children talk their way through the problems, using verbal mediation, or whether they are more apt to simply use mental imagery to work to the solution.
- Observe whether children need to touch the stimulus book to aid in their problem solving. Touching the stimuli may help some children visualize the solution.
- Although this test is not timed, examine whether children process the information slowly, carefully, and methodically, or whether they work more quickly and impulsively.
- Note whether children attend to part of the stimuli but miss other essential parts to successfully complete the matrix.
- Make note of signs of frustration or anxiety, especially when the problems become more complex.
- Note whether children's problem solving includes trying each of the given possible solutions one by one or first attempting to come up with a solution and then checking the row of choices to find the solution that they had created.

Picture Concepts

The materials needed to administer Picture Concepts include the *Administration and Scoring Manual,* Stimulus Book 1, and the record form. Administer both sample items to all children. Then begin with Item 1 for children ages 4–5 (and for those suspected of intellectual deficiency) and with Item 8 for children ages 6–7. During Picture Concepts, children are presented with two or three rows of pictures and then choose one picture from each row to form a group with a common characteristic.

Children can respond to an item by pointing, naming, or stating the corresponding numbers of the chosen pictures. If a child selects more than one picture in a single row, then you may direct them as often as necessary to pick one item in each row (the specific prompts are listed in the *Administration and Scoring Manual*). If a child asks the name of a picture, you may provide the name. Record responses simply by circling the number of the child's response. However, also record additional verbiage that the child includes during his or her response. Rapid Reference 2.13 lists behaviors to note during this subtest.

≡Rapid Reference 2.13

Behaviors to Note on Picture Concepts

- Note any statement that explains the concept by which the child grouped the pictures. Explanations are especially valuable for understanding errors. For example, errors that are made because a child consistently groups by matching color may indicate very concrete thinking, whereas errors made because a child described an elaborate, unusual way to connect two objects may indicate something completely different.

- Note when errors seem to be due to children always selecting pictures in the same location (e.g., one above the other). Such a pattern may be due to lack of motivation or lack of understanding of the subtest demands.

- Note whether and how children respond when the items become more abstract and difficult. Do they take a guess when uncertain or do they prefer to state, "I don't know" and move on?

- Note how rapidly a child responds to each item. Some children may be impulsive in responding, whereas others may be more careful and methodical in their processing of the items.

Symbol Search

Along with the appropriate Symbol Search form, examiners need two No. 2 lead pencils without erasers, a stopwatch, the *Administration and Scoring Manual,* and the record form for administration of this subtest. Prior to beginning the subtest, children must complete sample items and practice items, both of which are not timed. Do not to skip any of the demonstration, even if the child appears to readily understand the task. The directions to the sample, practice, and test items are lengthy and require multiple rehearsals so that you will be able to complete them while maintaining rapport with the child. A minimum of paraphrasing is acceptable while you read the directions; make every attempt to state them verbatim from the *Administration and Scoring Manual.* Don't begin the task until the child clearly understands the directions.

The timing of 120 seconds should be exact. Some children may purposefully or inadvertently skip items — remind them to go in order and not skip any. Other children may appear to stop the task before the 120-second time limit is up — remind them to keep going until they are told to stop. Rapid Reference 2.14 lists several behaviors to note during administration of Symbol Search.

≡Rapid Reference 2.14

Behaviors to Note on Symbol Search

- Note how the child handles the pencil. Is there pressure? Is the pencil dropped? Does the child seem coordinated?
- Observe attention and concentration. Is the child's focus consistent throughout the task, or does it wane as time goes on?
- Look to see whether children check each row of symbols only once or whether they go back and recheck the row of symbols in an item more than once. Obsessive concern with detail may be noted.
- Make note of the child's response style. Impulsivity and reflectivity are usually observable in this task.
- Consider whether children are utilizing their visual memory well. Watch eye movements to determine whether the child is moving back and forth several times between the Target and Search Groups before making a choice.
- Observe whether a child's response rate is consistent throughout the subtest. Note the number of items answered during each of the four 30-second intervals within the 120-second time limit.

Coding

Along with the appropriate Coding form, you need two No. 2 lead pencils without erasers, a stopwatch, the *Administration and Scoring Manual,* and the record form for administration of this subtest. If a child is left-handed, be prepared to place an extra Coding response key to the right of the child's response sheet so that the child may have an unobstructed view of the Coding key (some left-handers' hand position will obstruct the key on the record form).

Similar to those of Symbol Search, the directions for Coding are very lengthy and contain a lot of important detail. Be prepared to look up from reading the directions to check that the child is following what is being said. Therefore, rehearse the directions well and read carefully to each child. During administration of the sample items, if the child makes any mistake, correct it immediately. If the child does not appear to understand the task after the sample items are completed, then give further instruction until the child clearly understands the task.

Once the 120-second subtest has begun, be an astute observer. Children are not to omit any item or complete all items of one type at a time, and if

≡Rapid Reference 2.15

Behaviors to Note on Coding

- Watching the eye movements of children taking the test can be very informative. Consistent glancing back and forth from the Coding key to the response sheet may be indicative of a poor memory or insecurity. In contrast, a child who uses the key infrequently may have a good short-term memory and remember number-symbol pairs readily.

- Impulsivity in responding may be observed when a child quickly but carelessly fills in symbols across the rows.

- Shaking hands, a tight grip on the pencil, or pressure on the paper when the child is writing may be indicative of anxiety.

- Fatigue, boredom, or inattention may become apparent as the Coding subtest progresses. Noting the number of symbols copied during 30-second intervals provides helpful behavioral information.

- Obsessiveness or attention to detail may be noted if children spend a significant amount of time trying to perfect each of the symbols that are drawn.

- Note whether children have difficulty understanding that they are to work quickly. This behavior may be related to immaturity.

they do this, direct them to, "Do them in order. Don't skip any." Some children appear to stop midway through the task — remind them to continue until you tell them to stop. Occasionally children appear frustrated at the end of the test because they were only able to complete a few lines; in such situations, reassure the child that most children are not able to complete the entire sheet. All of the aforementioned behaviors are worthy of noting. As discussed in Rapid Reference 2.15, glean clinical information about problem-solving style, planning, and memory during this subtest.

Picture Completion

To administer Picture Completion, you need Stimulus Book 2, along with the *Administration and Scoring Manual,* the record form, and a stopwatch. Children are allowed a maximum of 20 seconds to solve each item.

Give sample Items A and B to all children administered this subtest. The samples are provided to ensure that children completely understand what is required of them before beginning the task. After the samples, children age 4 begin with Item 1, children age 5 begin with Item 4, and children ages 6–7 begin with Item 7. Several queries are allowed as often as necessary throughout the subtest to clarify a child's response. The Don't Forget box on this page lists the Picture Completion queries. Examiners sometimes err in administering this subtest by forgetting to query a child at the necessary times, so be sure to review these queries before beginning.

Consider either verbal or nonverbal responses acceptable answers. However, if a child's nonverbal response is correct, but his or her verbal response is incorrect, consider the answer spoiled and give no credit. Some children respond to the question "What part is missing?" by giving a verbal response, but others are more comfortable with pointing. Record *PC* when children point correctly and *PX* when they point incorrectly. Consistent nonverbal (e.g., pointing) responses are worth noting. Rapid Reference 2.16 lists other behavioral observations to note during administration of this subtest.

Object Assembly

Object Assembly requires examiners to manipulate many materials at once: puzzles, a stopwatch, the *Administration and Scoring Manual,* and a record form. Accurate timing is essential; allow children only 90 seconds for each

DON'T FORGET

Picture Completion Queries

Response Type	Example	Query for Clarification
Ambiguous or incomplete	*Fuzzy part*	"Show me where you mean." (to leg missing on bear)
Names the pictured object	*Bear*	"Yes, but what is missing?" (to leg missing on bear)
Mentions part that is off the page	*Bear's chair*	"A part is missing *in* the picture. What is it that is missing?" (to leg missing on bear)
Mentions an unessential part	*Bear's jacket*	"Yes, but what other part is missing?" (to leg missing on bear)

≡*Rapid Reference 2.16*

Behaviors to Note on Picture Completion

- The speed at which a child responds is noteworthy. A reflective individual may take more time in responding (but most likely can respond within the 20-second time limit), whereas an impulsive individual may respond very quickly but incorrectly.
- Note whether the child is persistent in stating that nothing is missing from the picture (rather than responding, "I don't know") because such a response style may reflect oppositionality or inflexibility.
- If nonverbal responses (pointing) are consistently observed, it may be evidence of a word retrieval problem in children. Although it is acceptable to give a nonverbal response, it is far more common to give a verbal response.
- Verbal responses that are imprecise (*the thingy that helps the boat move*) or overly elaborative (*elongated piece of wood that is carefully placed on each side of the boat which are used by boaters to help propel the boat through the water*) are also noteworthy.
- Note whether children give responses that consistently indicate a focus on details.
- After individuals have been redirected (i.e., *Yes, but what is the most important part that is missing?*), it is important to note whether they still continue to respond with the same quality of response. This persistence in approach may be indicative of a lack of understanding of the task or inflexibility in thinking.

item, and although bonus points are not awarded, be sure to record exact completion times. Although there are no sample items on Object Assembly, Items 1 and 2 contain two trials and examiners demonstrate the assembly of these puzzles before children are instructed to complete it themselves. If children do not correctly assembly the puzzles in Items 1 or 2 on their first attempt, then you again demonstrate the correct assembly before giving children a second trial.

Young children often do not understand the concept of being timed and needing to work as quickly as they can. During the subtest, if a child hesitates or seems to merely be playing with the pieces, remind them to "Work as fast as you can." For each item, tell the child in the instructions what item the assembled puzzle will be. If a child asks again what the item is during the subtest, it is acceptable to remind them.

The handling of materials needed for this subtest while keeping a child's attention has been greatly simplified in this version of the WPPSI. Unlike the WPPSI-R, this version of Object Assembly requires no layout shield (which was utilized to prevent children from seeing the puzzle before the examiner arranged it). To set up each item, simply place the puzzle pieces number-side up, in sequential order in your hand. Then line them up numerically from your left to your right. Place pieces with numbers having a single underline in the first row and place those with two underlines in the second row. Then to expose the pieces, flip the pieces from top to bottom (not right to left). If children turn pieces over during an item, unobtrusively turn them back over again.

Make careful behavioral observations during this subtest because much can be gleaned from this test beyond the final score. Some children, for example, will almost completely have the puzzle solved but then become frustrated and mix up the pieces to start totally anew. Rapid Reference 2.17 lists possible behaviors to note during administration of Object Assembly.

⟰Rapid Reference 2.17

Behaviors to Note on Object Assembly

- As on other performance subtests, observe how the child handles the puzzle pieces. Motor coordination and hand preference may be noted on this test.
- Note problem-solving approach (trial-and-error versus systematic planned approach), which can be discerned by observing the child's approach to the task.
- Note the speed at which children proceed. Do children appear impulsive and careless but quick, or are they careful, slow, and methodical?
- Note whether children can piece together parts but cannot get the whole. For example, some children will be able to assemble the front and back of the cow separately but cannot figure out how to connect them.
- Note when children verbalize what the object is but are unable to construct it correctly; this may be indicative of integration difficulties or problems with motor output.
- Observe and note behaviors indicative of obsessiveness with details on this test (as with Block Design). Some children may spend unnecessary time trying to get each of the pieces perfectly aligned.
- Observe how children handle frustration. Some may insist that you have not given them all the pieces. Yet other children merely appear to give up well before the time limit has expired.

CAUTION

Common Pitfalls in Administering Verbal Subtests

Information

- Defining words if asked by child
- Forgetting to give required prompts to an incomplete answer or to responses identified with an asterisk
- Being unaware that neutral queries may be given to Information responses that are incomplete or ambiguous

Vocabulary

- Not recording exact verbal responses
- Forgetting to provide the correct response for Items 1 and 2 when necessary
- Not querying vague or incomplete responses appropriately
- Spelling the words if asked

Word Reasoning

- Forgetting to administer Samples A and B to all children
- Forgetting to administer Sample C before Item 10
- Forgetting to say, "Let's try another one" to cue a child that you are beginning a new item
- Forgetting to automatically repeat preceding clues when administering the second and third clues
- Forgetting to record an R on the record form if a clue is repeated
- Forgetting to repeat each clue one time only if so requested or after approximately 5 seconds with no response
- Giving a child longer than 5 seconds to respond

Comprehension

- Forgetting to provide the correct response for Items 1 and 2 when necessary
- Neglecting to write down the exact verbal response
- Forgetting to query responses that are difficult to score or are noted with Q
- Explaining the meaning of a word if asked

Similarities

- Forgetting to administer Trial 2 of Items 1 or 2 when necessary
- Forgetting to emphasize the word *both* when reading instructions
- Forgetting to query responses that are difficult to score or are noted with Q
- Overquerying or underquerying vague responses

(continued)

Receptive Vocabulary
- Forgetting to circle a child's response for every item
- Forgetting to provide the correct response if necessary for Item 1

Picture Naming
- Forgetting to provide the correct response if necessary for Item 1
- Forgetting to query marginal responses, generalized responses, functional descriptions, and hand gestures
- Forgetting to provide the additional specific query for Item 9 if necessary

CAUTION

Common Pitfalls in Administering Performance Subtests

Block Design
- Forgetting to administer Trial 2 when necessary on Items 1–6
- Neglecting to give the correct number or type of blocks for an item
- Placing the model in an incorrect position
- Correcting block rotations more than two times
- Remembering to administer items in reverse order until credit is obtained on two consecutive designs if a child fails *either* trial of Item 6 (for a 4- to 7-year-old who begins with Item 6)
- Forgetting to administer Samples A and B before beginning Part B
- Forgetting to model Item 13 as well as present the stimulus picture
- Forgetting to record completion time (or recording it incorrectly)

Matrix Reasoning
- Forgetting to administer sample items to all children
- Forgetting to prompt the child as often as necessary by saying "Show me which one"
- Forgetting to circle the child's responses for all items
- Forgetting to follow the stop rule
- Incorrectly discontinuing too early

Picture Concepts
- Forgetting to administer the sample items to all children
- Forgetting to provide the correct grouping concept on Samples A and B when necessary

- Forgetting to circle the child's response from each row of items
- Forgetting to prompt the child to pick one picture from each row as often as necessary

Symbol Search

- Proceeding with task before the child clearly understands what is required
- Burying head in manual while reading directions
- Forgetting to turn the page for the child when he or she reaches the end of a page
- Not paying attention to child and allowing him or her to skip over items
- Forgetting to record the completion time

Coding

- Losing rapport with the child by burying head in administration manual while reading Coding's long directions
- Proceeding with task before the child clearly understands what is required
- Not paying attention to child and allowing him or her to skip over items
- Forgetting to place an extra response booklet to the right of the child's response booklet when a left-handed child has an obstructed view of the key
- Forgetting to record the completion time

Picture Completion

- Forgetting to time items (20s limit)
- Forgetting to administer sample items to all children
- Forgetting to note pointing with PC and PX
- Forgetting to give allowed queries as often as necessary
- Forgetting to give the correct response to Items 1 and 2 if the child doesn't give the correct response

Object Assembly

- Forgetting to tell the child what the pieces make in the introduction to each item
- Administering more puzzles than needed (discontinue after three consecutive failures)
- Neglecting to turn over puzzle pieces if they are not face up
- Forgetting to count the number of junctures correctly completed at the time limit when allowing a child to work beyond the time limit
- Incorrectly counting the number of completed junctures

TEST YOURSELF

1. **You have to test a 6 1/2-year-old girl, believed to have below-average intelligence, who is also suspected of having a language disorder. Which Wechsler scale should be administered?**

   (a) The WPPSI-III, because it has a more adequate floor for lower-functioning children.

   (b) The WPPSI-R, because it has a larger normative sample.

   (c) The WISC-IV, because it was developed from a more sound theoretical base than the WPPSI-III.

   (d) The WPPSI-III, because it was specifically designed to assess children with mental retardation.

2. **It is never appropriate to have the parent of a 3-year-old child accompany you to the test room because the parent may be distracting to the child.** True or False? _____

3. **You are explaining to a parent how to describe the testing to their 7-year-old child; the following is a good example of what the parent may say to the child:**

   (a) You will be tested by the doctor for about 2 or 3 hours.

   (b) If you finish all of the tests, even the hard tests, you will get a treat.

   (c) You just have to play with the nice doctor for a little bit. She'll let you pick the game you want to play.

   (d) You are going to look at some puzzles, play with some blocks, be asked some questions, and do other activities like that.

4. **You are scheduled to test a 5-year-old girl with cerebral palsy. What are some ways that you may need to adapt the testing to accommodate her?** _____

5. **While administering the Similarities subtest, you realize that if the child obtains a 0 score on the next item he or she will have reached the discontinue rule. The response the child gives to this question, even after a query, seems to fall right between a 0-point and 1-point response. You should**

   (a) take an extra few minutes to reread all of the responses in the 0-point and 1-point category while the child waits patiently.

   (b) continue administering further items until you are sure that the discontinue criteria has been met.

(c) count it as a 0-point response because the child was so close to meeting the discontinue rule.

(d) give the child the benefit of the doubt and score it as a 1-point response.

6. **If a child stops during the middle of a timed test to ask you a question, it is important to immediately stop timing and resume the timing only when the child's question has been answered.** True or False?

7. **You can query virtually any verbal response that the child gives if you feel that it is vague, incomplete or ambiguous.** True or False?

8. **Jake is being administered a subtest and asks for an item to be repeated. On which of the following subtests would that procedure be allowed?**

(a) Object Assembly

(b) Word Reasoning

(c) Vocabulary

(d) Block Design

Answers: 1. a; 2. False; 3. d; 4. Extend or eliminate time limits, administer only the Verbal scale if she has severe motor difficulties, allow nonverbal or a written response if she has severe expressive difficulties; 5. b; 6. False; 7. True; 8. c.

Three

HOW TO SCORE THE WPPSI-III

TYPES OF SCORES

Administration of the WPPSI-III results in three types of scores: raw scores, scaled scores, and standard score composites (IQs and quotients). The raw score is the first score that you will encounter. It is simply the total number of points earned on a single subtest. Alone, the raw score is meaningless because it is not a norm-referenced score. To interpret a child's raw score, convert it into a standard score (either a scaled score, IQ, or other composite). The various metrics for each type of Wechsler standard score are listed in Rapid Reference 3.1. Individual subtests produce scaled scores with a mean of 10 and a standard deviation of 3 (ranging from 1 to 19 for most subtests). The IQs and other composites have a mean of 100 and a standard deviation of 15 (ranging from about 45–50 to 150–160 for most WPPSI-III scales).

Because intellectual ability in the general population is distributed on a normal curve, most children earn scores on these tests that are within 1 standard deviation from the mean. About 66 of every 100 children tested earn IQs or indexes between 85 and 115. A greater number of children (about 95%) earn scores that are from 70 to 130 (2 standard deviations from the mean). The number of children earning extremely high scores (above 130) is only about 2.2%, and the number earning very low scores (less than 70) is also about 2.2%.

≡Rapid Reference 3.1

Metrics for Standard Scores

Type of Standard Score	Mean	Standard Deviation	Range of Values
Scaled Score	10	3	1–19
Verbal IQ (V-IQ)	100	15	49–150 (ages 2-6 to 3-11)
			46–155 (ages 4-0 to 7-3)
Performance IQ (P-IQ)	100	15	48–150 (ages 2-6 to 3-11)
			45–155 (ages 4-0 to 7-3)
Full Scale IQ (FS-IQ)	100	15	41–155 (ages 2-6 to 3-11)
			40–160 (ages 4-0 to 7-3)
General Language Composite (GLC)	100	15	51–150 (ages 2-6 to 3-11)
			45–152 (ages 4-0 to 7-3)
Processing Speed Quotient (PSQ)	100	15	46–150 (ages 4-0 to 7-3)

STEP BY STEP: HOW THE WPPSI-III IS SCORED

Raw Scores

Each of the items of a subtest contributes directly to the raw score. The scoring for most of the WPPSI-III subtests is not complex and can be readily done, but there are a few subtests (mainly on the Verbal Scales) in which subjectivity presents constant thorns to the examiner during the scoring process. Pointers for proper scoring of tricky subjective responses are discussed later in this chapter. Most examiners who can do simple addition (with or without the aid of counting on fingers and toes) can calculate the subtests' raw scores. The Caution box on page 69 notes errors that examiners make in the calculation of raw scores.

Scaled Scores

Converting the raw scores obtained from the WPPSI-III to scaled scores is a simple process. The materials needed to complete this process are as follows: (a) child's chronological age, (b) child's raw scores on all subtests, and (c) A.1 from the *WPPSI-III Administration and Scoring Manual* (Wechsler, 2002). After you transfer the raw scores from the inside of the record form to the front cover, begin the conversion to scaled scores. In the appropriate table (determined by the child's chronological age), look up the child's raw score and find its corresponding scaled score equivalent. Write the scaled score equivalents in the appropriate boxes on the front of the record form. First record all scaled scores in one column, then record each of the scaled scores in the appropriate IQ column (either Verbal or Performance) or other composite score column (either Processing Speed or General Language).

CAUTION

Common Errors in Raw Score Calculation

- Neglecting to add points earned from the first few items that weren't administered to the total raw score
- Neglecting to add the points recorded on one page of the record form with the points recorded on the next (e.g., WPPSI-III Comprehension lists the first 15 questions on one page and the last 5 on the next)
- Forgetting to subtract the number of incorrect responses from correct responses on Symbol Search
- Neglecting to multiply the number of correct junctures by the designated number on Object Assembly
- Transferring total raw scores incorrectly from inside the record form to the front page of the record form
- Miscalculating the raw score sum via an addition mistake
- Including points earned on items that were presented after the discontinue criterion was met

CAUTION

Common Errors in Obtaining Scaled Scores

- Miscalculating a sum when adding scores to obtain the raw score or the sum of scaled scores
- Writing illegibly, leading to errors
- Using a score conversion table that references the wrong age group
- Misreading across the rows of the score conversion tables
- Forgetting to write the scaled scores down in all the columns of all composites

IQs and Other Standard Scores

Obtaining the IQs and factor indexes is next in the process of score conversion. Carefully follow the following steps to obtain accurate scores.

Converting Scaled Scores to IQs

1. Calculate the sum of the appropriate subtest scaled scores for the Verbal and Performance IQs. For ages 2-6 to 3-11 , the Verbal scale typically consists of Receptive Vocabulary and Information, and the Performance scale typically consists of Block Design and Object Assembly. For ages 4-0 to 7-3, the Verbal scale typically consists of Information, Vocabulary, and Word Reasoning, and the Performance scale typically consists of Block Design, Matrix Reasoning, and Picture Concepts. See the Don't Forget box on page 71 for a important considerations to remember when summing supplemental subtest scaled scores.

2. For children ages 2-6 to 3-11, calculate the sum of scaled scores for the Full Scale by summing all subtests comprising the Verbal and Performance scales (four subtests total). For children ages 4-0 to 7-3, calculate the sum of scaled scores for the Full Scale by summing all subtests comprising the Verbal and Performance scales plus Coding (seven subtests total).

3. If the appropriate subtests have been administered, calculate the General Language (GL) sum of scaled scores by adding Receptive

Vocabulary and Picture Naming (for all ages). For children ages 4-0 to 7-3, also calculate the Processing Speed (PS) sum of scaled scores by adding Symbol Search and Coding.

4. Transfer the scores for the three scales (plus the GL and PS if the appropriate subtests were administered) to the *Sum of Scaled Scores to Composite Score Conversions* table that has separate columns for sums of scaled scores and composite scores.

DON'T FORGET

Things to Remember About Supplemental Subtest Scores

- Be careful not to sum supplemental subtests with the core subtests to determine Verbal, Performance, or Full Scale scores unless they were substituted for a core subtest.

- Note that supplemental subtest scaled scores are recorded in parentheses to remind examiners that they are separate from the core subtests.

5. For each scale, determine the appropriate IQ (and composite) based on the sum of scaled scores. See Tables A.2 to A.10 of the *WPPSI-III Administration and Scoring Manual* (Wechsler, 2002).

6. Record the percentile ranks and confidence intervals for each of the scales, which are also found in Tables A.2 to A.10 of the *WPPSI-III Administration and Scoring Manual* (Wechsler, 2002).

Special Considerations for IQs With Subtest Raw Scores of Zero

When you are converting raw scores to scaled scores and IQs, subtest raw scores of zero deserve special consideration. The problem with a raw score of zero is that you cannot determine what the child's true ability to perform on the test is. A zero raw score does not indicate that a child lacks a particular ability, but it does mean that the particular subtests did not have enough low-level easy items (floor items) to adequately assess the child's skills. For children ages 2-6 to 3-11, unless children obtain raw scores greater than zero on at least one of the Verbal subtests, do not derive the Verbal IQ. Likewise, if more than one zero raw score on Performance subtests is obtained, then do not derive the Performance IQ. If a child ages 2-6 to 3-11 obtains three or

DON'T FORGET

Subtests Included in WPPSI-III Composites

Verbal IQ		Performance IQ		General Language Composite		Processing Speed Quotient	Full Scale IQ	
Ages 2-6 to 3-11	Ages 4-0 to 7-3	Ages 2-6 to 3-11	Ages 4-0 to 7-3	Ages 2-6 to 3-11	Ages 4-0 to 7-3	Ages 4-0 to 7-3 only	Ages 2-6 to 3-11	Ages 4-0 to 7-3
Receptive Vocabulary	Information	Block Design	Block Design	Receptive Vocabulary	Receptive Vocabulary	Coding	Receptive Vocabulary	Block Design
Information	Vocabulary	Object Assembly	Matrix Reasoning	Picture Naming	Picture Naming	Symbol Search	Block Design	Information
	Word Reasoning		Picture Concepts				Information	Matrix Reasoning
							Object Assembly	Vocabulary
								Picture Concepts
								Word Reasoning
								Coding

four raw scores of zero of the Full Scale subtests, do not compute a Full Scale IQ. Do not derive the GLC if the total of the raw scores are zero.

For children ages 4-0 to 7-3, unless children obtain raw scores greater than zero on at least one of the Verbal subtests, do not derive the Verbal IQ or the Full Scale IQ. Likewise, if more than 2 zero raw scores on Performance subtests are obtained, then do not derive the Performance IQ or the Full Scale IQ. If a child ages 4-0 to 7-3 obtains raw scores of zero on both Processing Speed subtests, do not calculate the PSQ, and if the total raw score for General Language subtests is zero, then do not calculate the GLC.

Prorating and Subtest Substitution Options

The WPPSI-III provides options for prorated scoring if the regular core subtests that comprise the Verbal or Performance IQ are not usable. This situation may occur if a subtest is spoiled during administration or if a special handicap makes the administration of a particular subtest inadvisable. For children ages 2-6 to 3-11, only the Full Scale IQ can be prorated; the Verbal IQ, Performance IQ, and General Language Composite cannot. Thus, for the youngest age group, if three of the four subtests contributing to the Full Scale are valid, then prorate the IQ by consulting Table A.11 of the *Administration and Scoring Manual* (Wechsler, 2002).

Verbal, Performance, and Full Scale IQs may be prorated for children ages 4-0 to 7-3. To prorate either Verbal or Performance IQs, you must have two valid subtests. To prorate the Full Scale IQ, you must have either five or six valid subtest scores. Prorate these IQs by consulting Table A.11 of the *Administration and Scoring Manual* (Wechsler, 2002). Be sure to record the abbreviation *PRO* in the margin of the record form to indicate that the score was prorated.

If you have administered the full battery of WPPSI-III subtests, then you may be able to substitute a supplemental subtest for a core one rather than prorating a score. The decision to substitute one subtest for another cannot be arbitrarily made. There must be a substantial reason supporting the choice to make the substitution. If a core subtest is spoiled or you are unable to administer a subtest because of a child's disability, then consider substituting a supplemental subtest for the core subtest. The decision to substitute Symbol Search for Coding may be made, for example, if Coding was spoiled

DON'T FORGET

Replacing Core WPPSI-III Subtests

Original Subtest	→	Replacement Subtest
Receptive Vocabulary	→	Picture Naming [a]
Block Design	→	Picture Completion, Object Assembly [b]
Information	→	Comprehension, Similarities [b]
Matrix Reasoning	→	Picture Completion, Object Assembly [b]
Vocabulary	→	Comprehension, Similarities [b]
Picture Concepts	→	Picture Completion, Object Assembly [b]
Word Reasoning	→	Comprehension, Similarities [b]
Coding	→	Symbol Search [b]

[a] Only for ages 2-6 to 3-11.
[b] Only for ages 4-0 to 7-3.

because of a child's fine motor impairment. Fine motor impairment is also valid reason to substitute Picture Completion for Block Design. If you are aware of such fine motor impairment before the testing, make the decision ahead of time to utilize Picture Completion in the Performance IQ because it minimizes the effect of the fine motor impairment. However, do not be tempted to substitute one subtest for another because a child performed better or worse on one or the other. The Don't Forget box above lists which subtests are acceptable substitutes for core WPPSI-III subtests.

Scoring Subtests Requiring Judgment

While administering the WPPSI-III, you will likely find (or may have discovered if you are an experienced tester) that the Verbal subtests elicit many more responses than are listed in the *Administration and Scoring Manual*. The multitude of responses obtained are interesting but are also frustrating when it comes to the process of scoring that involves subjective judgment. Although The Psychological Corporation (2002) has sought to objectify as much as possible the responses on Vocabulary, Similarities, Comprehension, and Information, the information in the *Administration and Scoring Manual* is not all-inclusive and can only be used as a general guide.

How often have you administered a test to a child who blurts out a beautiful 1.5 point answer, seeming to fit neither in the neat 2-point or 1-point category listed in the *Administration and Scoring Manual*? This type of borderline response may be frustrating, but by having a clear understanding of the general scoring criteria provided in the manual, you can judge how to score any response. The general scoring criteria for WPPSI-III Verbal subtests are found in the *WPPSI-III Administration and Scoring Manual* (The Psychological Corporation, 2002) on page 88 for Vocabulary, page 128 for Comprehension, and page 159 for Similarities.

Consider some basic rules while scoring Verbal subtests. One is that a child cannot be penalized for poor grammar or improper pronunciation. Although grammar and pronunciation are important to note for clinical reasons, the content of what a child says is most important for scoring a response. Another rule is that long, elaborate answers are not necessarily worth more points than are short, concise ones. Some children have a tendency to respond in paragraph form, which leads to two or three answers rolled into one. If this occurs, either spontaneously or after a query, determine (a) whether the response has been spoiled, (b) which part of the response was intended as the final response, and (c) which part of the response is worth the highest number of points. If a child reveals a fundamental misconception in his or her long elaborate response, then the entire response may be spoiled and the response should be scored as zero. If a child's response contains many answers but none spoils the response, query further. Sometimes the last answer is clearly intended as the final response. In such a case, simply score the final response. Other times the second or third response is intended as the actual response. When uncertain, ask the child to clarify his or her response. For clarification purposes ask, "You said, _____, _____, and _____. Which one was your answer?" In some instances children state that their *entire* long response was what they had intended as their answer, and imbedded in that long response are 0-, 1-, and 2-point answers. In such a case, if no answer spoiled part of the long response, then simply score the *best* response.

SUBTEST-BY-SUBTEST SCORING KEYS

Rapid References 3.2 and 3.3 list important specific points to remember when you are scoring each of the WPPSI-III subtests. We do not review all the nuances of scoring each part of the tests here, but we do cover areas that commonly cause difficulty for examiners.

Rapid Reference 3.2

Keys to Scoring Verbal Subtests

Information

- On first 6 items, if child points to the correct picture but says an incorrect verbal response, the item is scored 0.
- Responses listed in the *Administration and Scoring Manual* are not all-inclusive. Give credit for responses that are of the same caliber as those in the manual.
- Add 1 point to the raw score for each of the unadministered reversal items.

Vocabulary

- Items 1–7 of Vocabulary are worth 0 or 1 point each, but the remaining items are worth 0, 1, or 2 points.
- Slang and regionalisms not in the dictionary are scored zero.
- Poor grammar is not penalized in scoring.
- Any meaning found in a standard dictionary is given credit.
- Utilize the general 0- to 2-point scoring criteria and the specific examples.
- Add 1 point to the raw score for each of the unadministered reversal items.

Word Reasoning

- Correct responses are awarded 1 point, regardless of whether the child needed one or three clues to get the answer right.
- Give credit to responses that are synonyms or specific brand names or objects.
- Add 1 point to the raw score for each of the unadministered reversal items.
- Do not award points for the sample items.

Comprehension
- Score Items 1 and 2 either 0 or 1 point, and score Items 3–20 either 0, 1, or 2 points.
- Use the specific scoring examples and the general 0-, 1-, and 2-point scoring criteria.
- If a child spontaneously improves his or her answer or improves the answer after a query, give credit for that improvement.
- Add 1 point to the raw score for each of the unadministered reversal items.

Similarities
- Similarities Items 1 and 2 are worth either 0 or 1 point credit each, and the remaining items are worth 0, 1, or 2 points each.
- Use the general 0- to 2-point scoring criteria and specific examples.
- Key to scoring is the degree of abstraction.

Receptive Vocabulary
- All items are worth 0 or 1 point.
- No response after 30 seconds, *don't know* responses, and incorrect responses are scored 0.

Picture Naming
- All items are worth 0 or 1 points.
- Give credit for correct responses that are mispronounced or misarticulated.
- Do not give credit for personalized responses, proper names, or fictional names.

≡Rapid Reference 3.3

Keys to Scoring Performance Subtests

Block Design
- For Items 1–6 of Block Design, successful completion within the time limit on the first trial earns 2 points, and success on the second trial earns 1 point.
- For Items 7–20, designs completed within the time limit are awarded 2 points.

(continued)

- Award 2 points per item for reversal items that are not administered.
- If a child correctly completes a design after the time limit has expired, no points are awarded (but note the child's performance).
- Award 0 points for partially completed designs.
- Rotations of designs of 30° or more are not penalized for Items 1–10 (Part A). However, rotations of designs of 30° or more on Items 11–20 are incorrect and scored 0 points.
- Gaps or misalignments greater than .25 inch are scored as incorrect (smaller gaps or misalignments are not penalized).

Matrix Reasoning

- Do not score sample items.
- All items are awarded either 1 or 0 points.
- Award 1 point per item for reversal items that are not administered.
- If a child does not respond or responds, "I don't know," award 0 points.

Picture Concepts

- Do not score the sample items.
- All items are awarded either 1 or 0 points.
- An item is correct only if correct pictures from all rows of the item are selected.
- Award 1 point per item for reversal items that are not administered.
- Incorrect responses and no responses after approximately 30 seconds are scored 0 points.

Symbol Search

- Careful placement of the Symbol Search template is necessary for accurate scoring.
- If a child has marked more than one box for the response to one item, score it 0. However, if the child clearly attempted to cross out an incorrect response and mark a correct response, then give credit.
- Skipped items are not counted toward the total.
- The number of correct items and the number of incorrect items are summed separately.
- The raw score is calculated by subtracting the number of incorrect items from the number correct.
- Only items completed before the 120-second time limit expired are counted toward the score.

Coding

- One point is given for each symbol correctly drawn within 120 seconds.
- Do not count sample items toward the final score.
- Use the Coding template to score the items.
- Symbols do not have to be drawn perfectly to obtain credit; they just must be recognizable.
- If a child has spontaneously corrected his or her drawing, give credit to the corrected drawing.
- Give the appropriate number of bonus points if a child completes all items correctly within the time limit.

Picture Completion

- Add 1 point to the raw score for each of the unadministered reversal items.
- If child responds with a correct description using a synonym or his or her own words, award 1 point.
- Award 1 point for items on which the child correctly pointed to the missing place.
- If the child's verbal response is incorrect, but the pointing response is correct, score 0.
- If the child doesn't respond within the 20-second time limit, score 0.

Object Assembly

- Count the number of correct junctures (where two pieces join) at the precise moment that the time limit expired to determine the score.
- Give credit for a juncture even if it is between two pieces that are separate from the rest of the puzzle.
- Give credit for junctures that have gaps or misalignments of less than or equal to .25 inch (award 0 points for larger gaps or misalignments).
- To obtain a raw score for Items 13 and 14, multiply the number of correct junctures by .5 (and round half-point scores upward).
- On Items 1 and 2, award 1 point if junctures are correctly joined on either Trial 1 or 2.

≡Rapid Reference 3.4

Minimum Hardware Requirements for the WPPSI™–III Scoring Assistant® and WPPSI™–III Writer™

- Windows® 95/98/2000/Me/NT 4.0 Workstation Operating System
- 100 MHz Pentium processor (166 MHz recommended)
- 32 MB RAM (64 MB recommended)
- 2 MB video card capable of 800 × 600 resolution (256 colors)
- 20 MB free hard disk space
- 3.5-inch floppy drive
- 50 MB temporary disk space for diskette installation
- CD-ROM drive recommended

COMPUTER SCORING PROCEDURES

Computer software is available assist in scoring the WPPSI-III. Rapid Reference 3.4 lists the minimum computer hardware requirements for both the scoring and interpretive software.

- The *WPPSI™–III Scoring Assistant*® (The Psychological Corporation, 2002b) generates concise score reports automatically from your PC after you simply enter raw scores. The program yields scaled scores, percentiles, age equivalents, composites, and confidence intervals, as well as a profile analysis. Discrepancy analysis for ability-achievement differences can be generated too. All WPPSI-III and WIAT-II scores can be graphed.
- The *WPPSI™–III Writer*™ (The Psychological Corporation, 2003) is an interpretive software program that allows you to produce individualized, comprehensive reports based on clients' score profiles. The program generates three types of reports: a nontechnical client report, a statistical report with graphs and tables, and a comprehensive interpretive report with narrative interpretations of WPPSI-III score levels, patterns, deviations, and background information along with tables and graphs.

TEST YOURSELF

1. While administering the Block Design subtest to Juan, several interruptions occur causing a recurring loss of her attention that, in your clinical judgment, has spoiled the subtest. Which subtest can you replace Block Design with in calculation of the Performance IQ?

   (a) Information

   (b) Picture Completion

   (c) Matrix Reasoning

   (d) Symbol Search

2. Because each WPPSI-III subtest begins at points that are calibrated for the individual child's chronological age, the raw scores are meaningful and interpretable without converting them to a standard score metric. True or False?

3. The best method of deciding when to substitute a supplemental WPPSI-III subtest for one of the core subtests in calculation of the IQs is to

   (a) wait to see which test the child performs the best on.

   (b) make an a priori decision to use one rather than the other, even before the subtests are administered.

   (c) flip a coin.

   (d) ask the child which one he or she liked better.

4. Shanea, age 3, is administered the WPPSI-III and obtains a raw score of 0 on Block Design and Object Assembly. You should

   (a) not calculate the Performance IQ.

   (b) calculate neither the Verbal IQ nor the Performance IQ.

   (c) calculate neither the Performance IQ nor the Full Scale IQ.

   (d) consider the entire WPPSI-III invalid.

5. Xander gives an elaborate response to the Vocabulary subtest, and you are unsure of what exactly his intended response is, so it is appropriate to ask him to specify what his intended answer was. True or False?

Answers: 1. b; 2. False; 3. b; 4. c; 5. True.

Four

HOW TO INTERPRET THE WPPSI-III

INTRODUCTION TO INTERPRETATION

This chapter is designed to simplify interpreting the large amount of scores and clinical data obtained from the WPPSI-III. Following the system of interpretation outlined in this chapter will help you organize the test data in systematic ways, leading to insightful interpretation. Each subtest is analyzed first, followed by a step-by-step method of interpreting the WPPSI-III from IQs through the profile of subtest scores. Emphasis is placed not only on interpretation of the numerical values obtained from each test but also on how these scores can (and indeed must) be integrated with background and behavioral information to yield interpretive hypotheses.

The key to accurate characterizing of children's strong and weak areas of functioning is to examine performances across several subtests, not individual subtest scores in isolation. We give general information and data about each individual subtest along with clinical and empirical information to help provide understanding about how each task contributes to the WPPSI-III. Although information on the unique qualities of each subtest is provided, the step-by-step fashion of interpretation outlined in this chapter provides a mechanism by which hypotheses about a child's performance can be tested when multiple subtests are examined together. The shared or overlapping abilities that encompass two or more subtests are crucial in creating a meaningful understanding of a child's cognitive abilities. Although we want examiners to be aware of the unique skills tapped by each single subtest, examination of the abilities shared by many WPPSI-III subtests is most informative.

CONSIDERATIONS ABOUT PROFILE INTERPRETATION

Before we present our approach to individual profile interpretation, we think it important to address some of the criticisms that have arisen from the approach we advocate (Kaufman, 1990a, 1994b; Kaufman & Lichtenberger, 1999, 2000, 2002; Lichtenberger, Broadbooks, & Kaufman, 2000). Kaufman (1994b) summarizes some of the critics' reviews of profile interpretation as well as IQ tests in general, and Kaufman and Lichtenberger (2002) address the same concerns about profile interpretation that we discuss in this chapter. In a review of our recent brief treatment of the WAIS-III (Kaufman & Lichtenberger, 1999) that presents an interpretive approach similar to the one here for the WPPSI-III, Flanagan and Alfonso (2000) stated that "although only positive comments can be made about the contribution of Kaufman's psychometric profile analysis approach to the advancement of Wechsler test interpretation, the field of cognitive assessment appears to be gradually moving beyond this method and encouraging the application of current empirically supported theories in the interpretation process" (p. 529). They go on to say, "although Kaufman and Lichtenberger offer several theoretical categorizations of WAIS-III subtests, they are not based on confirmatory factor analyses or other empirical validation methods within a given paradigm" (p. 530). Flanagan and Alfonso conclude, "notwithstanding the authors' cautionary statements regarding certain aspects of their interpretive approach, the [book's] major limitation may well prove to revolve around the fact that well-validated and contemporary theories of the structure of intelligence were not applied more vigorously in their interpretation guidelines" (p. 531).

Flanagan and Alfonso are critical of exactly which hypotheses should be interpreted, but they are not critical of the notion of profile interpretation per se. Indeed, the approach that Flanagan and her colleagues embrace involves the interpretation of a diversity of Broad and Narrow Abilities from the perspective of Gf-Gc theory (e. g., Flanagan, McGrew, & Ortiz, 2000). In contrast to Flanagan and Alfonso's moderate criticisms of our approach, Glutting, McDermott, and their colleagues have leveled severe criticisms not only of our approach but also of any type of profile interpretive system (e.g., McDermott, Fantuzzo, & Glutting, 1990). These critics of profile interpretation have gained support for their position from some professionals, as evidenced by a review of our *Essentials* book on the WISC-III and WPPSI-R (Kaufman & Lichtenberger, 2000): "Were readers of this book to fully embrace its contents, they might fall prey to delusions of profile overinterpretation" (Schaefer, 2002, p. 395).

Flanagan and Alfonso's (2000) comments stem from their belief that the Kaufman-Lichtenberger approach to profile analyses is antiquated because it does not revolve around the recent and strongly validated Cattell-Horn-Carroll (CHC) theory (Kaufman & Lichtenberger, 2002; McGrew & Flanagan, 1998). In contrast, adherents of the McDermott-Glutting critique such as Schaefer (2002) believe that any interpretation that goes beyond reliable global scores represents too much interpretation. In light of both the moderate and severe criticisms, we again reviewed the approach we advocate for interpreting Wechsler tests.

After pondering and discussing our approach, we concluded that the Kaufman-Lichtenberger method of Wechsler test interpretation is sound and defensible. One of the strongest arguments waged against our approach was that it does not have enough psychometric support in terms of factor-analytic data. The support for Flanagan and McGrew's cross-battery approach necessarily comes from group data because factor analysis depends on correlation coefficients obtained for groups of individuals. Similarly, the arguments advocated against profile interpretation by McDermott and Glutting are psychometric in nature and derived from group data. Although psychometric methods based on group data are important, they should not be deified as the only criterion. The approach we advocate examines each *individual*, not the performance of a *group*. The procedures that we present in our individual profile interpretation often have empirical support, but if not, they have either theoretical or clinical backing.

We are looking for unique approaches to address individual profiles. The validity that comes from group data may never be available for the individual profile approach that we advocate. For example, consider WISC-III or WAIS-III Digit Span. If you were to factor analyze the separate components of Digit Span in a factor analysis, Digits Forward and Digits Backward are almost always going to load together. However, this fact does not invalidate the practice at looking at the difference between them for an individual. Most people do in fact perform better on Digits Forward than on Digits

Backward. Thus, it is very noteworthy and clinically informative when an individual scores higher on Digits Backward or when the typical Forward-Backward discrepancy is unusually large.

We have never advocated interpreting a Wechsler profile or any other IQ test profile *in isolation*. Certainly, such a practice would be of questionable validity and of questionable ethical practice. Our interpretive approach stresses the importance of finding multiple sources of data to support a hypothesis that is based on a pattern of subtest scores. We probably cannot find a better support for our system than the following comments made by Anastasi and Urbina (1997) in a footnote to a McDermott-Glutting study: "One problem with several of the negative reviews of Kaufman's approach is that they seem to assume that clinicians will use it to make decisions based solely on the magnitude of scores and score differences. While it is true that the mechanical application of profile analysis techniques can be very misleading, this assumption is quite contrary to what Kaufman recommends, as well as to the principles of sound assessment practice" (p. 513).

In spite of our personal belief in the individual profile interpretation approach outlined in this book, we do recognize that some clinicians may feel more comfortable stopping short of developing hypotheses about what abilities underlie a pattern of subtest scores, whereas others prefer to rely only on hypotheses that have empirical support from group data. For the former group of nonbelievers who oppose any type of subtest interpretation, we recognize that both Step 6 (determining significant strengths and weaknesses in the subtest profile) and Step 8 (hypothesis generation) will be of little value. However, even without these two interpretive steps, the remaining steps offer an empirically based method of profile attack for the child's WPPSI-III global standard scores (IQs, PSQ, GLC). For the group of critics who are comfortable with profile interpretation, but only as it applies to empirically validated hypotheses, we recommend that they conduct all eight interpretive steps, but when identifying meaningful hypotheses they should limit these hypotheses to the ones that pertain to the CHC Broad and Narrow Abilities.

ANALYSIS OF EACH SUBTEST

Empirical, cognitive, and clinical data are provided for each of the WPPSI-III subtests. In the section on empirical analysis, subtest specificity and general intelligence (*g*-loadings) are described. A summary of cognitive abilities that each subtest is believed to measure is provided in the cognitive analysis section. An analysis of clinical considerations is presented in the final section.

Empirical Analysis

The empirical analyses of the WPPSI-III subtests are based on data from its standardization samples.

Loadings on the General Factor

How well each subtest measures general intelligence or *g* is determined, for our purposes, by the loadings on the unrotated first factor in principal components analysis. (We conducted these analyses ourselves.) Factor loadings of .70 or greater are considered good measures of *g*, loadings of .50 to .69 are deemed fair *g* loadings, and loadings below .50 are usually considered poor. Rapid Reference 4.1 reports data on the subtests' *g* loadings.

The strongest *g* loadings on the WPPSI-III were found in the Verbal subtests. For ages 4-0 to 7-3, the three Core Verbal subtests were the strongest measures of *g* (Information at .84, Word Reasoning at .84, and Vocabulary at .80). Both of the Core Verbal subtests for ages 2-6 to 3-11 were also good measures of *g*. On the Performance scale, the highest *g* loadings for ages 4-0 to 7-3 were found on Picture Completion and Matrix Reasoning. All other Performance subtests at this age and both Performance subtests for ages 2-6 to 3-11 were fair measures of *g*. There were no poor measures of *g* for either age group. For both broad age groups, all Verbal subtests, including the ones that constitute the GLC, had *g* loadings greater than .75. In contrast, none of the Performance or PSQ subtests had a *g* loading higher than .72. As a rule of thumb with few exceptions, WPPSI-III Verbal subtests had good *g* loadings whereas WPPSI-III Performance and Processing Speed subtests had fair *g* loadings.

The meaningfulness of *g* loadings, or the general intelligence concept, has been debated (Jensen, 1998; Neisser, 1998). We do know that this value represents how well the subtests "hang together" psychometrically. However, what is debatable is the theoretical construct that underlies the *g* value. Thus, a subtest with a strong *g* loading should not be interpreted as *the* representation of a child's level of cognitive ability.

≋Rapid Reference 4.1

WPPSI-III Subtests as Measures of General Ability (*g*)

Ages 2-6 to 3-11

Good measures of *g*		Fair measures of *g*		Poor measures of *g*
Information	.87	Object Assembly	.67	None
Picture Naming	.87	Block Design	.62	
Receptive Vocabulary	.84			

Ages 4-0 to 7-3

Good measures of *g*		Fair measures of *g*		Poor measures of *g*
Information	.84	Block Design	.68	None
Word Reasoning	.84	Picture Concepts	.67	
Vocabulary	.80	Symbol Search	.64	
Similarities	.78	Object Assembly	.59	
Picture Naming	.78	Coding	.51	
Receptive Vocabulary	.77			
Comprehension	.77			
Picture Completion	.72			
Matrix Reasoning	.70			

Note. For our purposes, g is determined by the loadings on the unrotated first factor in the principal components analyses that we conducted based on intersubtest correlations presented in the WPPSI-III Technical and Interpretive Manual. Factor loadings of .70 or greater are considered good measures of g, loadings of .50 to .69 are deemed fair g loadings, and loadings below .50 are considered poor.

Specificity of Subtests

The unique proportion of reliable variance of each subtest is referred to as *subtest specificity*. This proportion of variance is that amount of reliable variance that is not shared with other subtests included in the test battery. When deciding whether it is feasible to interpret the unique abilities or traits attributed to a subtest, you should take into account the subtest specificity. In addition to subtest specificity, the error variance must be taken into account when deciding whether to interpret a subtest's unique characteristics. Generally, if about

25% or more of the total variance is specific and the specific variance exceeds the error variance, then interpretation of specific abilities may be done.

The specificity for each subtest was statistically calculated via an uncomplicated technique. We obtained the shared variance for each subtest (we used the squared multiple correlation) and then subtracted this common variance from the subtest's reliability coefficient. The result of this calculation is the reliable unique variance (subtest specificity). To determine whether a task's uniqueness should be interpreted, we then compared the error variance for the subtest (one minus the reliability) to the specificity.

Rapid Reference 4.2 lists each subtest's specificity and error variance and also includes (in the note) the rules for distinguishing between ample and adequate specificity. Although no WPPSI-III subtests have inadequate specificity and most subtests have ample specificity, these results do not mean that examiners should routinely interpret each subtest's unique abilities. As mentioned earlier, the first plan of attack when examining a child's subtest profile is to create hypotheses from the shared abilities of many subtests (see the section entitled, "Step by Step: How to Interpret the WPPSI-III."). Interpretation of unique abilities is usually the last resort, after attempts to group subtests together have come up empty.

ABILITIES SHARED BY TWO OR MORE SUBTESTS

In this chapter we present numerous abilities that are hypothesized to underlie diverse groupings of WPPSI-III subtests, organized according to the structure of the Information Processing Model (Silver, 1993). In this framework, each hypothesized ability is categorized into one of three groups: (a) input, which contains abilities involving the type of information that is to be handled (e.g., visual or auditory stimuli); (b) integration-storage, which contains abilities that involve processing and memory components; and (c) output, which represents how individuals express their response (e.g., motor coordination or verbal expression). The Don't Forget box on page 91 summarizes the information processing model.

The basic two-category organization (Verbal and Performance) of subtests is the same across all Wechsler tests. However, many new organizational models have been proposed to interpret the Wechsler subtests, including the four-factor structure proposed in the test manuals for the WISC-IV and WAIS-III and the three-factor organization of the WPPSI-III for ages 4 and

≡Rapid Reference 4.2

WPPSI-III Subtests Categorized by Specificity
Ages 2-6 to 3-11

Subtests with Ample Specificity	Specificity	Error Variance	Subtests with Adequate Specificity
Block Design	.61	.15	None
Object Assembly	.59	.13	
Receptive Vocabulary	.33	.09	
Information	.29	.08	
Picture Naming	.26	.11	

Ages 4-0 to 7-3

Subtests with Ample Specificity	Specificity	Error Variance	Subtests with Adequate Specificity	Specificity	Error Variance
Picture Concepts	.51	.09			
Coding	.46	.16	Vocabulary	.24	.11
Object Assembly	.46	.16	Picture Naming	.23	.13
Matrix Reasoning	.45	.10	Word Reasoning	.21	.09
Picture Completion	.43	.10			
Block Design	.38	.16			
Similarities	.35	.05			
Symbol Search	.33	.17			
Receptive Vocabulary	.30	.13			
Comprehension	.28	.12			

Note. Subtests with ample specificity have specific variance that (a) reflects 25% or more of the subtest's total variance (100%) and (b) exceeds the subtest's error variance. Subtests with adequate specificity have specific variance that (a) reflects between 15% and 24% of the subtest's total variance and (b) exceeds the subtest's error variance. Subtests with inadequate specificity have specific variance that either (a) is less than 15% of the subtest's total variance or (b) is equal to or less than the subtests error variance.

Specific variance is obtained by subtracting the squared multiple correlation from the subtest's reliability. Error variance is obtained by subtracting the subtest's reliability from 1.00.

DON'T FORGET

Information Processing Model

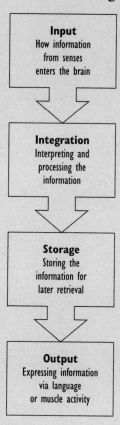

Input
How information from senses enters the brain

Integration
Interpreting and processing the information

Storage
Storing the information for later retrieval

Output
Expressing information via language or muscle activity

above. In the Subtest-by-Subtest Analysis, several hypothesized abilities are listed under each subtest, many of which come from theoretical reorganizations of the Wechsler subtests. We do not provide an in-depth discussion of theoretical and research-based recategorizations of the WPPSI-III, but this information is readily available for other Wechsler scales (see Flanagan et al., 2000; Kaufman, 1994b; Sattler, 2001). Provided here is a basic outline of different methods of recategorizing the Wechsler subtests, most notably Guilford (1967), Horn (1989; Cattell & Horn, 1978), Carroll (1997), and Bannatyne (1974; see Rapid References 4.3 through 4.8).

Rapid Reference 4.3

Broad Abilities of the Cattell-Horn-Carroll (CHC) Model Measured by WPPSI-III Subtests

Subtest	Fluid Ability (Gf)	Crystallized Ability (Gc)	Broad Visual-ization (Gv)	Long-Term Storage and Retrieval (Glr)	Broad Speediness (Gs)
Information		X			
Word Reasoning	X	X			
Vocabulary		X			
Similarities	X	X			
Picture Naming		X		X	
Receptive Vocabulary		X			
Comprehension		X			
Picture Completion			X		
Matrix Reasoning	X		X		
Block Design	X		X		
Picture Concepts	X	X			
Symbol Search					X
Object Assembly	X		X		X
Coding					X

Note. CHC categorizations are based on our clinical understanding of the theory, not factor-analytic data and were validated by an expert on CHC theory (Dawn Flanagan, personal communication, January 29, 2003).

Rapid Reference 4.4

Narrow Abilities of the Cattell-Horn-Carroll (CHC) Model Measured by WPPSI-III Subtests

Subtest	General Information	Language Development	Lexical Knowledge	Induction	Naming Facility	Flexibility of Closure	Spatial Relations	Visual-ization	Perceptual Speed	Rate of Test-Taking	Closure Speed
Information	X										
Word Reasoning		X	X	X							
Vocabulary		X	X								
Similarities		X	X								
Picture Naming		X	X		X						
Receptive Vocabulary		X	X								
Comprehension	X	X									
Picture Completion	X					X					
Matrix Reasoning				X							
Block Design							X	X			

(continued)

Rapid Reference 4.4 (continued)

Narrow Abilities of the Cattell-Horn-Carroll (CHC) Model Measured by WPPSI-III Subtests

Subtest	General Information	Language Development	Lexical Knowledge	Induction	Naming Facility	Flexibility of Closure	Spatial Relations	Visual-ization	Perceptual Speed	Rate of Test-Taking	Closure Speed
Picture Concepts				X							
Symbol Search									X	X	
Object Assembly							X				X
Coding										X	

Note. Cattell-Horn-Carroll (CHC) categorizations are based on our clinical understanding of the theory, not factor-analytic data., and were validated by an expert on CHC theory (Dawn Flanagan, personal communication, January 29, 2003).

Rapid Reference 4.5

Definitions of Gf-Gc Broad and Narrow Stratum Abilities of the Cattell-Horn-Carroll (CHC) Model

Ability (Code)	Definition
Crystallized intelligence (Gc)	Acquired knowledge that is primarily verbal or language based
General information (KO)	Range of general knowledge
Language development (LD)	General development of the understanding of words, sentences, and paragraphs (not requiring reading) in spoken native language skills
Lexical knowledge (VL)	Extent of vocabulary that can be understood in terms of correct word meanings
Fluid intelligence (Gf)	Ability to form and recognize concepts, draw inferences, comprehend implications, problem solve, extrapolate, and reason
Induction (I)	Ability to discover the underlying characteristic that governs a problem or a set of materials
Long-term storage and retrieval (Glr)	Ability to store information in and fluently retrieve new or previously acquired information from long-term memory
Naming facility (NA)	Ability to rapidly produce names for concepts when presented with a pictorial or verbal cue
Visual processing (Gv)	Ability to generate, perceive, analyze, synthesize, store, retrieve, manipulate transform and think with visual patterns and stimuli
Flexibility of closure (CF)	Ability to identify a visual figure or pattern embedded in a complex visual array, when knowing in advance what the pattern is

(continued)

Rapid Reference 4.5 (continued)

Definitions of Gf-Gc Broad and Narrow Stratum Abilities of the Cattell-Horn-Carroll (CHC) Model

Ability (Code)	Definition
Spatial relations (SR)	Ability to rapidly perceive and manipulate visual pattern or to maintain orientation with respect to objects in space
Closure speed (CS)	Ability to quickly combine disconnected, vague, or partially obscured visual stimuli or patterns into a meaningful whole
Visualization (Vz)	Ability to mentally manipulate objects or visual patterns and to see how they would appear under altered conditions
Processing speed (Gs)	Ability to fluently and automatically perform cognitive tasks
Rate of test-taking (R9)	Ability to rapidly perform tests that are relatively easy or that require very simple decisions
Perceptual speed (P)	Ability to rapidly search for and compare visual symbols presented side or separated in a visual field

Note. Broad abilities are in highlighted boxes. Definitions are from Flanagan, McGrew, and Ortiz (2000).

≡ *Rapid Reference 4.6*

Guilford's Operations and Contents

Operations (Intellectual Processes)	Description
Cognition (C)	Immediate awareness, recognition, or comprehension of stimuli
Memory (M)	Retention of information in the same form in which it was stored
Evaluation (E)	Making judgments about information in terms of a known standard
Convergent production (N)	Responding to stimuli with the unique or best answer
Divergent production (D)	Responding to stimuli where the emphasis is on a variety or quality of response (associated with creativity)

Contents (Nature of the Stimuli)	Description
Figural (F)	Shapes or concrete objects
Symbolic (S)	Numerals, single letters, or any coded symbol
Semantic (M)	Words and ideas that convey meaning
Behavioral (B)	Primarily nonverbal, involving human interactions with a stress on attitudes, needs, thoughts, and so on

CLINICAL CONSIDERATIONS

In addition to understanding the psychometric qualities of the subtests and the shared abilities, carefully consider clinical factors for subtest interpretation. We provide clinical factors related to each subtest based on our clinical experience and relevant literature (Kamphaus, 1993; Kaufman, 1994b; Kaufman & Lichtenberger, 2002; Sattler, 2001; Zimmerman & Woo-Sam, 1973). Although we provide a wide variety of clinical considerations, these suggestions are merely hypotheses to consider. To provide the best interpretation of any particular piece of clinical evidence, use your preferred theoretical framework.

≡ Rapid Reference 4.7

Classification of WPPSI-III Subtests in Guilford's Model

Subtest	Cognition	Memory	Evaluation	Convergent-Production
Verbal				
Information		Semantic		
Similarities	Semantic			
Vocabulary	Semantic			
Comprehension			Semantic	
Word Reasoning			Semantic	Semantic
General Language				
Receptive Vocabulary	Figural			Semantic
Picture Naming	Figural	Semantic		
Performance				
Picture Completion	Figural		Figural	
Matrix Reasoning			Figural	Figural
Block Design	Figural		Figural	
Object Assembly	Figural		Figural	
Picture Concepts			Semantic	Figural
Processing Speed				
Coding			Figural	Figural
Symbol Search			Figural	Figural

Note. Subtests are interpreted according to Guilford's (1967) original structure of intellect model based on Meeker's (1969) categorizations of traditional Wechsler subtests, Kaufman and Kaufman's (1977) categorizations of McCarthy subtests that resemble some new WPPSI-III subtests, and our own clinical judgment.

≡ Rapid Reference 4.8

Classification of WPPSI-III Subtests
According to Bannatyne's Model

WPPSI-III Subtest	Verbal Conceptualization Ability	Spatial Ability	Sequential Ability	Acquired Knowledge
Similarities	X			
Word Reasoning	X			
Comprehension	X			
Vocabulary	X			X
Information				X
Receptive Vocabulary				X
Picture Naming				X
Picture Concepts	X			
Picture Completion		X		
Block Design		X		
Object Assembly		X		
Matrix Reasoning		X		
Coding			X	

Note. Matrix Reasoning, Receptive Vocabulary, Picture Naming, and Word Reasoning represent our classifications based on an understanding of Bannatyne's model.

Little empirical validation exists for the diverse clinical hypotheses suggested by many clinicians. The process of clinical interpretation is complex and demands that individual pieces of data *not* be considered in isolation. Because the process that each clinician goes through in making inferences about data is somewhat idiosyncratic, even the best clinicians may disagree on hypotheses generated from any particular piece of clinical data (Lipsitz, Dworkin, & Erlenmeyer-Kimling, 1993).

SUBTEST-BY-SUBTEST ANALYSIS

Abilities denoted with an asterisk (*) are *unique* to the particular subtest being discussed. CHC is an abbreviation for the Cattell-Horn-Carroll model.

Verbal Subtests

Information
Ages 2-6 to 3-11 — Core subtest, V-IQ, FS-IQ
Ages 4-0 to 7-3 — Core subtest, V-IQ, FS-IQ

Information: Abilities Shared With Other Subtests
Input
  Achievement
  Auditory perception of complex verbal stimuli (understanding questions)
  Simple verbal directions (Information Items 1–8)
  Auditory-vocal channel
  Visual perception of complete meaningful stimuli (Information items 1-6)
Integration-Storage
  Acquired knowledge (Bannatyne)
  Crystallized intelligence — Gc (CHC broad ability)
  Culture-loaded knowledge
  Fund of information
  General information (CHC narrow ability)
  Long-term memory
  Memory (primarily), mostly of semantic stimuli (Guilford)
  Verbal comprehension
  *Range of general factual knowledge
Output
  Simple vocal response
  Visual-motor coordination (Information Items 1–8)

Information: Influences Affecting Subtest Scores
  • Alertness to the environment
  • Cultural opportunities at home
  • Foreign language background
  • Intellectual curiosity and striving
  • Interests
  • Outside reading

- Richness of early environment
- School learning

Information: Clinical Considerations

- Items are generally nonthreatening and emotionally neutral.
- Rationalizations and excuses may be produced in response to this test (i.e., "That isn't important").
- Effortless, automatic responding facilitates good performance. Children with chronic anxiety may suffer early failures and depressed scores in general.
- Retrieval difficulties may be revealed on this test when successes on harder items are preceded by failures on easy items.
- Alertness to the environment in addition to formal schooling together are the source of most of the factual knowledge needed for success.
- Unnecessary detail and trivial responses may suggest obsessiveness.
- Intellectual ambitiousness can be reflected in high scores and is often coupled with high Vocabulary scores.
- A perfectionistic approach may be evident when no response is preferred to an imperfect answer.
- Bizarre or odd responses can shed light on a child's mental state. For example, a response such as *There are 1,000 days in a week* may warrant exploration to assess mental functioning or to assess whether the child is taking the test seriously.
- Problems with numbers may lower scores substantially for younger and lower functioning children. Numbers or number concepts are measured by Items 9, 12, 17, and 28.

Vocabulary

Ages 2-6 to 3-11 — Not administered
Ages 4-0 to 7-3 — Core subtest, V-IQ, FS-IQ

Vocabulary: Abilities Shared With Other Subtests

Input

Auditory perception of simple verbal stimuli (understanding single words)
Visual perception of complete meaningful stimuli (Vocabulary Items 1–5)
Visual-vocal channel (Vocabulary Items 1–5)

Integration-Storage
    Acquired knowledge (Bannatyne)
    Cognition of semantic stimuli (Guilford)
    Concept formation
    Crystallized Intelligence — Gc (CHC broad ability)
    Degree of abstract thinking
    Fund of information
    General ability
    Language development (CHC narrow ability)
    Learning ability
    Lexical knowledge (CHC narrow ability)
    Long-term memory
    Verbal comprehension
    Verbal concept formation
    Verbal conceptualization (Bannatyne)
    Word knowledge
    *Oral vocabulary
Output
    Simple vocal expression (Vocabulary Items 1–5)
    Verbal expression

Vocabulary: Influences Affecting Subtest Scores

- Cultural opportunities at home
- Foreign language experience
- Intellectual curiosity and striving
- Interests
- Outside reading
- Richness or early environment
- School learning

Vocabulary: Clinical Considerations

- Repression may lead to poor performance by pushing out of consciousness any word meanings that are even mildly conflict-laden. Repression may also impair the acquisition of new word meanings as well as recall of specific words on the Vocabulary subtest.

- As in Information, high scores relative to other Verbal subtests can reflect intellectual ambitiousness or stress for achievement in the child's life.
- The content presented in children's responses lends itself to analysis regarding the child's fears, guilt, preoccupations, feelings, interests, background, cultural milieu, bizarre thought processes, perseveration, and clang associations (hat-cat, thief-leaf). Themes in response content may occur also in conjunction with Comprehension or Similarities, as well as during spontaneous conversation during the assessment.
- Perseveration is sometimes evidenced when individuals give the same opening line for each response (e.g., *Polite, that's a hard one to define . . .*).
- Distinguish responses that are overlearned, almost book-like definitions from responses driven by intellectual vigor and personalization of the responses with current experiences.
- The open-ended nature of the Vocabulary responses allow you to glean information about children's verbal fluency, not just word knowledge. Some words are easily defined by one-word synonyms, but some children may give excessive verbiage in their responses or may give responses in a roundabout manner.
- Hearing difficulties may become apparent. Because the words are presented in isolation, there is no context by which help to understand the word.
- Evaluate level of abstract thinking in Vocabulary items. Responses may be abstract (microscope is "an instrument") or more concrete (courage is "like when you save someone from a fire").

Word Reasoning
Ages 2-6 to 3-11 — Not administered
Ages 4-0 to 7-3 — Core subtest, V-IQ, FS-IQ

Word Reasoning: Abilities Shared With Other Subtests
Input
    Understanding long questions
    Understanding words

Integration-Storage
  Acquired knowledge (Bannatyne)
  Cognition of semantic stimuli (Guilford)
  Convergent-production (Guilford)
  Crystallized Intelligence — Gc (CHC broad ability)
  Degree of abstract thinking
  Decentration (Piagetian ability to focus on all pertinent attributes)
  Fluid intelligence — Gf (CHC broad ability)
  Fund of information
  Induction (CHC narrow ability)
  Language development (CHC narrow ability)
  Learning ability
  Lexical knowledge (CHC narrow ability)
  Long-term memory
  Reasoning (verbal)
  Simultaneous processing
  Synthesis (part-whole)
  Verbal comprehension
  Verbal concept formation
  Verbal conceptualization (Bannatyne)
  *Integration of sequentially presented auditory stimuli
Output
  Simple verbal expression

Word Reasoning: Influences Affecting Subtest Scores
  • Ability to respond when uncertain
  • Attention span
  • Cultural opportunities at home
  • Flexibility
  • Foreign language experience
  • Intellectual curiosity and striving
  • Interests
  • Outside reading
  • Richness or early environment
  • School learning

Word Reasoning: Clinical Considerations

- Repression may impair the acquisition of new word meanings as well as recall of specific words on the subtest.
- High scores relative to other Verbal subtests can reflect intellectual ambitiousness or stress for achievement in the child's life.
- Themes in children's responses lend themselves to analysis regarding the child's fears, guilt, preoccupations, feelings, interests, background, cultural milieu, bizarre thought processes, and perseveration. Themes in response content may occur also in conjunction with Vocabulary, Comprehension, or Similarities, as well as during spontaneous conversation during the assessment.
- Perseveration is sometimes evidenced when children give the same opening line for each response (e.g., *That's a hard clue to figure out . . .*) or when children give the same answer for many items.
- Hearing difficulties may become apparent for children who only focus on part of the auditory stimuli. Children may only hear part of the clue or only clearly hear the clue that is repeated once or twice.
- Attentional difficulties may also become apparent if a child consistently responds to only part of the clues. For example, the child may repeatedly attend to the first clue, or perhaps only the last clue may catch the child's attention.
- Risk-taking behavior is displayed by children who continually respond to the first clue, even if their initial answers tend to be wrong. This type of quick responding may also denote impulsivity, just as reflective children are likely to wait until all clues have been given before offering their first response.

Comprehension

Ages 2-6 to 3-11 — Not administered
Ages 4-0 to 7-3 — Supplemental subtest

Comprehension: Abilities Shared With Other Subtests
Input
   Auditory perception of complex verbal stimuli (understanding questions)

Integration-Storage
  Achievement
  Cognition of semantic stimuli (Guilford)
  Crystallized Intelligence — Gc (CHC broad ability)
  Culture-loaded knowledge
  Evaluation
  General information (CHC narrow ability)
  Language development (CHC narrow ability)
  Reasoning (verbal)
  Verbal comprehension
  Verbal conceptualization (Bannatyne)
  *Demonstration of practical information
  *Evaluation and use of past experiences
  *Knowledge of conventional standards of behavior
Output
  Verbal expression

Comprehension: Influences Affecting Subtest Scores
- Cultural opportunities at home
- Flexibility
- Negativism (e.g., *Dogs shouldn't have to wear tags*)
- Overly concrete thinking

Comprehension: Clinical Considerations
- A stable and emotionally balanced attitude and orientation is necessary for success on this subtest. Any type of maladjustment may lower scores.
- A high score on Comprehension alone is not enough evidence to interpret strong social adjustment. Corroborating evidence must be obtained from clinical observations, background information, or adaptive behavior inventories.
- Responses offer clues about a disturbed child's social-adaptive functioning in practical, social situations. However, be cautious about generalizing from single-issue questions to the complexities of the real world.

- When responses appear overlearned, stereotypical, or parroted, test the limits to determine level of real understanding and reasoning ability.
- Like responses to Similarities and Vocabulary, responses to Comprehension may vary in their degree of abstractness. Ability to think in abstract terms (e.g., *we need to be on time to be responsible*) is distinct from more concrete types of responses (*we need to be on time so you don't miss the school bus*).
- All Comprehension questions allow querying for clarification of responses. Analyze how children respond to follow-up questioning. Do they become defensive? Are they inflexible and unable to move beyond their original response? There are clinically relevant bits of information obtainable from observing the difference between someone who is spontaneously able to produce 2-point responses versus someone who needs constant structure and prodding.

Similarities

Ages 2-6 to 3-11 — Not administered
Ages 4-0 to 7-3 — Supplemental subtest

Similarities: Abilities Shared With Other Subtests

Input
    Auditory perception of simple verbal stimuli (understanding simple words)
    Distinguishing essential from nonessential detail
    Understanding words
Integration-Storage
    Achievement
    Cognition of semantic stimuli (Guilford)
    Concept formation
    Crystallized intelligence — Gc (CHC broad ability)
    Degree of abstract thinking
    Fluid intelligence — Gf (CHC broad ability)
    Language development (CHC narrow ability)
    Lexical knowledge (CHC narrow ability)

Logical abstractive (categorical) thinking
Reasoning (verbal)
Verbal comprehension
Verbal concept formation
Verbal conceptualization (Bannatyne)
*Logical classification (verbal stimuli)
Output
Much verbal expression

Similarities: Influences Affecting Subtest Scores

- Flexibility
- Interests
- Negativism (e.g., *they're not alike*)
- Overly concrete thinking

Similarities: Clinical Considerations

- Evaluate degree of abstractness; responses may be *abstract* (tables and chairs are "furniture"), *concrete* (dogs and cats "have paws"), or *functional* (books and newspapers are "for reading").
- Glean clinically rich information from the nature of the verbal response. Note overelaboration, overly general responses, overly inclusive responses, or self-references. Overelaboration may suggest obsessiveness. Overly inclusive responses may suggest a thought disorder. Self-references are unusual during Similarities and may be indicative of personal preoccupation.
- Obsessive children may provide responses that vary in quality by embedding a 2-point response among 1- or 0-point responses; this may lead to unusually high scores, as long as no response spoils the answer.
- Examine the pattern of responses. A child who earns a raw score by accumulating several 1-point responses may differ substantially in potential from a child who earns the same raw score with some 2-point and 0-point responses. The child who mixes the 2s and 0s probably has a greater capacity for excellent performance.
- Creativity may be exhibited in trying to come up with the relationship between two concepts. Sometimes visual imagery may be

used. The creativity doesn't invariably mean a wrong response (like Comprehension).

- Correct responses on the easier items may simply reflect over-learned, everyday associations rather than true abstract thought.
- Children who miss the first or second items administered provide the opportunity to see how they benefit from feedback. The examiner gives an example of a correct answer if the child doesn't provide a perfect answer to the first 2 items administered. Children who catch on quickly to these prompts demonstrate flexibility and adaptability. On the other hand, rigidity or poor learning ability may be evident if the child continues to insist that certain pairs are "not alike."
- Formal learning is less emphasized than is "new problem solving" (Horn's fluid classification). The child's task is to relate to verbal concepts, but the individual concepts tend to be simple and well known (even the hardest items use common concepts such as *asleep, heavy,* and *sweet*).

Receptive Vocabulary
Ages 2-6 to 3-11 — Core subtest, V-IQ, FS-IQ, GLC
Ages 4-0 to 7-3 — Optional subtest, GLC

Receptive Vocabulary: Abilities Shared With Other Subtests
Input
    Simple verbal directions
    Understanding words
    Visual motor channel
    Visual perception of complete meaningful stimuli
Integration-Storage
    Acquired knowledge (Bannatyne)
    Cognition of semantic stimuli (Guilford)
    Convergent production (Guilford)
    Crystallized intelligence — Gc (CHC broad ability)
    Figural evaluation (Guilford)
    Fund of information
    Language development (CHC narrow ability)

Learning ability
Lexical knowledge (CHC narrow ability)
Long-term memory
Verbal comprehension
Verbal concept formation
Verbal conceptualization (Bannatyne)
Word knowledge
*Receptive vocabulary

Output
Simple motor response

Receptive Vocabulary: Influences Affecting Subtest Scores

- Cultural opportunities at home
- Foreign language experience
- Intellectual curiosity and striving
- Interests
- Outside reading
- Richness or early environment
- School learning
- Visual-perceptual problems

Receptive Vocabulary: Clinical Considerations

- Perseveration is sometimes evident when children point to the picture in the same location for each response (e.g., always points to the upper right-hand picture).
- A child's spontaneous verbalizations can provide additional information about why he or she responded in a certain manner.
- The closed-ended nature of the Receptive Vocabulary responses allows you to glean information only about children's word knowledge, not verbal fluency. However, some children may give excessive verbiage in addition to their pointing response, which will allow you to evaluate verbal fluency too.
- Hearing difficulties may become apparent because the stimulus words are presented in isolation and there is no context by which to help the child understand the word. Clues to hearing difficulties include responses in which a child is randomly guessing or

repeatedly responding, "I don't know." In addition, be alert for children who tend to respond to pictures that sound like the stimulus word but are conceptually different (e.g., hearing *microscope* rather than the stimulus word, *telescope*); these children may be responding incorrectly because they misheard the stimulus word.

Picture Naming
Ages 2-6 to 3-11 — Supplemental subtest, GLC
Ages 4-0 to 7-3 — Optional subtest, GLC

Picture Naming: Abilities Shared With Other Subtests
Input
  Simple verbal directions
  Visual perception of complete meaningful stimuli
  Visual-vocal channel
Integration-Storage
  Acquired knowledge
  Crystallized knowledge — Gc (CHC broad ability)
  Figural cognition (Guilford)
  Figural evaluation (Guilford)
  Language development (CHC narrow ability)
  Lexical knowledge (CHC narrow ability)
  Long-term storage and retrieval (CHC broad ability)
  Semantic content (Guilford)
  Verbal concept formation
  Word knowledge
  *Naming facility (CHC narrow ability)
  *Visual recognition with verbal expression
Output
  Simple vocal expression

Picture Naming: Influences Affecting Subtest Scores
  • Cultural opportunities
  • Intellectual curiosity and striving
  • Richness of early environment
  • School learning
  • Visual-perceptual problems

Picture Naming: Clinical Considerations

- Children who consistently give more global than specific responses to pictured items (e.g., *vehicle* rather than *car*, *utensil* rather than *fork*) may be attempting to make the task more challenging or may be trying to impress the examiner.
- Children who talk their way around an answer rather than giving a simple one-word response may have word retrieval difficulties or may tend to be long-winded (e.g., *the big orange thing you get on Halloween, you know, it's all squishy inside and you can make it have a scary face or something*).
- Children who respond frequently by gesturing may have word retrieval difficulties, may have expressive difficulties, or may be shy.
- Responses that are personalized (e.g., *My daddy has a whistle just like that*) may indicate immaturity or egocentric thinking.
- Children whose responses frequently require querying to clarify the answer may warrant further assessment of expressive language abilities.
- Note frequent mispronunciation or misarticulation on this subtest. Patterns such as dropping first consonants or stuttering may be observed.

WPPSI-III Performance Subtests

Block Design
Ages 2-6 to 3-11 — Core subtest, P-IQ, FS-IQ
Ages 4-0 to 7-3 — Core subtest, P-IQ, FS-IQ

Block Design: Abilities Shared With Other Subtests
Input
    Auditory perception of complex verbal stimuli (following directions)
    Visual-motor channel
    Visual perception of abstract stimuli (designs-symbols)
Integration-Storage
    Cognition and evaluation of figural stimuli (Guilford)
    Concept formation
    Fluid intelligence — Gf (CHC broad ability)

Perceptual organization
Planning
Reproduction of models
Simultaneous processing
Spatial (Bannatyne)
Spatial relations (CHC narrow ability)
Spatial visualization
Speed of mental processing
Synthesis (part-whole relationships)
Trial-and-error learning
Visual processing — Gv (CHC broad ability)
*Analysis of whole into component parts (analytic strategies)
*Nonverbal concept formation
*Visualization (CHC narrow ability)
Output
Visual-motor coordination

Block Design: Influences Affecting Subtest Scores
- Cognitive style (field dependence-field independence)
- Flexibility
- Visual-perceptual problems
- Working under time pressure (less of a problem with WPPSI-III than with WPPSI-R because time bonuses for perfect performance have been eliminated)

Block Design: Clinical Considerations
- Note completion times and how often a child scores 0 points because she or he ran out of time. Although there are no bonus points earned for quick performance on the WPPSI-III, slow completion of the designs may indicate obsessive concern with detail or reflectivity.
- Visual-perceptual problems are often apparent on this subtest. If a low score occurs, the input of the visual material may be related to inaccurate perception rather than due to problem-solving ability or motor output. Testing the limits can often help to determine whether the child is having perceptual difficulties or other problems.

- Interpret scores in light of problem-solving approaches that were observed. Some children use trial and error, whereas others use a systematic and planned approach. Factors such as rigidity, perseveration, speed of mental processing, carelessness, self-concept, cautiousness, and ability to benefit from feedback affect the test.
- Some children may have little motivation to try and give up easily; others learn as they take the test and sometimes catch on just when they discontinue. In such cases, testing the limits by administering further items can be of great clinical value (although any extra items administered beyond the discontinue rule cannot be counted in the score).

Matrix Reasoning
Ages 2-6 to 3-11 — Not administered
Ages 4-0 to 7-3 — Core subtest, P-IQ, FS-IQ

Matrix Reasoning: Abilities Shared With Other Subtests
Input
    Visual perception
    Distinguishing essential from nonessential detail
    Visual-motor channel
Integration-Storage
    Broad visualization — Gv (CHC broad ability)
    Convergent-production (Guilford)
    Figural cognition (Guilford)
    Figural evaluation (Guilford)
    Fluid intelligence — Gf (CHC broad ability)
    General ability
    Holistic (right-brain) processing
    Induction (CHC narrow ability)
    Learning ability
    Nonverbal reasoning
    Perceptual organization
    Reasoning
    Simultaneous processing
    Spatial ability (Bannatyne)
    Spatial visualization

Synthesis
*Analogic reasoning
*Nonverbal problem solving with no time limit
Output
Simple (verbal) or nonverbal (pointing) response
Visual organization

Matrix Reasoning: Influences Affecting Subtest Scores
- Ability to respond when uncertain
- Cognitive style (field dependence, field independence)
- Color blindness (for some items, the use of several colors may confuse color-blind individuals)
- Flexibility
- Motivation level
- Negativism (e.g., *None of them go there*)
- Overly concrete thinking
- Persistence
- Visual-perceptual problems

Matrix Reasoning: Clinical Considerations
- Because this subtest is not timed, response times may vary widely from child to child or from item to item for a given child. Those who are mentally retarded or neurologically impaired may take longer to respond. Impulsivity may be indicated by extremely quick, incorrect responses. Failure to respond within a reasonable amount of time (45 seconds) is of potential diagnostic value, because it may be indicative of reflective style, obsessiveness, or confusion.
- Some items have complex visual stimuli. Children with visual-perceptual problems may display stimulus overload in attempting to input the multicolored, spatially complex items. Note differences in responding to the first 17 items that picture objects as stimuli versus the last 12 items that are geometric shapes and designs.
- Approaches to solving the Matrix Reasoning items vary from child to child. Some children tend to respond with a trial-and-error approach by testing each of the possible choices one by one.

Others may use a more planful, holistic approach to the problem, first mentally creating a solution to fill in the *?* and then searching the given responses to see whether one matches the solution they had envisioned. Because many children in the 4- to 7-year age range have not yet achieved the developmental stage of concrete operations, much less the formal operations that do not emerge until about age 11 years, this WPPSI-III subtest tends to be solved more concretely, via trial-and-error, than abstractly. For the Wechsler scales designed for older-age children and adults, the reverse tends to be true.

- Perseveration may be apparent on this subtest if a child repeatedly chooses the same number response for each item (e.g., number 3).
- Rule out color blindness as a potential cause for poor performance. If such information is not offered spontaneously by the child's parents, consider probing for information on color blindness if there is less difficulty on items that depend on form (e.g., Items 18, 21, 23, 25, 27, 28) versus those that depend on color (e.g., Items 19, 20, 22, 24, 29).
- Indecisiveness (e.g., *it is either 1 or 3*) may indicate insecurity or need for feedback. Analysis of errors on Matrix Reasoning may indicate visual neglect if there is a differential frequency of errors on items in a given sector of visual space.
- If a child's impulsive choice matches the details of the stimulus rather than completing the overall pattern, cognitive rigidity may be underlying the child's responses.

Picture Concepts
Ages 2-6 to 3-11 — Not administered
Ages 4-0 to 7-3 — Core subtest, P-IQ, FS-IQ

Picture Concepts: Abilities Shared With Other Subtests
Input
    Distinguishing essential from nonessential detail
    Visual perception
    Visual motor channel
    Simple directions (following directions)

Integration-Storage
  Convergent production (Guilford)
  Concept formation
  Crystallized intelligence — Gc (CHC broad ability)
  Decentration (Piagetian ability to focus on all pertinent attributes)
  Figural cognition (Guilford)
  Figural evaluation (Guilford)
  Fluid intelligence — Gf (CHC broad ability)
  General ability
  Holistic (right-brain) processing
  Induction (CHC narrow ability)
  Language development
  Learning ability
  Logical abstractive (categorical) thinking
  Nonverbal reasoning
  Perceptual organization
  Reasoning
  Semantic content
  Simultaneous processing
  Verbal concept formation
  Verbal conceptualization (Bannatyne)
  Verbal reasoning
  Visual association
  Visual organization
  *Logical classification (visual stimuli)
Output
  Simple (verbal) or nonverbal (pointing)

Picture Concepts: Influences Affecting Subtest Scores

- Ability to respond when uncertain
- Concentration
- Creativity
- Flexibility
- Negativism (e.g., *None of them go together*)
- Overly concrete thinking
- Persistence
- Visual-perceptual problems

Picture Concepts: Clinical Considerations
- Children who are mentally retarded or neurologically impaired may take longer to respond to items. Impulsivity may be indicated by extremely quick, incorrect responses. Failure to respond within a reasonable amount of time (30 seconds) is of potential diagnostic value because it may be indicative of reflective style, obsessiveness, or confusion.
- Some children choose their answer with a trial-and-error approach by testing each of the possible choices from one row one by one with the choices from the other row. Others may use a more planful approach to the problem, first quickly scanning all the choices and then searching the given responses again to find the best match. As was discussed for Matrix Reasoning, children in the WPPSI-III age range are more likely to use a trial-and-error rather than an abstract approach for solving Picture Concepts items.
- Perseveration may be apparent on this subtest if a child repeatedly chooses the pictures placed in the same location for each item (e.g., the first picture in the first row and the first in the second).
- Use a child's verbalizations during responding to understand the logic behind how problems were solved.
- There is a strong verbal component to this test for children ages 6 to 7 years, as evidenced by the results of factor analysis and clinical experience. Examine children's patterns of errors to determine whether their verbal reasoning may be related to difficulties or successes.
- Indecisiveness (e.g., *this one either goes with 1 or 3*) may indicate insecurity or need for feedback.

Symbol Search
Ages 2-6 to 3-11 — Not administered
Ages 4-0 to 7-3 — Supplemental subtest, PSQ

Symbol Search: Abilities Shared With Other Subtests
Input
Auditory perception of complex verbal stimuli (following directions)
Distinguishing essential from nonessential details

Encoding information for further cognitive processing
Visual-motor channel
Visual perception of abstract stimuli (designs-symbols)
Integration-Storage
Convergent production and evaluation of symbolic stimuli (Guilford)
Figural evaluation (Guilford)
Learning ability
Perceptual organization
Planning
Short-term memory (visual)
Spatial visualization
Speed of mental processing
Visual memory
*Perceptual speed (CHC narrow ability)
*Speed of visual search
Output
Broad speediness — Gs (CHC broad ability)
Clerical speed and accuracy
Paper-and-pencil skill
Processing speed
Rate of test taking (CHC narrow ability)
Visual-motor coordination

Symbol Search: Influences Affecting Subtest Scores

- Anxiety
- Attention-concentration
- Concentration
- Distractibility
- Obsessive concern with accuracy and detail
- Persistence
- Visual-perceptual problems
- Working under time pressure

Symbol Search: Clinical Considerations

- As in the subtests that contribute to P-IQ, visual impairment should be ruled out before a low Symbol Search score is interpreted.

- As noted in the Administration chapter of this book, it is important to be an astute observer during this task because many observed behaviors can help to interpret the Symbol Search score. Concentration, distractibility, obsessive concern with detail, impulsiveness, reflectivity, motivation level, visual-perceptual problems, or anxiety are just some of the factors that may be inferred to be related to a child's performance on Symbol Search.
- A learning curve may be present on this test. Children who begin to answer later items more quickly may have developed a plan or strategy after completing earlier items. To note whether speed of responding is in fact increasing, it is a good idea to routinely track how many items were answered during each of the four 30-second intervals during the subtest.
- Because many young children are not motivated to beat the clock, so to speak, observe whether a child's poor performance is due to his or her lack of motivation (or lack of understanding) to work quickly.
- Visual memory ability can sometimes be inferred from observations on this task. Some children may look at the Target symbol only once and then find the response in the Search Group, and others may look back and forth several times between the Target and Search groups before marking *?* or the matching symbol. The repeated referring back and forth between the symbols may be indicative of poor visual memory (or of insecurity).
- After the entire test has been administered, you may test the limits to help discern why certain responses were made. Point to some items answered correctly and some that were wrong, and ask the child to explain why they choose *?* or the matching symbol.

Coding

Ages 2-6 to 3-11 — Not administered
Ages 4-0 to 7-3 — Core subtest, FS-IQ, PSQ

Coding: Abilities Shared With Other Subtests

Input

Auditory perception of complex verbal stimuli (following directions)

Encoding information for further cognitive processing
Visual-motor channel
Visual perception of abstract stimuli (designs-symbols)

Integration-Storage

Convergent production and evaluation of figural stimuli (Guilford)
Integrated brain functioning (verbal-sequential and visual-spatial)
Learning ability
Perceptual organization
Planning
Reproduction of models
Sequential (Bannatyne)
Sequential processing
Short-term memory (visual)
Visual memory
*Visual sequencing

Output

Broad speediness — Gs (CHC broad ability)
Clerical speed and accuracy
Paper-and-pencil skill
Rate of test taking (CHC narrow ability)
Visual-motor coordination
*Psychomotor speed

Coding: Influences Affecting Subtest Scores

- Anxiety
- Attention-concentration
- Concentration
- Distractibility
- Obsessive concern with accuracy and detail
- Persistence
- Visual-perceptual problems
- Working under time pressure

Coding: Clinical Considerations

- Visual or motor impairment must be ruled out before interpreting a low score.

- Children who have demonstrated perfectionistic or compulsive tendencies prior to Coding should be told during the sample items that they need to copy the symbols legibly but not perfectly.
- Changes in rate of responding during the subtest can be related to motivation, distraction, fatigue, boredom, and so forth. Thus, as for Symbol Search, it is a good idea to routinely note the number of symbols copied during each of the four 30-second periods within the 120-second limit.
- Astute observation is key to interpreting scores on this subtest. Include the following in your interpretation of the score: coordination (grip on the pencil), attention-concentration, distractibility, motivation level, visual perceptual problems (rotating or distorting symbols), perfectionistic tendencies, perseveration (copying the same symbol for a whole line), or anxiety.
- Some children search for each shape in the key as they fill in every item, unable to remember that the star is first and the square is last. This behavior could be indicative of memory or sequencing problems.
- Short-term visual memory deficits may be evident if children keep referring back to the key before copying symbols (or these individuals may be insecure). Those who have memorized several pairs of symbols are likely to have a good visual memory (if they aren't making errors in their responses).
- Testing-the-limits procedures can be used to help to determine what caused a low Coding score. After the entire WPPSI-III is administered, use these procedures. To see how well a child can attend to, process, and remember the shapes and which symbols they are paired with, present a series of stars, circles, triangles, crosses, and squares drawn in one column and then randomly present each of the marks that corresponds with the shapes and ask the child to match as many of the marks that they can remember with the corresponding shapes (see Figure 4.1). Additionally you can attempt to measure how many symbols can be recalled regardless of the shapes, by asking the child to write as many of the different symbols as they can recall. Errors in

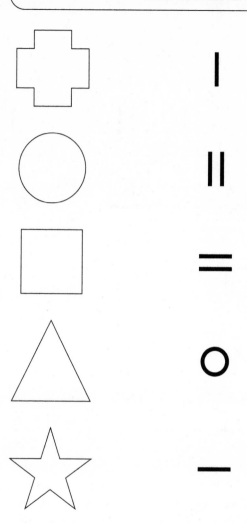

Figure 4.1 Suggested procedures for testing the limits on WPPSI-III Coding.

Directions: For each of the shapes in the first column, instruct the child to point to the mark in the second column that goes with the shape. If the child prefers, you may have the child draw the marks inside the shapes.

rotation, distortion, or inversion may occur. If the child cannot draw, you may present him or her with a sheet containing 15 symbols (5 target symbols and 10 foils) and ask the child to either point to or mark with a pencil the symbols that he or she

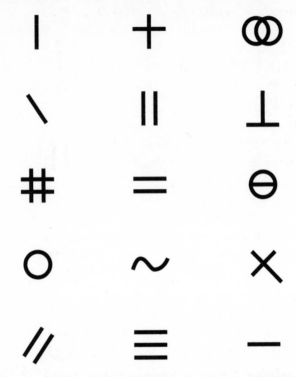

Figure 4.2 Additional procedures for testing the limits on WPPSI-III Coding.

Directions: Instruct the child to point to (or mark through) the symbols that he or she remembers seeing during the Coding subtest.

remembers seeing (see Figure 4.2). A final procedure to employ is to ask the child how he or she remembered which symbol went with which shape. Sometimes children are able to articulate that they verbally encoded the symbols or used another sort of strategy. Thus, performance on each of these testing-the-limits procedures will help to decipher why a subject earned a particular score, whether it be due to memory ability or lack of an efficient problem solving strategy.

Picture Completion
Ages 2-6 to 3-11 — Not administered
Ages 4-0 to 7-3 — Supplemental subtest

Picture Completion: Abilities Shared With Other Subtests

Input

Simple verbal directions

Visual-motor channel

Visual perception of meaningful stimuli (people and things)

Integration-Storage

Cognition and evaluation of figural stimuli (Guilford)

Distinguishing essential from nonessential details

General information (CHC narrow ability)

Holistic (right-brain) processing

Perceptual organization

Simultaneous processing

Spatial (Bannatyne)

Visual intelligence — Gv (CHC broad ability)

Visual organization without essential motor activity

*Flexibility of closure (CHC narrow ability)

*Visual recognition without essential motor activity

Output

Simple motor or vocal (pointing or one word response)

Picture Completion: Influences Affecting Subtest Scores

- Ability to respond when uncertain
- Alertness to the environment
- Cognitive style (field dependence-field independence)
- Concentration
- Negativism (e.g., Nothing is missing)
- Working under time pressure

Picture Completion: Clinical Considerations

- Although this subtest is timed, usually the 20-second limit pro-vides ample time for children who are neither mentally retarded nor neurologically impaired. Implusivity may be indicated by extremely quick, incorrect responses. Failure to respond within the limit is of potential diagnostic value because even reflective children typically respond within the limit.

- Verbal responses are more common than nonverbal responses on this Performance task, especially because Samples A and B teach the task by asking for verbal responses and the directions for subsequent items ask, "What part is missing?" rather than asking the child to point to the missing part. Although nonverbal responses are also considered correct, the frequency of such responses should be evaluated and may possibly be indicative of word retrieval problems. Verbal responses that are imprecise or vague may also be indicative of word retrieval problems. In preschool age children, nonverbal or vague verbal responses may occur more frequently.
- Negativity or hostility may be noted in persistent "Nothing is missing" responses.
- Obsessiveness or concentration problems may be evident in responses that are focused on trivial details of a picture (e.g., the fingernail polish on the hand). Similarly, confabulatory responses or responses indicating that something not in the picture is missing (e.g., the child's mother is missing) are of clinical interest. Giving trivial or confabulatory responses several times during the subtest is of potential diagnostic interest, especially because examiners are instructed to redirect individuals the first time they give a trivial response or a confabulatory response.

Object Assembly
Ages 2-6 to 3-11 — Core subtest, P-IQ, FS-IQ
Ages 4-0 to 7-3 — Supplemental subtest

Object Assembly: Abilities Shared With Other Subtests
Input
  Simple verbal directions
  Visual-motor channel
  Visual perception of meaningful stimuli (people-things)
  Integration-Storage
  Cognition and evaluation of figural stimuli (Guilford)
  Fluid intelligence — Gf (CHC broad ability)
  Holistic (right-brain) processing

Perceptual organization
Planning ability
Reasoning (nonverbal)
Simultaneous processing
Spatial (Bannatyne)
Spatial relations (CHC narrow ability)
Speed of mental processing
Synthesis (part-whole relationships)
Trial-and-error learning
Visual processing — Gv (CHC broad ability)
*Ability to benefit from sensory-motor feedback
*Anticipation of relationships among the parts
*Closure speed (CHC narrow ability)
Output
Broad speediness — Gs (CHC broad ability)
Visual-motor coordination

Object Assembly: Influences Affecting Subtest Scores

- Ability to respond when uncertain
- Cognitive style (field dependence, field independence)
- Experience with puzzles
- Flexibility
- Persistence
- Visual-perceptual problems
- Working under time pressure (less of a problem with WPPSI-III than with WPPSI-R because time bonuses for perfect performance have been eliminated)

Object Assembly: Clinical Considerations

- Although no bonus points are awarded for quick performance on the WPPSI-III, reflectivity or obsessive concern with detail can be noted with slower completion times or with puzzle completions beyond the time limits.
- How children manipulate the puzzle pieces is informative. Problem-solving approach may be noted: trial and error versus a systematic and insightful attack, impulsive versus reflective

cognitive style, and carelessness versus cautiousness. Rigidity or perseveration may be evident (trying repeatedly to put the same puzzle piece in the same wrong place). Motor coordination, concentration, persistence, and speed of processing may all be inferred from behaviors and performance on this subtest.

- Input problems may be present if objects are constructed upside down or at an angle.
- Integration problems are demonstrated when separate groups of pieces are assembled, but the child cannot get the whole. At times children insist that a piece is missing from the puzzle when they cannot completely integrate the given pieces.
- Output or coordination problems are evident when the child aligns the puzzle pieces correctly but too far apart or inadvertently misaligns a piece or two while adding pieces to complete the puzzle.
- Children who try to turn the puzzle pieces over before the examiner is done arranging the puzzle pieces may be revealing impulsivity, insecurity, or low moral development, or they may be testing the limits of the examiner.

STEP BY STEP: HOW TO INTERPRET THE WPPSI-III PROFILE

This section provides a systematic way to approach and interpret the WPPSI-III profile. Rather than just grabbing randomly at scores that may look interesting, our approach leads you carefully from the most global score to the most specific. Through this process, you will determine the most meaningful hypotheses about the child's abilities.

Interpretation of WPPSI-III profiles evolves through eight steps. The first step looks at the most global score, FS-IQ. Steps 2 and 3 deal with the Verbal and Performance IQs and their discrepancy. Step 4 examines subtest scatter, Step 5 computes differences between the P-IQ and PSQ (only for children ages 4-0 to 7-3), and Step 6 addresses the strengths and weaknesses in the subtest profile. Step 7 determines whether the GLC warrants interpretation, and Step 8 helps you generate hypotheses about the child's strong and weak abilities. The practical meaningfulness of the IQs is examined throughout the steps. This step-by-step method is a recipe that can be followed like a cookbook, but clinicians may also deviate from the recipe and use clinical information to reject empirical rules in favor of alternative interpretations of the data. To create an in-depth understanding of each child's peaks and valleys of abilities, combine theory, clinical skill, and knowledge of the instrument.

Each of the steps of interpretation of the WPPSI-III profile is explained in the following pages. However, these steps are also summarized in worksheet form (see the WPPSI-III Interpretive Worksheet in Appendix A). The illustrative samples of how to use the various steps in the interpretive process will utilize the data from Ophelia's profile (see Table 4.1). Ophelia is a 6 year, 1 month old girl who was referred for an assessment because of her parents' concern about how to best help her develop her cognitive strengths. (All of the illustrative cases presented in this book have had the identifying information changed to protect the confidentiality of the clients.) Ophelia's profile is also presented in the last chapter of this book to demonstrate how to translate the empirical framework into an actual clinical case.

Step 1: Interpret Full Scale IQ

The WPPSI-III FS-IQ is the most reliable score obtained on the test. It has a mean split-half coefficient of .95 for children ages 2-6 to 3-11 and .97 for children ages 4-0 to 7-3. The stability coefficient for the FS-IQ at all ages is .91, and the standard error of measurement at each of the nine age levels is about 3 IQ points. Due to these strong psychometric qualities, the FS-IQ should be considered first in interpretation of the profile. Consider not only the single FS-IQ value, but also the confidence interval, percentile rank, and descriptive category that you entered on the Record Form. As with the confidence interval, we encourage examiners to include in a case report the child's descriptive category or category range. For example, if a child's FS-IQ is 108 and the confidence interval is 104 to 112, then the child is functioning at the average to high average level of intelligence. Using descriptive categories and confidence intervals facilitates accurate communication between professionals and laypeople and avoids pigeonholing the child. This approach helps to communicate that there is error surrounding a child's obtained score, which puts the score in perspective. Rapid Reference 4.9 shows a completed example of Step 1 of the WPPSI-III Interpretive Worksheet.

Table 4.1 Wechsler Preschool and Primary Scale of Intelligence–Third Edition

WPPSI-III Profile for Ophelia, Age 6-1

Composite Scale	Standard Score	90% Confidence Interval	Percentile Rank	Qualitative Description
Verbal IQ	116	110–120	86	High average
Performance IQ	119	112–124	90	High average
Processing Speed Quotient	104	96–111	61	Average
Full Scale IQ	120	115–124	91	Superior
General Language Composite	113	106–118	81	High average

Verbal Subtests	Scaled Score	Percentile Rank	Performance Subtests	Scaled Score	Percentile Rank
Information	13	84	Block Design	12	75
Vocabulary	11	63	Matrix Reasoning	16	98
Word Reasoning	15	95	Picture Concepts	11	63
Comprehension	9	37	Picture Completion	11	63
Similarities	13	84	Object Assembly	11	63

General Language Subtests			Processing Speed Subtests		
Receptive Vocabulary	15	95	Symbol Search	10	50
Picture Naming	10	50	Coding	12	75

We encourage examiners to look at the FS-IQ first, but the interpretive process certainly does not stop there. In fact, in progressing through the rest of the steps, examiners may find that the FS-IQ is meaningless and is therefore rendered uninterpretable. If there are large differences between the Verbal and Performance IQs or too much scatter among the subtests, then the importance of the FS-IQ is diminished. Additional factors such as fatigue, anxiety, or cultural background may also affect the interpretability of the FS-IQ.

A child's abilities can rarely be captured accurately via one number (or even three IQ values). Thus, it is inappropriate to attribute too much weight

≡Rapid Reference 4.9

Step 1: Interpret the Full Scale IQ

Scale	IQ	90% or 95% Confidence Interval (circle one)	Percentile Rank	Descriptive Category
Full Scale	120	115-124	91	High Average-Superior
Performance	119	112-124	90	High Average-Superior
Verbal	116	110-120	86	High Average-Superior

⇩

to the FS-IQ alone. To understand the complex nature of cognitive functioning, consider many different abilities rather than just looking at a summary of those abilities, as is done when focusing exclusively on the FS-IQ.

Step 2: Is the Verbal IQ Versus Performance IQ Discrepancy Significant?

One level below the interpretation of the global FS-IQ is the comparison between Performance and Verbal IQs. In this step of WPPSI-III interpretation, you need to compute the size of the difference between the P-IQ and V-IQ and determine whether the discrepancy is large enough to be statistically significant. For the purposes of this calculation, the size rather than the direction of the difference is what is important.

The WPPSI-III *Administrative and Scoring Manual* (Wechsler, 2002, Table B.1) only gives values for statistical significance between the V-IQ and P-IQ at the .05 and .15 levels. However, we feel that the .15 level is too liberal for most testing purposes because it contains too much built-in error. The WPPSI-III Interpretive Worksheet (Appendix A) presents difference values at the .01 and .05 levels individual age groups as well as the average across age groups. Overall for all ages, at the .01 level, a 14-point discrepancy between the Verbal and Performance IQs is necessary for significance, and at the .05 level a 10-point discrepancy is needed. You have the option of using either the average value or the value for the appropriate age group, depending on your clinical preference. Rapid Reference 4.10 shows a completed example of Step 2 of the WPPSI-III Interpretive Worksheet.

It is up to each individual examiner to decide the level of confidence (and error) that he or she is willing to accept. However, when difference scores are considered, the level of confidence should at least be at the 95% level. The purpose of calculating the difference scores in the profile is to generate useful hypotheses. To allow flexible interpretation, the 95% level of confidence may provide more information than does the conservative level of 99%.

If no significant difference is found between the WPPSI-III V-IQ and P-IQ, then you can assume that overall the child's verbal and nonverbal skills are fairly evenly developed (which is what we have done in Ophelia's case).

≡Rapid Reference 4.10

Step 2: Is the Verbal IQ Versus Performance IQ Discrepancy Significant?

V-IQ	P-IQ	Difference	Age Group	Significant (p<.01)	Significant (p<.05)	Not Significant	Is there a significant difference?
116	119	3	2:6-3:5	15+	12-14	0-11	YES (NO)
			3:6-4:5	14+	11-13	0-10	
			4:6-4:11	13+	10-12	0-9	
			5:0-5:5	12+	9-11	0-8	
			5:6-6:11	13+	10-12	0-9	
			7:0-7:3	12+	9-11	0-8	
			All Ages	14+	10-13	0-9	

⇩

Step 2 Decision Box		
If the answer to Step 2 is NO, there is not a significant difference between the V-IQ and P-IQ	⇨	First explain the meaning of the scales not being significantly different. Then **Skip to Step 4.**
If the answer to Step 2 is YES, there is a significant difference between the V-IQ and P-IQ	⇨	Continue on to **Step 3.**

⇩

The Step 2 decision box in the WPPSI-III Interpretive Worksheet tells you that you may now skip to Step 4, as the third step considers whether the discrepancy is abnormally large. Obviously, if the difference is not large enough to be statistically significant, it is not going to be abnormally large.

Step 3: Is the Verbal IQ Versus Performance IQ Discrepancy Abnormally Large?

In this step we ask whether the size of the difference found in Step 2 is abnormally large — but only if it was found to be statistically significant in the previous step. To be considered abnormally large, the difference must be so large that it is rare among the normal population.

Nearly all children have some sort of discrepancy between their Verbal and Performance IQs and sometimes that discrepancy is large, even for normal children. On average, nearly *half* of the children in the WPPSI-III standardization sample (48.6%) displayed V-P IQ discrepancies of at least 10 points, with almost *one third* of the children (30.6%) earning discrepancies of 14 or more points. As noted in Step 2, V-P IQ differences of 10 and 14 points are statistically significant at the .05 and .01 levels, respectively. Indeed, the *mean* discrepancy is 11.3 points for children who scored higher on the Performance Scale (P-IQ > V-IQ) and 11.0 points for children with the reverse profile (V-IQ > P-IQ). Thus, it is common for normal young children to display significant discrepancies between their WPPSI-III Verbal and Performance IQs, similar to previous findings with the Wechsler scales at all age ranges, including adults (Kaufman, 1994b; Kaufman & Lichtenberger, 2002).

Because statistically significant differences are not necessarily abnormal, we must investigate how large a discrepancy must be to be abnormally large. How frequently a discrepancy occurs in the normal population is presented in Table B.2 in Appendix B of both WPPSI-III manuals (The Psychological Corporation, 2002; Wechsler, 2002). The data provided in Step 3 of the WPPSI-III Interpretive Worksheet show that for a V-IQ versus P-IQ discrepancy on the WPPSI-III to be considered abnormal (e.g., occurring in 15% or less of the normal population), a 20-point difference between the IQs must be present, regardless of the direction of the difference. In addition to the extreme 15%, we present the extreme 10%, 5%, 2%, and 1% in the WPPSI-III Interpretation Worksheet (Appendix A) so that examiners can determine more exactly how rare a given discrepancy is. These different levels of abnormality correspond to V-P IQ discrepancies — regardless of direction — of 23, 28, 33, and 36 points, respectively.

The WPPSI-III manuals also report discrepancy data in Table B.2 for groups in the WPPSI-III standardization sample with differing FS-IQ ranges. The most noteworthy findings are the following: (a) the smallest discrepancies, regardless of direction, were found for children who earned FS-IQs below 80 (mean = 9.9); (b) the largest discrepancies were identified for those with FS-IQs between 110 and 119 (mean = 12.1); and (c) children with relatively low FS-IQs (less than 90) tended to favor the Performance IQ (P-IQ > V-IQ), but the reverse pattern was not true for children with relatively high IQs (110+). Regarding the latter finding, children with IQs below 80 averaged P > V of 11.8 points versus V > P of only 7.9 points. For those earning FS-IQs of 80–89, mean P > V was 10.9 versus mean V > P of 9.8 — the same trend, but less extreme. (Note that the mean discrepancies reported in this section are only for individuals who had at least some discrepancy in their V- and P-IQs. The tables in the WPPSI-III manuals that pertain to V-P IQ differences exclude the approximately 4% of young children with V = P.)

If an abnormally large difference exists between a child's verbal and nonverbal abilities, then address and interpret that discrepancy. Interpret an abnormally large discrepancy even if scatter exists within the IQs. As the Step 3 decision box explains, if the size of the discrepancy is *normal*, then examine the scatter in the IQs in Step 4. However, if there is an abnormally large discrepancy, then you may proceed directly to Step 5.

Step 4: Is the V-IQ Versus P-IQ Discrepancy Interpretable?

Before interpreting any significant discrepancies found in Step 2, you need to further investigate the V-IQ and P-IQ. Sometimes one or both of the IQs are not interpretable because they do not represent unitary abilities. Step 4 provides a process for examining whether the V-IQ versus P-IQ discrepancy is interpretable in a practical and clinical sense. However, if an abnormally large discrepancy between the Verbal and Performance IQs was revealed in Step 3, then you should skip Step 4 because the abnormally large discrepancy will be interpreted regardless of whether scatter is present in the IQs. Some examiners prefer to complete Step 4 no matter what in order to gain a better understanding of how the IQs are functioning.

The amount of scatter among the three Verbal subtests that compose the V-IQ for 4- to 7-year-olds (only two subtests for those less than 4 years) indicates how variable or diverse a child's abilities are within the verbal domain. If an abnormal amount of scatter is present across subtest scores, denoting substantial intersubtest variability, assume that a global verbal ability is *not* responsible for the child's scaled scores. Similarly, if an unusually large amount of scatter is present among the Performance subtests, then the P-IQ is not very meaningful or interpretable.

For children ages 4-0 to 7-3, determine the amount of scatter among the three subtests that are used in the calculation of V-IQ by computing the difference between the highest and lowest of the three scaled scores. To determine the size of the difference required to denote abnormal scatter, we examined the cumulative frequency distributions presented in Appendix B of both WPPSI-III manuals for intersubtest scatter (Table B.6). According to these data, about 27% of children had differences of 4 or more points between the highest and lowest of their three V-IQ subtests, and about 13% of children had differences of 5 or more points. The latter value meets our scatter criterion of occurring about 15% or less in the normal population, so *consider scatter on the Verbal scale abnormal if the difference is 5 points or more.*

For the three P-IQ subtests, data in the manuals reveals that about 20% of children had discrepancies of 6 or more points and about 11% had scaled-score differences (high minus low) of 7 points. The value of 7 therefore corresponds to abnormal scatter. After determining whether scatter among the Verbal subtests is abnormal, then undertake a similar process to calculate the scatter among the three subtests of the P-IQ. If the difference between the highest and lowest of the three P-IQ subtests is 7 points or greater, consider the Performance Scale to have abnormally large scatter.

For children ages 2-6 to 3-11, scatter within V-IQ and P-IQ is simply the difference between the two subtests that constitute each scale. A 4-point scaled-score difference (or greater) between Information and Receptive Vocabulary is needed for abnormal scatter in V-IQ and a difference of at least 6 points is needed for Block Design versus Object Assembly to denote abnormal P-IQ scatter. Scatter of this size on either the Verbal or Performance scale occurred in about 15% or fewer of the children ages 2–6 to 3–11 tested on the WPPSI-III (Wechsler, 2002, Table B.4). Rapid Reference 4.11 shows a completed example of Step 4 of the WPPSI-III Interpretive Worksheet.

≡ Rapid Reference 4.11

Step 4: Is Verbal Versus Performance IQ Discrepancy Interpretable?

A.) Is there abnormal Verbal scatter for ages 4-0 to 7-3?

	High Scaled Score of 3 V-IQ Subtests	Low Scaled Score of 3 V-IQ Subtests	High-Low Difference	Abnormal Scatter	Not Abnormal	Is there abnormal scatter?
Ages 4-0 to 7-3	15	11	4	5 or more	0-4	YES (NO)

B.) Is there abnormal Performance scatter for ages 4-0 to 7-3?

	High Scaled Score of 3 P-IQ Subtests	Low Scaled Score of 3 P-IQ Subtests	High-Low Difference	Abnormal Scatter	Not Abnormal	Is there abnormal scatter?
	16	11	5	7 or more	0-6	YES (NO)

⇩

Step 4 Decision Box				
If the answers to both Step 4 questions (A and B) are **NO**	⇨	then V-IQ **versus** P-IQ discrepancy is interpretable	⇨	Explain the meaningful difference between V-IQ & P-IQ. **Then go to Step 5.**
If the answers to either Step 4 question (A or B) are **YES**	⇨	then do **not** interpret the V-IQ **versus** P-IQ difference	⇨	Examine the strengths and weaknesses in **Step 5.**

⇩

Note: If there is a significant difference between the component parts of the Full Scale IQ (i.e., the Verbal IQ and the Performance IQ or significant subtest scatter), the Full Scale IQ should not be interpreted as a meaningful representation of the individual's overall performance.

If you find an abnormal amount of scatter on the Verbal scale, then the V-IQ probably does not reflect a unitary construct for the child, so don't interpret the V-IQ. Similarly, if you find abnormally large scatter on the Performance Scale, then the P-IQ does not represent a unitary construct, so don't interpret the P-IQ.

Therefore, if either the Verbal or Performance IQ is uninterpretable because of the variability within the scale, then the difference between these scales is also uninterpretable. The discrepancy between the V-IQ versus P-IQ does not meaningfully represent a difference in global verbal versus nonverbal intelligence if either of the global IQs does not represent unitary factors. If abnormally large scatter is *not* present, then consider the scales unitary and interpret the difference between them. However, if the discrepancy between the Verbal and Performance scales is not interpretable, then the most meaningful representation of a child's abilities may be in their individual relative strengths and weaknesses on the WPPSI-III (Step 7) and in the hypotheses derived from the overall pattern of their subtest scores (Step 8) .

Interpreting the Global Verbal and Nonverbal Dimensions

If you are able to interpret the Verbal and Performance IQs, you should explore a variety of interpretive hypotheses. These hypotheses may be derived from clinical, theoretical, or research-based information, or some combination of these. In this section we provide an outline of some of the possible interpretations; more thorough discussion of these hypotheses is available elsewhere (Flanagan, McGrew, & Ortiz, 2000; Kaufman, 1994b; Kaufman & Lichtenberger, 2002; Prifitera & Saklofske, 1998). Chapter 6 of this book also reviews some research on Verbal-Performance patterns that are typically found in populations such as children with mental retardation and children who are gifted.

The WPPSI-III *Technical and Interpretive Manual* offers some general guidelines on how the Verbal and Performance IQs may be interpreted. The V-IQ is "a measure of acquired knowledge, verbal reasoning and comprehension" and is a "more refined, purer measure of verbal comprehension, than the WPPSI-R VIQ" (The Psychological Corporation, p. 135). In contrast, the P-IQ is "a measure of fluid reasoning, spatial processing, attentiveness to detail, and visual-motor integration" (The Psychological Corporation, p. 136). These general descriptions provided by the publisher of the WPPSI-III are clearly related to the widely respected concepts of Horn, Cattell, and Carroll that we describe in the following section.

Fluid and Crystallized Theory

Horn and Cattell (1966, 1967) distinguished between two broad concepts, Crystallized Intelligence (Gc) and Fluid Intelligence (Gf). Learning that is dependent on a child's school-acquired knowledge and acculturation is categorized as Gc, whereas one's ability to solve novel problems that do not depend on formal schooling or acculturation are categorized as Gf (Cattell & Horn, 1978). The original Gc-Gf theory put forth by Horn and Cattell was subsequently expanded and refined by Horn (1989) to include roughly eight abilities that provide "purer" measures of intellectual abilities. Besides Gc and Gf, Horn's expanded theory comprises abilities such as short-term acquisition and retrieval (SAR or Gsm), broad speediness (Gs), broad visualization (Gv), quantitative thinking (Gq), auditory processing (Ga), and long-term storage and retrieval (Glr). The pure tests of fluid ability (Gf) do not include variables such as processing speed, visualization, memory, or Gc but do focus on reasoning (Horn, 1989, 1991; Kaufman & Horn, 1996). The pure tests of crystallized ability (Gc) minimize the effects of short-term memory and fluid reasoning and focus on knowledge and comprehension.

Tasks that call for "fluent visual scanning, Gestalt Closure, mind's eye rotations of figures and ability to see reversals" are categorized as Gv (Horn, 1989, p. 80), whereas tasks that require basic immediate recall of stimuli are categorized as SAR (Horn & Hofer, 1992). Tasks that relate to "carefulness, strategies (or metacognition), mood (such as depression), and persistence" are measures of Gs (Horn, 1989, p. 84).

The theories of Horn and Cattell have been applied to the Wechsler scales many times, initially by Matarazzo (1972) and subsequently by many others (Flanagan et al., 2000; Kaufman, 1994b; Kaufman & Lichtenberger, 2002). Carroll (1993, 1997) expanded the Gf-Gc taxonomy even further, postulating many specific abilities that are subsumed under the broad cognitive domains of Gf, Gc, Gv, and so forth. Ultimately, the theories of Horn and Carroll were merged to form the Cattell-Horn-Carroll (CHC) theory (Flanagan et al., 2000). To categorize each WPPSI-III subtest, we considered carefully the work of Horn (1989, 1991), Carroll (1997), Kaufman (1994b), Woodcock (1990), and Flanagan et al. (2000).

We list the broad abilities according to CHC theory for each WPPSI-III subtest in Rapid Reference 4.3. The very specific or narrow CHC abilities (Flanagan et al., 2000) measured by the WPPSI-III subtests are listed in Rapid Reference 4.4. These abilities are the "Narrow Stratum I" abilities first postulated by Carroll (1993). These subtest categorizations, initially made based on our interpretation of the CHC model, were validated by Dawn Flanagan (personal communication, January 29, 2003). Definitions of both the broad and narrow CHC abilities are provided in Rapid Reference 4.5.

As discussed in chapter 1, Wechsler did not design his subtests based on Gf-Gc theory — or on any theory, for that matter. Thus, it is not surprising that the WPPSI-III Verbal and Performance subtests and scales are complex and cannot be *cleanly* broken apart into the pure Gc and Gf factors (see Kaufman, 1994b). Several Verbal subtests are related to Gc and Gf, and some Performance subtests are related to Gf, Gv, or Gs (see Rapid References 4.3 and 4.4). Although some authors feel comfortable categorizing Wechsler's subtests into only one of Horn's expanded theory broad categories (e. g., Flanagan et al.,

2000), it is our belief that some Wechsler subtests are best classified as measuring more than one aspect of Horn's theory. For example, Similarities has a Gc component (language ability) and a Gf component (using reasoning to figure out the similarity); Word Reasoning also has components of Gc and Gf, whereas Block Design and Object Assembly have Gv as well as Gf components.

The factor analyses of WPPSI-III Supplemental and Core subtests exemplify the fact that the subtests are not pure measures of Gc, Gf, or Gs. For example, as noted in chapter 1, Picture Concepts loaded about equally well on both Processing Speed and Verbal factors at age 4 but was primarily a Performance task at age 5 and primarily a Verbal subtest at ages 6–7 (see Table 1.1).

Picture Concepts' stimuli all correspond to verbal concepts, which likely explains why its three highest correlations were with Verbal subtests (Similarities, Word Reasoning, and Information) and its three lowest were with Performance (or Processing Speed) subtests. Table 4.2 shows the WPPSI-III subtests with the highest and lowest correlations with Picture Concepts for ages 4-0 to 7-3.

The types of tasks included among the highest and lowest correlates of Picture Concepts (Table 4.2) make it clear why this subtest was more of a Verbal than a Performance subtest at ages 4-0 to 4-11 and 6-0 to 7-3 in the factor analyses of Core and Supplemental subtests. Less clear is why it loaded on the Processing Speed factor for 4-year-olds (as well as Verbal factor), especially

Table 4.2 Subtests With Highest and Lowest Correlations With Picture Concepts

Subtest	r
Highest	
Word Reasoning	.51
Similarities	.51
Information	.49
Lowest	
Block Design	.41
Object Assembly	.39
Coding	.32

Note. Coefficients are from *WPPSI-III Technical and Interpretive Manual* (Table 5.1).

when its lowest correlation was with Coding (.32). The 30-second time limit for Picture Concepts items may account for its association with Processing Speed at ages 4-0 to 4-11 — but not for children ages 5-0 to 7-3 — because the time limit may not be as much of an issue for children in the older portion of the WPPSI-III age range. Or perhaps the cognitive demands of Coding and Symbol Search are higher for 4-year-olds than for older children, increasing its relationship to Picture Concepts for that age group. Confirmatory factor analyses help determine whether Picture Concepts' multiple loadings affect the construct validity of the WPPSI-III. Results of the analyses showed no significant differences between the model that allows Picture Concepts to load on *both* the Verbal and Performance factors and the model that places Picture Concepts *only* on the Performance factor. Therefore, although the placement of Picture Concepts on the WPPSI-III's Performance factor seems to be supported by the confirmatory analyses, interpretation of Picture Concepts (and the P-IQ) must include an understanding of its Gf, Gs, and Gc components.

Clearly the WPPSI-III subtests are complex in terms of their underlying abilities (e.g., Gc, Gf, Gv, Gs). It is possible that one factor is a stronger driving force in determining one child's test score on a subtest, whereas a different factor may best explain another child's performance on the same subtest. Therefore, before automatically interpreting a subtest as a measure of any particular theoretical construct, you should consider background information, behavioral observations, and supplementary test scores for supportive data.

Step 5: Is the Performance IQ Versus Processing Speed Quotient Discrepancy Interpretable?

The PSQ is a new composite on the WPPSI-III, which can only be calculated if the supplemental Symbol Search subtest is administered (in addition to the Core Coding subtest). A child's speed of responding can affect performance on other scales, such as the P-IQ. Processing speed has been shown to be sensitive to clinical conditions such as ADHD, learning disabilities, and traumatic brain injuries (e. g., Donders, 1996). Although most of this type of research has been based on school-age children and adolescents, it is likely that noting whether a child's performance on the WPPSI-III PSQ is significantly higher or lower than the P-IQ will facilitate the clinical interpretation of very young children as well.

Before examining the difference between scores on the Processing Speed and Performance scales, determine whether the P-IQ is a unitary construct that can be interpreted. If you completed Step 4, then you have already made that determination. If the P-IQ was found to be interpretable, then continue with the present Step; *if not, then proceed directly to Step 6.*

If you opted to skip Step 4 (because Step 3 revealed abnormal scatter between V-IQ and P-IQ), then determine now whether the P-IQ is unitary. Follow the instructions in Step 4 on pages 135–136 for P-IQ (skip the computations for V-IQ). If the P-IQ includes an abnormal amount of subtest scatter, then it cannot be interpreted; *proceed to Step 6.* If P-IQ is interpretable, then continue with this step.

Now determine whether the PSQ is a unitary construct by examining the scaled-score difference between Coding and Symbol Search. If the difference is abnormally large (i.e., equal to or greater than 5 points), then the PSQ is not a unitary construct and should not be interpreted. If abnormal scatter exists in either the PSQ or the P-IQ, then the difference between the two composite scores should not be interpreted. However, if Coding and Symbol Search are not abnormally different from one another, then interpret the PSQ.

If *both* the PSQ and the P-IQ are unitary constructs, then interpret the difference between the two composites. For the overall sample, a PSQ-P-IQ discrepancy of 13 points is significant at the .05 level and a discrepancy of 17 points is significant at the .01 level. Rapid Reference 4.12 shows a completed example of Step 5 of the WPPSI-III Interpretive Worksheet using data for Ophelia.

The base rate data in Appendix B of both WPPSI-III manuals (Table B.2) provide information about how common (or abnormal) PSQ > PIQ and PIQ > PSQ discrepancies are for the total sample of children ages 4-0 to 7-3 and separately by FS-IQ range, and they present data on the average magnitude of these standard-score differences. Overall, regardless of the direction of the discrepancy, standard-score differences of 21 or more points occur rarely (about 15% of the time) in the normal population, and the value of 21 points denotes abnormal discrepancies for both P-IQ > PSQ and PSQ > P-IQ. In addition, the average discrepancy for children who scored higher on P-IQ is about 11 points, the same mean for children who scored higher on PSQ. However, when the size of abnormal discrepancies is examined separately by IQ range, then an interesting pattern emerges. Children with IQs

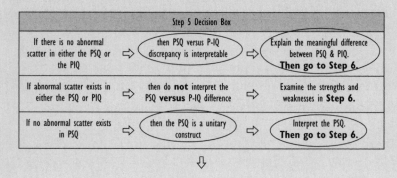

Rapid Reference 4.12

Step 5: Is the Performance IQ Versus Processing Speed Quotient Discrepancy Interpretable?

(complete only for children ages 4-0 to 7-3)

A.) Is there Abnormal Scatter in the PSQ

Coding Scaled Score	Low Scaled Score of 3 V-IQ Subtests	High-Low Difference	Abnormal Scatter	Not Abnormal	Is there abnormal scatter?
12	10	2	4 or more	0-3	YES (NO)

B.) Is the PIQ vs. PSQ discrepancy significant?

P-IQ	PSQ	Difference	Abnormal Scatter	Significant (p<.01)	Significant (p<.05)	Not Significant	Is there a significant difference?
119	104	15	4 or more	17+	13-16	0-12	(YES) NO

Step 5 Decision Box		
If there is no abnormal scatter in either the PSQ or the PIQ	⇒ then PSQ versus P-IQ discrepancy is interpretable	⇒ Explain the meaningful difference between PSQ & PIQ. **Then go to Step 6.**
If abnormal scatter exists in either the PSQ or PIQ	⇒ then do **not** interpret the PSQ **versus** P-IQ difference	⇒ Examine the strengths and weaknesses in **Step 6.**
If no abnormal scatter exists in PSQ	⇒ then the PSQ is a unitary construct	⇒ Interpret the PSQ. **Then go to Step 6.**

⇩

below 90 more often have large discrepancies in favor of the PSQ, but the reverse pattern is true for higher-functioning children (IQs of 110+). Table 4.3 summarizes this pattern.

For children with IQs under 90, the stronger performance on speeded tests than on P-IQ subtests likely reflects the fact that the P-IQ requires higher-level cognitive processes such as nonverbal reasoning and problem solving; tasks that measure such processes are more challenging to children with low IQs. In contrast, the large discrepancies in favor of P-IQ for children with IQs

Table 4.3 Mean PSQ > PIQ and PIQ > PSQ Discrepancies, by Ability Level

	IQ Level		
	< 89	90–109	110+
PSQ > PIQ	12	11	11
PIQ > PSQ	8	11	13

Note. These data are based on data presented in Table B.2 in both WPPSI-III manuals.

over 109 likely reflect their strong reasoning skills (perhaps at the expense of processing information quickly). The sections that follow contain information that will help in understanding and interpreting the PSQ.

Processing Speed Quotient: Clinical Considerations

As in interpretation of the other composite scores, to interpret the PSQ accurately you should consider and integrate multiple sources of data. The most obvious interpretation of the PSQ is, of course, processing speed. However, other factors may also come into play when children respond to Coding and Symbol Search — for example, fine-motor coordination, motivation, attention-concentration, anxiety, distractibility, reflectiveness, compulsiveness, visual memory, planning ability, or ability to process abstract symbols (see the Don't Forget box on page 146).

The types of speeded performance measured by the two subtests of the PSQ differ to some extent. *Mental* speed is tapped considerably during Symbol Search, whereas *psychomotor* speed is primarily tapped during Coding. Either or both of these aspects of speed can influence a child's score on the PSQ. The effect of fine-motor coordination is also important to consider in evaluating performance on this composite. Observe children as they hold the pencil. Awkward, clumsy grips and pencil strokes that are not fluid may be indicative of poor fine-motor coordination. Also observe children's fine-motor coordination while they manipulate blocks or puzzle pieces during Block Design and Object Assembly. Visual-perceptual problems may also be evident by observing how a child draws the symbols during Coding, the types of errors made during Block Design and Object Assembly, and possible distortions during Picture Completion.

Noncognitive factors may affect a child's performance on the PSQ; for example, level of motivation, anxiety, attention-concentration, and perfectionism may all play a role in performance. Some children have more of a reflective, careful style of processing information and are therefore reluctant to work quickly. Other children with perfectionistic tendencies may work very slowly and carefully to ensure that they do not draw any of the symbols inaccurately on Coding or make a messy slash mark on Symbol Search. Anxiety may interfere with a child's ability to remain continually focused on the task at hand, as may poor attention-concentration or distractibility. Examiners need to be good clinicians to discern which (if any) behaviors had a substantial effect on a child's obtained PSQ. These inferences are particularly important for children who perform relatively poorly on one or both PSQ subtests because the educational implications are quite different for children who earn identical PSQ scores if the likely explanation for one child is behavioral (e.g., anxiety or low motivation) and for the other child it is a cognitive weakness.

But good observation skills are needed to understand children's possible strong or weak abilities, not just their behaviors. Good or poor planning ability may be especially evident on the Symbol Search subtest wherein children are required to efficiently handle abstract symbols. If children have good planning abilities, you may see better performance on Symbol Search than on Coding, but if they are poor in planning ability, Symbol Search may be weaker. Both Coding and Symbol Search can be enhanced by strong visual-memory skills. If children can remember either the target symbols in Symbol Search or the pairs of symbols and numbers in Coding without having to repeatedly look back at the key, then they will be able to perform more efficiently and will earn relatively high scores; in contrast, children with poor visual memory are likely to refer back to the Symbol Search targets or the Coding key very frequently, thereby losing valuable time and earning a low PSQ.

Processing Speed Quotient: Empirical Considerations
The WPPSI-III factor-analytic data support the underlying importance of children's abilities to handle abstract symbols during the Processing Speed subtests. In fact, the data indicate that Matrix Reasoning loads together with Symbol Search and Coding through age 5-11 (see Table 4.4). However, because Matrix Reasoning has no time limits, the connection between Matrix Reasoning and the Processing Speed subtests is something other than speed. Perhaps at ages 4-0 to 5-11 the cognitive demands to process the abstract

Table 4.4 Factor Loadings for Matrix Reasoning Derived From Exploratory Analysis With Core and Supplemental WPPSI-III Subtests

Age	Verbal	Performance	Processing Speed
4-0 to 4-11	.16	.19	**.39**
5-0 to 5-11	.12	**.36**	**.30**
6-0 to 7-3	.26	**.59**	-.09

Note. Loadings ≥ .30 are in bold. Loadings are from *WPPSI-III Technical and Interpretive Manual* (Table 5.4).

symbols of Coding and Symbol Search are greater than at older age levels, increasing the relationship of PSQ to Matrix Reasoning for younger children.

Correlations between Matrix Reasoning and the two Processing Speed subtests across the six age bands reveal fairly consistent relationships between Matrix Reasoning and Symbol Search but inconsistent relationships between Matrix Reasoning and Coding. The median correlation between Matrix Reasoning and Symbol Search was .50 (ranging from .44 to .52). In contrast, the Coding-Matrix Reasoning correlations varied widely, ranging from .12 to .55. The smallest Coding-Matrix Reasoning correlations (< .25) were found for the two oldest age groups, but the correlations for the other four age groups were substantially higher, ranging from .40 to .55 (see Table 4.5). Thus, the demands of processing abstract symbols during Symbol Search

Table 4.5 Matrix Reasoning's Correlations With Processing Speed Subtests and Processing Speed Quotient (PSQ) Across Six Separate Age Groups

	Correlations With Matrix Reasoning						
	Ages 4-0 to 4-5	Ages 4-6 to 4-11	Ages 5-0 to 5-5	Ages 5-6 to 5-11	Ages 6-0 to 6-11	Ages 7-0 to 7-3	Median
Symbol Search	.44	.52	.52	.48	.50	.50	.50
Coding	.41	.44	.55	.40	.22	.12	.41
PSQ	.47	.55	.60	.48	.40	.35	.48

Note. Coefficients are from *WPPSI-III Technical and Interpretive Manual* (Tables A.4, A.5, A.6, A.7, A.8, and A.9).

likely drive the moderate relationship with Matrix Reasoning throughout the entire WPPSI-III age range. Similarly, the moderate Matrix Reasoning-Coding relationships in the four youngest age groups may be driven by the demands to process the abstract Coding symbols. However, Matrix Reasoning's relationship with Coding is dramatically lessened when children reach age 6, perhaps because the task of dealing with Coding's symbols has become automatic and is no longer even moderately complex for older children.

Step 6: Determine Significant Strengths and Weaknesses in the Subtest Profile

The first steps of WPPSI-III interpretation involve examination of the global scores, but in Step 6 you examine the fine details of the subtest profile. Each child is unique, and this level of profile analysis makes a child's special characteristics come to light as you create hypotheses about each particular child's strong and weak areas of cognitive functioning. We first review some empirical guidelines.

An *ipsative* comparison is one that examines how well a child is performing on each subtest relative to his or her own average score. The ipsative comparison is quite different from the comparison between an individual's subtest scores and

DON'T FORGET

Possible Interpretations of the Processing Speed Quotient

- Processing speed
- Ability to process abstract visual symbols
- Visual-motor coordination
- Motivation
- Attention-concentration
- Anxiety
- Distractibility
- Reflectiveness
- Compulsiveness
- Visual memory
- Planning ability

the normative mean. When we compare each of an individual's subtest scores to the mean of all of his or her subtest scores, we discover what *relative* strengths and weaknesses a person has, regardless of how they compare to the normative group. For example, a developmentally delayed child may earn a scaled score of 10 on one subtest, which is in the Average range compared to the normative group, but when comparing this score of 10 to the *child's mean* subtest score of 7, that scaled score is considered a personal relative strength.

To compare individual subtest scaled scores to a mean scaled score, you first need to calculate the child's mean scaled score. For the WPPSI-III, we recommend that you use the mean of *all subtests administered* as your base of comparison. In our previous books on interpretation of Wechsler tests, we advocated using separate Verbal and Performance means if a child's V-P IQ discrepancy was abnormally large. However, with this latest Wechsler test, we decided to use mean of all the WPPSI-III subtests administered as the base of comparison for every subtest because (a) many subtests are supplementary or optional and examiners are likely not to administer all of them; (b) some subtests are not clearly Verbal or Performance within the WPPSI-III classification system (e.g., Coding); and (c) for the youngest age group, the separate Verbal and Performance scales comprise only two subtests apiece. Although our steps use the one mean, if examiners are more comfortable using separate Verbal and Performance means when an abnormally large V-P IQ difference is present (i.e., 20 points or more), we feel that approach is also acceptable.

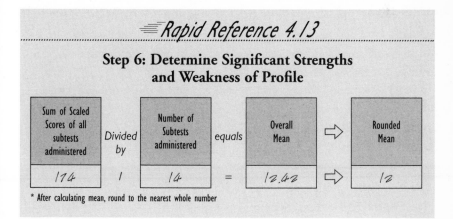

≡*Rapid Reference 4.13*

Step 6: Determine Significant Strengths and Weakness of Profile

Sum of Scaled Scores of all subtests administered	Divided by	Number of Subtests administered	equals	Overall Mean	⇨	Rounded Mean
174	÷	14	=	12.42	⇨	12

* After calculating mean, round to the nearest whole number

Rapid Reference 4.13 shows a completed example of how to calculate the mean used in Step 6 of the WPPSI-III Interpretive Worksheet.

To prevent calculation errors, we suggest that after you compute the mean to the nearest tenth and then round the mean to the nearest whole number (Rapid Reference 4.13 and 4.14). See Kaufman (1994b, pp. 125–128) for a review of some of the controversial issues surrounding various methods of calculating subtest strengths and weaknesses.

After the scaled scores have been recorded in the WPPSI-III Interpretive Worksheet, then calculate the difference between each of the administered subtests and the rounded mean or means. Note with a plus sign (+) or minus sign (-) whether each subtest falls above or below the subtest mean (see this step exemplified with Ophelia's case in Rapid Reference 4.14 and with 3-year-old Antonio's case in Rapid Reference 4.15). Mark those subtests that fall above the mean with a positive valence and those falling below with a negative valence.

The next part of Step 6 determines whether the size of the difference between each scaled score and the rounded mean of all subtest scaled scores is large enough to be interpreted meaningfully (we will use the word *significant* even though technically the values we provide are not based on conventional statistical significance but on frequency of occurrence in the normal population; see Kaufman, 1994b, chapter 3, for an in-depth discussion of this and related topics). We provide the sizes needed in the WPPSI-III Interpretive Worksheet (Appendix A), which are based on the values from the extreme 10% listed in Table B.5 of both WPPSI-III manuals. The values presented in the WPPSI-III manuals are exact values, but for simplicity, we prefer to use rounded values. If you wish, you may refer to the WPPSI-III manuals for exact values, although the rounded values are sufficient to calculate the strengths and weaknesses, and they minimize the risk of clerical error and reduce dependency on tables.

If the difference between each scaled score and the individual's mean is large enough to be significant, then consider it a strength (if significantly above the mean) or weakness (if significantly below the mean). On the WPPSI-III Interpretive Worksheet, denote the strengths and weaknesses by the letters *S* and *W*, respectively. However, if scaled scores do not differ significantly from the appropriate mean, consider them chance fluctuations. Do not interpret nonsignificant differences as strengths or weaknesses per se, but utilize them to support hypotheses (see Step 8).

≡Rapid Reference 4.14

Step 6: Determine Significant Strengths and Weaknesses of Profile for Ages 4-0 to 7-3.

Verbal Subtest	Scaled Score	Rounded Mean	Difference[b]	Size of Difference Needed for Significance	Strength or Weakness (S or W)	Percentile Rank (See Table 4.6)
Information	13	12	+1	±3		84
Vocabulary	11	12	-1	±3		63
Word Reasoning	15	12	+3	±3	S	95
Comprehension	9	12	-3	±3	W	37
Similarities	13	12	+1	±3		84
Receptive Vocabulary	15	12	+3	±3	S	95
Picture Naming	10	12	-2	±3		50
Performance Subtest						
Block Design	12	12	0	±4		75
Matrix Reasoning	16	12	+4	±4	S	98
Picture Concepts	11	12	-1	±4		63
Symbol Search	13	12	+1	±4		84
Coding	14	12	+2	±4		91
Picture Completion	11	12	-1	±4		50
Object Assembly	11	12	-1	±4		75

Difference[b] = Subtest scaled score minus appropriate rounded mean

One of the additional components of Step 6 is converting the scaled scores to percentile ranks (see Rapid References 4.14 and 4.15). Many people are not familiar with the scaled score's mean of 10 and standard deviation of 3, but are likely to understand the commonly used percentile rank. In writing the interpretation of test results section of a report, the metric of percentile rank can be very useful in communicating to parents and professionals alike. We provide percentile ranks for the scaled score values in Table 4.6.

≡ Rapid Reference 4.15

Step 6: Determine Significant Strengths and Weaknesses of Profile.

Sum of Scaled Scores of all subtests administered	Divided by	Number of Subtests administered	equals	Overall Mean	⇨	Rounded Mean
45	/	14	=	9	⇨	9

* After calculating mean, round to the nearest whole number

Strengths and Weaknesses for Ages 2-6 to 3-11

Verbal Subtest	Scaled Score	Rounded Mean	Difference[b]	Size of Difference Needed for Significance	Strength or Weakness (S or W)	Percentile Rank (See Table 4.6)
Receptive Vocabulary	10	9	+1	±3		50
Information	6	9	-3	±3	W	9
Picture Naming	11	9	+2	±3		63
Performance Subtest						
Block Design	8	9	-1	±4		25
Object Assembly	10	9	+1	±4		50

Step 7: Is the General Language Composite Interpretable?

Reporting and interpreting the GLC is not necessary for every child. The GLC was developed primarily for children ages 2-6 to 3-11 and also for those older children with potential language delays (The Psychological Corporation, 2002). The goal of the GLC was to "provide clinicians with a well-normed screening measure that could indicate the possible need for additional assessment of language development" (Diane Coalson, personal communication, November 21, 2002).

Table 4.6 National Percentile Ranks and IQs Corresponding to Scaled Scores

Percentile Rank	Scaled Score	Corresponding IQ
99.9	19	145
99.6	18	140
99	17	135
98	16	130
95	15	125
91	14	120
84	13	115
75	12	110
63	11	105
50	10	100
37	9	95
25	8	90
16	7	85
9	6	80
5	5	75
2	4	70
1	3	65
0.5	2	60
0.1	1	55

To determine whether the GLC should be reported and interpreted, answer the following two questions for children ages 2-6 to 3-11:

A. Is Receptive Vocabulary or Picture Naming a significant strength or weakness (see Step 6)?

B. Are differences between Receptive Vocabulary and Picture Naming small enough to be considered *normal* (i. e., not abnormally large)?

Then for children ages 4-0 to 7-3 ask a third question:

C. Is GLC significantly different from V-IQ?

Interpret the GLC for children ages 4-0 to 7-3 if the answers to Questions A, B, and C are all *yes,* and interpret the GLC for children ages 2-6 to 3-11 if the answers to questions A and B are *yes.*

An affirmative response to Question A indicates that a significant strength or weakness is present in Receptive Vocabulary, Picture Naming, or both. This variation from a child's average performance, which was determined in Step 6, tells you that there is something unique happening in the child's language abilities that warrants further investigation.

An affirmative answer to Question B indicates that Receptive Vocabulary and Picture Naming are not abnormally different from one another, indicating that the GLC can be considered a unitary construct that can be meaningfully interpreted. From Table B.4 in both WPPSI-III manuals, differences of 4 or more points occurred about 15% of the time for children ages 2-6 to 3-11 and the same value was found for ages 4-0 to 7-3. Therefore, discrepancies of 4 or more points are needed between Receptive Vocabulary and Picture Naming to denote abnormal scatter; conversely, differences of 0-3 points indicate *normal* variability and produce *yes* answers to Question B.2 for both age groups.

Finally, an affirmative answer to Question C for children ages 4-0 to 7-3 indicates that a child's general verbal ability is significantly different from his or her overall language development, again warranting further investigation of language skills. For the purposes of this analysis, the .05 level is sufficient. This value equals 11 points for children ages 4-0 to 7-3. This comparison is not made for ages 2-6 to 3-11 because for very young children *both* the two-subtest V-IQ and the two-subtest GLC include Receptive Vocabulary; hence, the contrast is meaningless.

Using the case of Ophelia, who earned V-IQ = 116, GLC = 113, Receptive Vocabulary = 15, and Picture Naming = 10, we walk through Step 7 in Rapid Reference 4.16. We have determined that because the GLC is not a unitary construct for Ophelia (the scatter between the two subtests is abnormally large), we do not report or interpret the GLC for her case.

The WPPSI-III's developers did not intend that the GLC be compared to the V-IQ, but they conceded that it is an interesting question (Diane Coalson, personal communication, November 21, 2002). As mentioned, the 50% overlap between V-IQ and GLC for very young children makes the V-IQ versus GLC comparison psychometrically and clinically senseless. "The GLC

≡Rapid Reference 4.16

Step 7: Interpret General Language Composite.

A.) Is Receptive Vocabulary or Picture Naming a significant relative strength or weakness?

Receptive Vocabulary	Picture Naming	Is either subtest a relative S or W?
S or W in Step 6?	S or W in Step 6?	YES NO

B.) Is the difference between Receptive Vocabulary and Picture Naming normal (i.e., not abnormally large)?

Receptive Vocabulary Scaled Score	Picture Naming Scaled Score	Difference	Abnormal Scatter	Normal Variability	Is there normal variability?
15	10	5	4 or more	0-3	YES NO

C.) Is GLC significantly different from V-IQ?

GLC	V-IQ	Difference	Significant (p<.05)	Not Significant	Is there a significant difference?
113	116	3	11+	0-10	YES NO

⇩

	Step 7 Decision Box
For Ages 2-6 to 3-11	↗ If A and B are YES, then interpret the GLC ↘ If A or B are NO, then don't interpret the GLC
For Ages 4-0 to 7-3	↗ If A, B, and C are YES, then interpret the GLC ↘ If A, B, or C are NO, then don't interpret the GLC

(Left margin: Ages 4-0 to 7-3)

only includes subtests that focus on language development through measurement of receptive and expressive vocabulary abilities. The V-IQ includes the Information subtest, which requires more extensive processing of language (in both the receptive and expressive arenas) with no visual stimuli. That is, the GLC does not provide as much breadth as the V-IQ in measuring verbal ability — it is focused on vocabulary ability" (Diane Coalson, personal communication, November 21, 2002). The differences between what V-IQ and GLC measure is more meaningful for ages 4 and above because of the inclusion of Word Reasoning in V-IQ and the elimination of any subtest overlap between the two global scores. Nonetheless, because both the V-IQ and GLC include measures of *word knowledge* (Vocabulary is a V-IQ subtest for ages 4-0 to 7-3), the comparison between these two global scores is probably of limited value for most children, regardless of age.

Any hypotheses borne from a child's GLC score should be supported with corroborating data from other sources (e. g., supplemental test results, behavioral observations, teacher or parent reports). Recall that the GLC mainly taps receptive and expressive vocabulary ability, and is more or less a screening tool. Further assessment of a child's language skills by a speech and language pathologist may be warranted if a child earns a low score on the GLC, even if it does not differ significantly from V-IQ.

Step 8: Generate Hypotheses About Strengths and Weaknesses in the WPPSI-III Profile

As mentioned at the beginning of this chapter, controversy exists about hypothesizing strong and weak abilities based on fluctuations in a child's subtest profile. We recognize that some examiners are not comfortable with this process of hypothesis generation, and for those examiners, Step 8 will be of no value. In our personal experience, however, the hypothesis-generation step is one of the most important in the process of test interpretation. Step 8 does not end with WPPSI-III scores, but rather *begins* with these scores. Meaningful hypothesis generation demands integration of data obtained from WPPSI-III strengths and weaknesses with that obtained from behavioral observations, background information, and supplemental testing in order to confirm or disconfirm hypotheses. When interpretations are validated by multiple pieces as data such as these, then strong and sensible recommendations can be made for intervention.

This step is designed to help create meaning from the relative strengths and weaknesses noted in Step 6. One of the challenges in creating hypotheses is to find abilities that are shared by two or more subtests rather than simply stating what the textbook definition of each single subtest purportedly measures. The potential problem with using definitions of single subtests is that when hypotheses are considered in isolation, there is risk of missing contradictory information that may be present. For example, when children earn a high score on WPPSI-III Matrix Reasoning, some examiners automatically state that such children have strong "novel problem solving" abilities. However, such a statement (when made in isolation) might neglect the relative trouble that was evidenced on Word Reasoning and Picture

Concepts, in addition to the comments that the parents made about their child's struggles with new concepts that are presented in school.

Your goal is to find information that is consistent across the entire profile. Support each strength and weakness with two or more subtests, and whenever feasible, with clinical observations, background information, and supplementary cognitive or achievement measures. Occasionally a profile may be totally flat, evidencing no relative strengths or weaknesses. Examination of such a flat profile will not likely provide a great deal of information in and of itself. In such cases, it may be necessary to administer supplemental subtests that measure abilities not well tapped by the WPPSI-III.

INTRODUCTION TO WPPSI-III SUBTEST INTERPRETIVE TABLES

Appendix B lists the abilities that are believed to underlie each WPPSI-III subtest (Appendix C is a shorter version of Appendix B that lists only the five subtests administered to children ages 2-6 to 3-11). The information included in the tables summarizes and reorganizes the material that was included in the subtest-by-subtest analysis at the beginning of this chapter. We are presenting a variety of interpretive systems in these tables, but there are many other potential models that examiners might find valuable depending on their interests and orientation. (For example, Ottem, 1999, presents a structural approach to categorizing WPPSI subtests for interpreting the profiles of language-impaired children.) The shared abilities tables that we have created are useful in facilitating the process of hypothesis generation. Influences that are shared by at least two WPPSI-III subtests are also presented in an organized manner in Appendices B and C.

The WPPSI-III Shared Abilities tables are organized according to the information-processing model: Input-Integration/Storage-Output. This model considers the following:

- What type of stimuli does the individual have to respond to?
- How is the information processed and remembered?
- How is the person required to respond?

Apart from the specific content of the task, it is important to consider aspects of the stimulus or response that may affect a child's performance on certain subtests. The shared abilities listed in Appendixes B and C provide a number of hypothesized abilities but are intended only as a good guideline. These lists are not exhaustive; thus, use them as a reference open to expansion. Take into consideration the individuality of each child and each testing situation when doing the necessary detective work in the process of profile analysis.

Reliability Coefficients of Shared Abilities

With each group of subtests listed in the shared abilities tables, the split-half and test-retest reliabilities are provided. These values are based on the average reliability values presented in the WPPSI-III manual (Wechsler, 1989) and on the intercorrelations among the subtests in each cluster. The formula for calculating the composite was applied (Tellegen & Briggs, 1967).

How to Use Information About Shared Abilities

What do you do with all the information provided about how abilities overlap various subtests? The next section provides you with a set of sequential guidelines of how to best utilize the information in Appendix B (and Appendix C) to generate hypotheses. We use Ophelia's profile to demonstrate how to use the guidelines to develop potential strong and weak abilities to investigate.

Guideline 1

Choose one of the strengths (S) or weaknesses (W) determined in Step 6. Write down all the shared abilities and influences that involve this subtest. For example, choose the first relative strength found in Ophelia's profile: Word Reasoning. Table 4.7 shows a subset of all the possible shared abilities for Word Reasoning written down together (this information was pulled from Appendix B), and beside this list of abilities are all other subtests that also may measure this ability.

Make special considerations when including shared abilities that tap the earliest items of the Information and Vocabulary subtests because each one requires different abilities for the earlier versus later items. The first few items of each task have stimuli that are pictorial in nature and require a child to point to the correct response (Information) or give a one-word response (Vocabulary). In contrast, the remaining higher-level items on Vocabulary and Information have auditory stimuli and require a vocal response.

Appendixes B and C list abilities measured by all items of these two subtests and also include a listing of abilities only measured by the first items that are pictorial in nature or require different cognitive processing — for example, these are listed as *I (1-6)*. Rapid Reference 4.17 lists the numbers of the items that are different from the rest of the subtest for each of these tasks. Like the other subtests listed in the shared abilities table, these specific items should also be pulled from Appendix B and written down (see Ophelia's case in Table 4.7).

Guideline 2

Evaluate each ability listed for the first strength or weakness (examined in Guideline 1) to determine how the child performed on the other subtest or subtests that also measure the identified abilities. In the process of deciding which abilities explain the strength or weakness, less stringent criteria are applied than are used for the process of determining significant strengths and weaknesses (in Step 6). Simply consider whether a person has scored above, below, or equal to his or her own mean score on all pertinent subtests for an ability. (This information has already been calculated in Step 6 and is recorded in the difference column on Step 6 of the WPPSI-III Interpretive Worksheet.) Then record this information on your list of shared abilities by writing the following notations next to each subtest (except the first several items of Information and Vocabulary):

- Minus sign (-), indicating performance below the child's mean subtest scaled score
- Plus sign (+), indicating performance above the child's mean subtest scaled score
- Zero (0), indicating performance exactly at the child's mean subtest scaled score

≡Rapid Reference 4.17

Pictorial Items That Require Special Consideration in Interpretation

WPPSI-III Subtest	Pictorial Items
Information	1–6
Vocabulary	1–5

Table 4.7 Example of List of Shared abilities for WPPSI-III Word Reasoning

Ability	Verbal Subtests							Performance Subtests						
	I	V	WR	C	S	RV	PN	BD	MR	PCon	SS	Cd	PC	OA
Input														
Auditory-vocal channel	I	V	WR	C	S									
Auditory perception of complex verbal stimuli	I		WR	C				BD			SS	Cd		
Understanding long questions	I		WR	C										
Integration-Storage														
Acquired knowledge (Bannatyne)	I	V	WR			RV	PN							
Cognition (Guilford)		V	WR	C	S	RV		BD	MR	PCon			PC	OA
Convergent production (Guilford)			WR			RV			MR	PCon	SS	Cd		
Crystallized ability (CHC)	I	V	WR	C	S	RV	PN			PCon				
Decentration			WR							PCon				
Fluid ability (CHC)			WR		S			BD	MR	PCon				OA

Fund of information	I	V	WR		RV		
Handling abstract verbal concepts		V	WR	S			
Induction			WR			MR	PCon

Note. I = Information; V = Vocabulary; WR = Word Reasoning; C = Comprehension; S = Similarities; RV = Receptive Vocabulary; PN = Picture Naming; BD = Block Design; MR = Matrix Reasoning; PCon = Picture Concepts; SS = Symbol Search; Cd = Coding; PC = Picture Completion; OA = Object Assembly; I (1–6)= First six Information items only; V (1–5) = First five Vocabulary items only.

When Items 1–6 of Information or 1–5 of Vocabulary are listed in the shared abilities table for special consideration, you do not write a plus, minus, or zero next to these part subtests. The reason this is not done is that a scaled score is not obtained just for the initial items of a subtest. Therefore, you cannot determine whether these items are above, below, or equivalent to the overall subtest mean. In Guideline 3 we discuss how to examine and integrate a child's performance on these items of a subtest, if necessary.

Again using Ophelia's example of her relative strength in Word Reasoning, Table 4.8 demonstrates how to fill in the +, -, or 0 next to the pertinent subtests. For example, in the first row, the auditory-vocal channel is listed as a hypothesized strong ability. The first subtest listed with this ability is Information, and because Ophelia's Information scaled score was higher than her overall mean subtest scaled score (see Rapid Reference 4.14), a + is placed next to the Information subtest (denoted by I+). Also listed with the auditory-vocal channel are Vocabulary, Comprehension, and Similarities. The appropriate pluses, minuses, or zeros are placed next to each of these subtests, according to whether Ophelia scored above, below, or equivalent to her own scaled score mean (e.g., V-, C-, S+). Table 4.8 demonstrates this process by showing a completed example of this process for the partial list of possible abilities measured by Word Reasoning.

CAUTION

When looking at whether a subtest is above, below, or equivalent to the mean subtest scaled score, do not write +, -, or 0 by pictorial items in the following subtests:

- Information (Items 1–6)
- Vocabulary (Items 1–5)

These items are only part of a subtest and do not represent entire subtest scaled score.

Guideline 3

Examine each ability written on the list (in Guideline 1) to determine whether it should be considered a strong or weak ability. In general, shared strengths are those in which a person has scored above his or her own mean score on all pertinent subtests, with at least one discrepancy reaching significance. However, there are exceptions to this general rule for shared abilities that are described in the Don't Forget box on page 161. Think of the rules of whether to accept or reject abilities as strengths or weaknesses of as rules of thumb rather than as rigid principles. At times, you may find that there is an overabundance of other clinical data from the background information, behavioral observations, or supplemental testing that support a shared ability as a strength or weakness (even if the guidelines in the Don't Forget box below are not met). If multiple sources of information indicate that a particular ability is worthy of interpretation, then accept that particular ability as an interpretable relative strength or weakness.

When Items 1–6 of Information or 1–5 of Vocabulary are listed in the shared abilities table for special consideration, examine them prior to making a judgment about whether an ability is a relative strength or weakness.

DON'T FORGET

Rules for Accepting and Rejecting Potential Hypotheses

Number of Subtests Constituting a Shared Ability	Rule for Interpreting Ability as a Strength[a]	Rule for Interpreting Ability as a Weakness[b]
2	• All subtests must be above the mean.	• All subtests must be below the mean.
3 or 4	• At least 2 or 3 subtests must be above the mean. • Only one subtest may be equivalent to the mean.	• At least two or three subtests must be below the mean. • Only one subtest may be equivalent to the mean.
5 or more	• At least 4 subtests must be above the mean. • Only one subtest may be equal to the mean or less than the mean.	• At least 4 subtests must be below the mean. • Only one subtest may be equal to the mean or greater than the mean.

[a]At least one subtest is a significant strength.
[b]At least one subtest is a significant weakness.

Table 4.8 Example of List of Shared abilities for Word Reasoning With +, -, 0 Completed From Ophelia's Profile

Ability	Verbal Subtests							Performance Subtests						
	I	V	WR	C	S	RV	PN	BD	MR	PCon	SS	Cd	PC	OA
Input														
Auditory-vocal channel	I+	V-	WR+	C-	S+									
Auditory perception of complex verbal stimuli	I+		WR+	C-				BD 0			SS+	Cd+		
Understanding long questions	I+		WR+	C-										
Integration-Storage														
Acquired knowledge (Bannatyne)	I+	V-	WR+			RV+	PN-							
Cognition (Guilford)		V-	WR+	C-	S+	RV+		BD 0	MR+	PCon-			PC-	OA-
Convergent production (Guilford)			WR+			RV+			MR+	PCon-	SS+	Cd+		
Crystallized ability (CHC)	I+	V-	WR+	C-	S+	RV+	PN-			PCon-				
Decentration			WR+							PCon-				
Fluid ability (CHC)			WR+		S+			BD 0	MR+	PCon-				OA-

Fund of information	I+	V-	WR+	RV+		
Handing abstract verbal concepts		V-	WR+	S+		
Induction			WR+		MR+	PCon-

Note. I = Information; V = Vocabulary; WR = Word Reasoning; C = Comprehension; S = Similarities; RV = Receptive Vocabulary; PN = Picture Naming; BD = Block Design; MR = Matrix Reasoning; PCon = Picture Concepts; SS = Symbol Search; Cd = Coding; PC = Picture Completion; OA = Object Assembly.

0 = subtest scaled score is equal to mean subtest scaled score

+ = subtest scaled score is above mean subtest scaled score

− = subtest scaled score is below mean subtest scaled score

- First, apply the rules for accepting and rejecting potential hypotheses that are listed in Don't Forget on page 161 to the other subtests listed with the hypothesized ability.
If a child has made two or more errors on Items 1–6 of Information or 1–5 of Vocabulary, then consider these first items as supportive evidence for a relative *weakness*.
- If a child has no errors on Items 1–6 of Information or 1–5 of Vocabulary, then consider these first items as supportive evidence for a relative *strength*.

In the example of Ophelia's case, she did not make errors on Items 1–6 of Information. Thus, any abilities associated with the first few items of these subtests may use her perfect performance on the first items as supportive evidence of a relative strength. However, she did make two errors on the first five Vocabulary items and then went on to obtain points for the higher-level, nonpictorial items. Thus, in an examination of any of the hypothesized weak

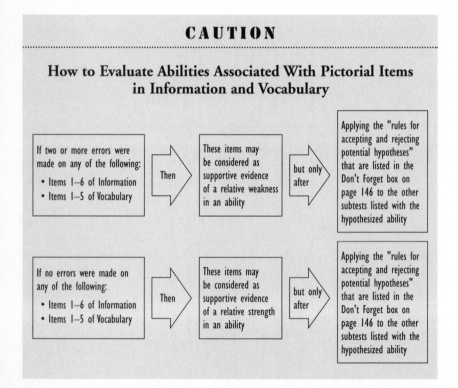

CAUTION

How to Evaluate Abilities Associated With Pictorial Items in Information and Vocabulary

If two or more errors were made on any of the following:
- Items 1–6 of Information
- Items 1–5 of Vocabulary

Then → These items may be considered as supportive evidence of a relative weakness in an ability → but only after → Applying the "rules for accepting and rejecting potential hypotheses" that are listed in the Don't Forget box on page 146 to the other subtests listed with the hypothesized ability

If no errors were made on any of the following:
- Items 1–6 of Information
- Items 1–5 of Vocabulary

Then → These items may be considered as supportive evidence of a relative strength in an ability → but only after → Applying the "rules for accepting and rejecting potential hypotheses" that are listed in the Don't Forget box on page 146 to the other subtests listed with the hypothesized ability abilities that have Items 1–5 of Vocabulary associated with them, her errors on these first items may provide supportive evidence of a relative weakness.

Table 4.9 shows how the rules of thumb have been applied to Ophelia's Word Reasoning example that we have been following. We consider each of the hypothesized abilities one by one to determine whether it may be deemed a relative strength. For example, the auditory-vocal channel is an ability that is hypothesized to underlie five subtests (Information, Vocabulary, Word Reasoning, Comprehension, and Similarities). Examination of the pluses, minuses, and zeroes next to these subtests show that three subtests are above the mean, and two are equivalent to the mean. The rules for accepting and rejecting potential hypotheses tell us that for an ability to be considered a strength when there are five or more subtests, at least four subtests must be above the mean, and only one subtest may be equal to or below the mean. These five subtests do not meet these criteria, so we cross it off the list and do not consider it as a possible strong ability (the fact that the auditory-vocal channel is neither a strength or weakness is denoted in the last column of Table 4.9 with *none*).

The second ability to consider with Ophelia's profile is "auditory perception of complex verbal stimuli." Six subtests are related to this ability. On four of the subtests, Ophelia earned scaled scores that were above her own mean (I+, WR+, SS+, and Cd+), one subtest was below her mean (C–), and the last subtest was equal to her mean (BD 0). Thus, again we would not consider *auditory perception of complex verbal stimuli* as a relative strength (denoted by *none* in the last column of Table 4.9).

The next ability to consider with Ophelia's profile is *understanding long questions*. Three subtests are noted to have this underlying ability. On two of the subtests, Ophelia earned scaled scores that were above the average subtest mean and on the third subtest her score was below the mean. Thus, because three subtests constituted this shared ability and two of those three were above the mean and one rebel subtest was below the mean, understanding long questions may not be considered a relative strength in her profile of abilities (*none* is marked in the last column).

We continue our examination of each ability listed in Appendix B that contains WR. Eventually we come to *convergent production,* which lists six subtests that are related to the ability. Five of these subtests are above Ophelia's mean and only one is below her mean. When we apply the rules for

Table 4.9 Example of List of Shared Abilities for Word Reasoning With Abilities Ruled in or out as Strengths Underlying Ophelia's Profile

Ability	Verbal Subtests							Performance Subtests							Strength or Weakness (S or W)
	I	V	WR	C	S	RV	PN	BD	MR	PCon	SS	Cd	PC	OA	
Input															
Auditory-vocal channel	I+	V-	WR+	C-	S+										none
Auditory perception of complex verbal stimuli	I+		WR+	C-				BD 0			SS+	Cd+			none
Understanding long questions	I+		WR+	C-											none
Integration-Storage															
Acquired knowledge (Bannatyne)	I+	V-	WR+			RV+	PN-								none
Cognition (Guilford)		V-	WR+	C-	S+	RV+		BD 0	MR+	PCon-			PC-	OA-	none
Convergent production (Guilford)			WR+			RV+			MR+	PCon-	SS+	Cd+			S
Crystallized ability (CHC)	I+	V-	WR+	C-	S+	RV+	PN-			PCon-					none
Decentration			WR+							PCon-					none

	I	V	WR	S	RV	BD	MR	PCon	OA	none
Fluid ability (CHC)			WR+	S+		BD 0	MR+	PCon-	OA-	none
Fund of information	I+	V-	WR+		RV+					none
Handling abstract verbal concepts		V-	WR+	S+						none
Induction			WR+				MR+	PCon-		none

Note. I = Information; V = Vocabulary; WR = Word Reasoning; C = Comprehension; S = Similarities; RV = Receptive Vocabulary; PN = Picture Naming; BD = Block Design; MR = Matrix Reasoning; PCon = Picture Concepts; Cd = Coding; PC = Picture Completion; OA = Object Assembly.

0 = subtest scaled score is equal to mean subtest scaled score

+ = subtest scaled score is above mean subtest scaled score

− = subtest scaled score is below mean subtest scaled score

Table 4.10 Example List of Shared Abilities for Comprehension With Abilities Ruled in or out as Weaknesses Underlying Ophelia's Profile

Ability	Verbal Subtests							Performance Subtests							Strength or Weakness (S or W)
	I	V	WR	C	S	RV	PN	BD	MR	PCon	SS	Cd	PC	OA	
Input															
Auditory-vocal channel	I+	V-	WR+	C-	S+										none
Auditory perception of complex verbal stimuli	I+		WR+	C-				BD 0			SS+	Cd+			none
Auditory perception of simple verbal stimuli		V-		C-	S+										none
Understanding long questions	I+		WR+	C-											none
Integration-Storage															
Achievement	I+	V-		C-	S+										none
Cognition (Guilford)		V-	WR+	C-	S+	RV+		BD 0	MR+	PCon-			PC-	OA-	none
Crystallized ability (CHC)	I+	V-	WR+	C-	S+	RV+	PN-			PCon-					none
Culture-loaded knowledge	I+			C-											none

	I	V	WR	C	S	RV	PN	BD	MR	PCon	SS	Cd	PC	OA	none
Evaluation (Guilford)				C-		RV+	PN-	BD 0	MR+	PCon-	SS+	Cd+	PC-	OA-	none
General ability	I+	V-		C-	S+			BD 0	MR+	PCon-					none
General Information (CHC)	I+			C-									PC-		none
Language development		V-	WR+	C-	S+	RV+	PN-			PCon-					none
Reasoning			WR+	C-	S+				MR+	PCon-				OA-	none
Reproduction of models								BD 0				Cd+			none
Semantic cognition (Guilford)		V-	WR+	C-	S+	RV+									none
Semantic content (Guilford)	I+	V-	WR+	C-	S+	RV+	PN-			PCon-					none
Verbal comprehension	I+	V-	WR+	C-	S+	RV+									none
Verbal conceptualization (Bannatyne)		V-	WR+	C-	S+	RV+				PCon-					none

Note. I = Information; V = Vocabulary; WR = Word Reasoning; C = Comprehension; S = Similarities; RV = Receptive Vocabulary; PN = Picture Naming; BD = Block Design; MR = Matrix Reasoning; PCon = Picture Concepts; SS = Symbol Search; Cd = Coding; PC = Picture Completion; OA = Object Assembly.

0 = subtest scaled score is equal to mean subtest scaled score
+ = subtest scaled score is above mean subtest scaled score
- = subtest scaled score is below mean subtest scaled score

accepting and rejecting hypothesis, we learn that convergent production may be considered a relative strength for Ophelia. Thus, on Table 4.9, an *S* has been written in the last column in the row that contains convergent production.

Guideline 4

Repeat Guidelines 1, 2, and 3 for every other significant strength or weakness (listed in Step 5). Shown in Table 4.10 is Ophelia's next relative subtest weakness, Comprehension (Rapid Reference 4.14). After filling in all of the pluses, minuses, and zeroes in the Shared Abilities Worksheet for the abilities underlying Comprehension, no hypothesized abilities that appear to be possible explanations for Ophelia's weakness in Comprehension. Consider whether the behavioral observations, background information, and supplemental test data shed any light on possible explanations for her relative weakness in Comprehension. Guideline 5 explains what to do in a situation in which no hypothesized abilities were uncovered. Chapter 7 provides a complete written case report of Ophelia's profile that integrates and interprets the various strengths and weaknesses.

Guideline 5

If no hypothesized strong or weak abilities are uncovered during the process of examining subtests' shared abilities, then consider interpreting the unique abilities that are presumably measured by significantly high or low scores on subtests. However, the primary focus in explaining the peaks and valleys in a subtest profile should be on shared abilities that link several subtests and that are also supported by background information, behavioral observations, and supplemental testing. Occasionally, however, no hypothesized strengths or weaknesses in abilities are apparent across subtests. Then consider interpretations that are specific to a particular subtest. The unique abilities (denoted with an asterisk) are listed in the subtest-by-subtest description of abilities listed earlier in this chapter.

Before interpreting the unique ability associated with a subtest, determine the amount of specificity of a subtest. As shown in Rapid Reference 4.2, all WPPSI-III subtests for both age groups have either ample or adequate amounts of specificity; hence, the unique abilities measured by all WPPSI-III subtests may be interpreted. However, do not automatically interpret a unique ability even if it has ample specificity. It is best to have other supportive evidence from background data, behavioral observations, or supplemental testing if you are interpreting a unique ability. Only acquiesce to an interpretation of a highly specific and unique strength or when all hypotheses involving shared abilities have proven useless.

 TEST YOURSELF

1. **The approach of test interpretation for the WPPSI-III advocated in this chapter requires examiners to focus on**

   (a) unique abilities of subtests.

   (b) shared abilities across two or more subtests.

   (c) shared abilities across two or more subtests plus behavioral observations.

   (d) shared abilities across two or more subtests plus behavioral observations, background information, and supplemental testing.

2. **You have been analyzing Annie's profile and have found that there are no abilities that are shared by two or more subtests. Before interpreting the unique ability for a specific subtest you should consider what?**

   (a) The g loadings

   (b) Throwing the entire assessment out

   (c) The amount of subtest specificity

   (d) The intercorrelations among all subtests

3. **The most reliable scale on the WPPSI-III is the**

   (a) Full Scale IQ.

   (b) Verbal IQ.

   (c) Performance IQ.

   (d) General Language Composite.

4. **In completing Step 3 of the WPPSI-III Interpretive Worksheet (Appendix A), you find that there is a 22-point discrepancy between Jose's Verbal IQ and Performance IQ. Because this is considered an abnormally large discrepancy,**

   (a) Jose should be deemed abnormal.

   (b) Jose's profile should be considered invalid.

(c) This unusually large discrepancy should be interpreted even if there is significant scatter in either the Verbal or Performance scales.

(d) You must check to see whether the level of abnormality reaches the extreme 1% to determine whether the large discrepancy is interpretable.

5. An ipsative comparison is one that

(a) compares an individual's scores to those in the child's normative age group.

(b) compares an individual's subtest scaled score to the mean of his or her own mean scaled score.

(c) should only be made on rare occasions.

(d) can only be made with children ages 4-0 to 7-3.

6. A hypothesis that a child has difficulty understanding pictorial stimuli may be supported if a young child has made many errors *only* on the first few items on which of the following WPPSI-III subtests?

(a) Information and Vocabulary

(b) Comprehension and Information

(c) Object Assembly and Block Design

(d) Picture Concepts and Picture Completion

7. The Rules for Accepting and Rejecting Potential Hypotheses for using the Shared Abilities tables in WPPSI-III profile interpretation should be considered rigid rules that are not ever to be broken. True or False?

8. The constructs central to Horn and Cattell's (1967) theory are

(a) Verbal and Performance IQ.

(b) Crystallized (Gc) and Fluid (Gf) Intelligence.

(c) Creativity and Practical Intelligence.

(d) Visual and Auditory Memory.

9. A low score on the General Language Composite may be interpreted as all of the following except

(a) indicative of possible language delay (warranting further evaluation).

(b) receptive and expressive language difficulty.

(c) verbal reasoning difficulty.

(d) poor speed of language processing.

10. The Verbal IQ and the General Language Composite

(a) provide the most important contrast in the WPPSI-III profile.

(b) should not be compared in children under age 4 because there is 50% overlap between the scales.

(c) are nearly interchangeable in children ages 4 and up because they both tap complex language abilities such as verbal reasoning.

(d) should be contrasted to determine if the Full Scale IQ is interpretable.

11. A low score on the Processing Speed Quotient may be interpreted as all of the following except

(a) fine-motor control difficulty.

(b) reflective processing style.

(c) poor visual memory.

(d) poor nonverbal reasoning.

12. The goal of the detective work involved in deciphering the strong and weak areas in the WPPSI-III profile is to find information that is consistent across the entire profile. True or False?

Answers: 1. d; 2. c; 3. a; 4. c; 5. b; 6. a; 7. False; 8. b; 9. c; 10. b; 11. d; 12. True.

Five

STRENGTHS AND WEAKNESSES OF THE WPPSI-III

S ince their inception, there have been many published opinions about the strengths and weaknesses of Wechsler instruments. In this chapter we have highlighted what we feel are the *major* strengths and weaknesses of the WPPSI-III.

OVERVIEW OF ADVANTAGES AND DISADVANTAGES OF THE WPPSI-III

The strengths and weaknesses of the WPPSI-III have been pulled from our and other professionals' clinical experience with the instrument and from portions of published reviews of the WPPSI-R (Bracken, 1992; Delugach, 1991; Glutting & McDermott, 1989; Kaufman, 1990b, 1992) that are applicable to the WPPSI-III (including weaknesses noted for the WPPSI-R that were addressed in the third edition). No published reviews of the WPPSI-III have appeared yet. The strengths and weaknesses of the WPPSI-III are organized by the following topics: test development, administration and scoring, reliability and validity, standardization, and interpretation. These topics are treated in Rapid References 5.1 through 5.5, respectively.

In our opinion, The Psychological Corporation took a bold approach to the revision of the WPPSI-R. Lowering the age range of the test and having separate subtest groupings for the two age groups were enormously beneficial changes for users of the test. In addition, many old subtests were dropped and new theoretically driven subtests were added, which also improved the clinical utility of the test. The WPPSI-III has several major strengths: The reliability is excellent for all IQ scales, stability coefficients for IQ scales are quite strong, factor analyses of the core battery offer good support of construct validity, and the standardization sample is well stratified. Perhaps the biggest strength of the WPPSI-III is the sensitivity of the test developers to published criticisms of its predecessor, the WPPSI-R. The previous version was criticized for including bonus points for speed on Object Assembly and Block Design, especially in view of young children's typical unawareness of the need to work quickly; for including difficult concepts in its test directions; for having a particularly cumbersome scoring system for one subtest (Geometric Design); for including Performance subtests that were quite unstable; and, in general, for being user-*un*friendly (see, for example, Kaufman, 1990b). The Psychological Corporation responded to all of these criticisms by eliminating bonus points for speed, getting rid of Geometric Design and generally improving scoring systems of most subtests, simplifying test directions for many tasks by deemphasizing difficult basic concepts (though several basic concepts still remain), improving the stability of Performance subtests (in part by eliminating unstable Mazes and adding stable Matrix Reasoning), and — in general — making the WPPSI-III much more user-friendly than previous editions of the test.

Despite these strong positives, the WPPSI-III has a few important negatives. The boldness of the test developers and their often sound rationales for adding and deleting subtests did not prevent the WPPSI-III from having an unbalanced test battery, one that includes among its 14 subtests (for ages 4–7) a total of three word knowledge tasks (Receptive Vocabulary, Picture Naming, and Vocabulary) and zero measures of short-term memory. Short-term memory is included in most theories of intelligence, such as Guilford's or CHC and is an especially important skill to assess for young children; this ability was measured by the WPPSI-R Arithmetic and Sentences subtests, and its absence from WPPSI-III core, supplemental, and optional subtests is disappointing. Also, one new Performance subtest (Picture Concepts), which was surprisingly included among the triad that contribute to P-IQ, does not have good factorial validity. It is largely a verbal task for ages 6-0 to 7-3, and it does not emerge as a Performance task for 4-year-olds in the analysis of core and supplemental subtests. The equivocal factor loadings for Picture Concepts would not have been a serious problem if the Performance Scale had included more subtests, as was true for the WPPSI-R, but with only three subtests contributing to P-IQ, this aberration is noteworthy.

≡Rapid Reference 5.1

Strengths and Weaknesses of WPPSI-III Test Development

Strengths

- The test publisher was sensitive to criticisms of the WPPSI-R — for example, by eliminating bonus points for speed on Block Design and Object Assembly, removing many basic concepts from test directions, and eliminating the unstable Mazes subtest.

- The test's artwork, including color, is appealing to young children.

- The tabbed format of the manual and bent cover are user friendly.

- The battery design with some core subtests, some supplemental, and others optional is useful for examiners who need to conduct a shorter battery due to time constraints.

- The addition of Matrix Reasoning, Symbol Search, and Coding to the battery enhances the continuity of measurement with other Wechsler third editions.

- The GLC subtests are very useful additions in assessing clinical populations.

- WPPSI-R's Geometric Design was wisely eliminated because it was very difficult to score accurately.

- The downward extension of Symbol Search was very well done.

Weaknesses

- The elimination of WPPSI-R Sentences and WPPSI-R Arithmetic in the Third Edition removed the measurement of a crucial skill in young children — auditory short-term memory. Memory is a key aspect in many theories of intelligence (e.g., Horn, Guilford, CHC).

- There is an overrepresentation of tests of word knowledge because of the addition of Receptive Vocabulary and Picture Naming to a battery that already included Vocabulary.

- Item 18 of Picture Completion is problematic because the correct answer (a child's missing tooth) is something that is commonly missing from a young child.

- The decision to include Coding in the FS-IQ is problematic for clinical populations with poor fine motor skills, and substituting Symbol Search is not a satisfactory solution.

≋Rapid Reference 5.2

Strengths and Weaknesses of WPPSI-III Administration and Scoring

Strengths

- Record forms are well designed and facilitate administration and scoring.
- Having separate record forms for the two age groups is beneficial because the groups are administered different sets of subtests.
- Having separate sections of the *Administration and Scoring Manual* for each age band simplifies administration.
- Inclusion of teaching, sample, and practice items facilitates administration to the youngest children.
- The liberal use of queries is allowed, which aids in the administration and scoring of the test to children with limited vocabularies or difficulty sustaining attention.
- Gaps, misalignments, and rotations are permitted (to a developmentally appropriate level) on Block Design and Object Assembly, which reduces the confounding effect in scoring of delays due to fine motor development.
- The administration of Object Assembly has been greatly simplified in comparison to its administration in the WPPSI-R.

Weaknesses

- Some of the directions include concepts that may be too advanced for some preschoolers (e.g., *same* is used in Coding and Symbol Search; *in order* and *skip* are used in Coding; and *top, up, down,* and *same* are used in Block Design).
- Directing a young child to "Work as fast as you can" may place undo stress on a young child who doesn't understand the concept of needing to work quickly.
- Creative children and others who think outside the box may be unfairly penalized on the Picture Concepts subtest because they can find creative and clever justifications for all sorts of pairs of pictures' going together.
- The smiley face on the star in Item 4 of Picture Naming is distracting for young children.
- It is unclear how to score Item 16 of Information if a child names six colors, three of which are colors of the rainbow and three of which are not.

≡ Rapid Reference 5.3

Strengths and Weaknesses of WPPSI-III
Reliability and Validity

Strengths

- Reliability coefficients for IQs are strong for both age groups. For ages 2-6 to 3-11, reliability coefficients ranged from .95 for Verbal and Full Scale IQs to .90 for Performance IQ. For 4-0 to 7-3 average reliability coefficients ranged from .97 for the Full Scale IQ to .89 for the Processing Speed Quotient.

- Stability coefficients for the composites are good (.84 to .92 for ages 2-6 to 3-11 and .87 to .93 for ages 4-0 to 7-3).

- Factor-analytic results offer generally good support for the construct validity of the battery across all age groups.

Weaknesses

- Although floors have been improved from the WPPSI-R, some subtests still have questionable floors. For example, the floor of Object Assembly is not good for children under 3 (raw scores of 1 translate to scaled scores of 5). For children ages 4 and above, five subtests have questionable floors at various ages: Symbol Search, Similarities, Comprehension, Coding, and Word Reasoning. The Don't Forget box on page 182 presents scaled-score equivalents for raw scores of 1 for these subtests.

- For 7-year-olds, the ceiling of Object Assembly is poor (maximum scaled score of 14), and the ceiling of Picture Naming is marginal (maximum scaled score of 16). Down through age 5-6, Object Assembly's ceiling is marginal (maximum scaled scores of 15 or 16).

- Object Assembly's average test-retest coefficients were below .75 for two of the three age groups listed (.74, .76, and .72).

- Although the factor-analytic results generally support the test's validity, the data indicate that Picture Concepts is decisively a Verbal test at ages 6-0 to 7-3 and has split loadings on the Verbal and Processing Speed factors at ages 4-0 to 4-11.

≡Rapid Reference 5.4

Strengths and Weaknesses of WPPSI-III Standardization

Strengths

- The age range was expanded to 2 years 6 months through 7 years 3 months (for the WPPSI-R the range was 3-0 to 7-3, and for the WPPSI the range was 4-0 to 6-6).

- The excellent, large normative group was well stratified to match Census data.

- Excellent methodologies for eliminating test bias were used for WPPSI-III item selection.

- The WPPSI-III/WIAT-II linking study provides valuable information that allows practitioners to identify discrepancies between aptitude and achievement while correcting for regression effects.

- Ten special group studies were conducted during the WPPSI-III's standardization, which enhances the scale's clinical utility.

Weaknesses

- No major weaknesses

≡ Rapid Reference 5.5

Strengths and Weaknesses of WPPSI-III Interpretation

Strengths

- Both manuals include several tables that facilitate interpretation, such as the size of the differences required for significance when comparing a child's single subtest score to his or her mean score and the frequency of occurrence of significant differences.

- The record form contains an area for calculation of strengths and weaknesses, as well as discrepancy comparisons for the global scales.

- The descriptive categories are conveniently located right on the record form.

- The WPPSI-III Technical and Interpretive Manual provides some interpretive guidelines for profile interpretation (The Psychological Corporation, 2002, pp. 134–141). For example, it discusses how to calculate discrepancy scores and how to compare scores on different composites.

- The WPPSI-III Technical and Interpretive Manual provides guidelines for comparing the WPPSI-III and WIAT-II (The Psychological Corporation, 2002, pp. 141–143). It reviews the simple-difference method and the predicted-difference method for comparing ability with achievement.

- A combination of old and new subtests provides a good measure of fluid reasoning on the WPPSI-III

Weaknesses

- The Technical and Interpretive Manual provides little research on minority assessment. When interpreting a test profile for a minority child, it is important to know how other members of a minority group perform, on average, and those data are not available in the manual.

- Interpreting Picture Concepts can be complicated at ages 4-0 to 4-11 and 6-0 to 7-3 because the factor-analytic data indicate that verbal variables influence performance.

- Interpreting Matrix Reasoning can likewise be complicated at age 4 (and to some degree at age 5) because this untimed test — inexplicably — has noteworthy factor loadings on the Processing Speed dimension when the factor analyses include both Coding and Symbol Search.

- The inclusion of different types of items on the same subtest complicates interpretation (e.g., picture and verbal items on Information and Vocabulary).

- Although the addition of seven new subtests and deletion of five old ones has strengthened the third edition of the WPPSI in many ways, these changes have also altered the meaning of the IQs, have produced an

(continued)

for children ages 4-0 to 7-3 (especially Matrix Reasoning, Word Reasoning, Picture Concepts, and Similarities). The fluid subtests are particularly useful for those examiners who rely on CHC theory for interpretation.

- The new Processing Speed Quotient offers the means for estimating the degree to which a child's speed of performance has affected his or her performance.
- The GLC can help tease out when poor expressive vocabulary, receptive vocabulary, or both are deflating other verbal subtest scores.

overrepresentation of tests of word knowledge, and have eliminated auditory short-term memory from its array of abilities. Hence, research on the previous versions of the WPPSI may not generalize to the WPPSI-III.

DON'T FORGET

Scaled Score Equivalents of Raw Scores of 1 for Subtests with Questionable Floors at Ages 4 and 5

Subtest	Ages 4-0 to 4-2	Ages 4-3 to 4-5	Ages 4-6 to 4-8	Ages 4-9 to 4-11	Ages 5-0 to 5-11
Symbol Search	7	7	6	5	—
Similarities	7	7	6	6	5
Comprehension	6	5	5	5	—
Coding	6	6	5	—	—
Word Reasoning	5	5	—	—	—

Note. This table lists only the subtests with questionable floors for children ages 4 and above. Subtests with questionable floors were considered those whose raw scores of 1 translate to scaled scores of 5 or higher.

TEST YOURSELF

1 **The WPPSI-III does not include the WPPSI-R Sentences and Arithmetic subtests, and, therefore, fails to measure what important ability?**

(a) Verbal reasoning

(b) Auditory short-term memory

(c) Visual memory

(d) Lexical ability

2. **The standardization sample of the WPPSI-III is poorly stratified and not adequately representative of U.S. Census data.** True or False?

3. **Creative children or children who can come up with clever justifications for all sorts of pairs of pictures going together may be penalized on which subtest?**

(a) Receptive Vocabulary

(b) Picture Naming

(c) Picture Concepts

(d) Similarities

4. **Although the ceilings of most WPPSI-III subtests are satisfactory, which subtests should be considered carefully in terms of ceiling effects during interpretation?**

(a) Picture Completion and Information

(b) Similarities and Picture Concepts

(c) Object Assembly and Picture Naming

(d) Symbol Search and Coding

5. **According to factor-analytic data, Picture Concepts — a Performance subtest — has strong Verbal loadings at some ages.** True or False?

6. **The poor floor for several of the WPPSI-III subtests has implications for testing what population?**

(a) Children identified as gifted

(b) Children with mental retardation

(c) Children with visual impairments

(d) Normal children between the ages of 6-6 and 7-3

(continued)

7. Together, Matrix Reasoning, Word Reasoning, Picture Concepts, and Similarities are particularly useful for assessing what CHC Broad Ability?

(a) Fluid Intelligence

(b) Crystallized Intelligence

(c) Processing Speed

(d) Visualization

8. Although many changes were made from the WPPSI-R to the WPPSI-III, most of the research on the WPPSI and WPPSI-R should be generalizable to the WPPSI-III. True or False?

Answers: 1. b; 2. False; 3. c; 4. c; 5. True; 6. b; 7. a; 8. False.

Six

CLINICAL APPLICATIONS
OF THE WPPSI-III

This chapter focuses on clinical applications of the WPPSI-III. Topics include practical use and application of WPPSI-III core, supplemental, and optional subtests; assessment of language development and disorders; clinical applications of the WPPSI-III measure of processing speed (PSQ); joint interpretation of IQ and achievement (i.e., WPPSI-III and WIAT-II); and assessment of both giftedness and mental retardation. As the literature on these topics is immense, we attempt only to highlight some of the major findings in this chapter, especially as they pertain to the WPPSI-III and WPPSI-R in particular and to preschool assessment in general. Because the WPPSI-III was recently published and does not yet have a large data base, we supplemented the data from the *WPPSI-III Technical and Interpretive Manual* (The Psychological Corporation, 2002, especially chapter 5) with results of research studies that featured the WPPSI-R and WPPSI and other instruments as well: the WISC-III and its predecessors at the ages of approximate overlap with the WPPSI-III (6–7 years), the McCarthy Scales of Children's Abilities (McCarthy, 1972), Kaufman Assessment Battery for Children (K-ABC; Kaufman & Kaufman, 1983), and recent editions of the Stanford-Binet (SB4; Thorndike, Hagen, & Sattler, 1986; and SB5; Roid, 2003).

USE OF THE WPPSI-III CORE, SUPPLEMENTAL, AND OPTIONAL SUBTESTS

The WPPSI-III offers many new features that we reviewed in chapters 1 and 5. The new test framework includes a core battery plus supplemental and optional subtests (see Figures 1.1 and 1.2 in chapter 1). We treat the important clinical question of when to administer some or all of the supplemental and optional subtests in this section; no clear guidelines are given in the WPPSI-III manuals regarding the administration of core, supplemental, and optional subtests.

In general, each child's individual needs will determine whether to administer supplemental and optional subtests in addition to the core battery. Consider a child's age, referral question, attention span, and verbal or motor deficits in deciding which battery to administer. Most clinicians recognize that the younger the children are, the shorter their attention spans. The Psychological Corporation recognized this fact and developed a WPPSI-III core battery for children ages 2-6 to 3-11 that is only four subtests long. Even the seven-subtest core battery for children ages 4-0 to 7-3 is short in comparison to the 10 mandatory WPPSI and WPPSI-R subtests for all children in the age range.

Even within the 2-6 to 3-11 age range, significant variability exists among children in their ability to maintain focus and attention during testing. Children who have been exposed to day care or preschool may more readily acclimate to the testing situation (which requires extended periods of sitting and focusing), whereas those who have not been in such situations may find the structure of the testing situation more foreign. Children of all ages who are referred for conduct disorders, hyperactivity, or attentional problems will likely challenge even the most experienced examiner during the administration of the core battery, not to mention any supplemental or optional subtests. Children who have language-related difficulties may not enjoy or attend well to language-related subtests, but it is these very children who require the administration of the optional and supplemental tasks that measure vocabulary, verbal reasoning, and verbal expression. Similarly, children with motoric or visual difficulties may not enjoy or attend well to subtests requiring visual perception or motor manipulation, but these types of non-core subtests need to be administered to assess the child's deficits.

WPPSI-III Battery for Ages 2-6 to 3-11

For children under age 4, the core battery consists of four subtests that required a median administration time of about 30 minutes for the standardization sample (Wechsler, 2002, Table 2.1). Picture Naming, which adds an average of about 5 minutes of testing time, is the only supplemental subtest. Because many young children are referred for language-related problems, spending the extra few minutes to administer Picture Naming is likely a wise choice. However, if the child has no suspected language difficulties or is functioning in the above-average range of intelligence, then Picture Naming is not necessary to administer. In addition, if poor attention is an issue for the child and language delays are of no concern, then do not add Picture Naming to the battery.

Whereas administration of Picture Naming adds the GLC to the child's profile of composite scores, this global score overlaps 50% with V-IQ, making its interpretation as a separate construct unclear. Whereas an additional composite score often aids interpretation, that is not usually true on the WPPSI-III for very young children; the extra GLC standard score may actually obscure or confuse the clinician's understanding of the abilities of children below age 4. When examiners do decide to administer Picture Naming to a child of 2-6 to 3-11, the main benefits are (a) interpreting the child's performance on this specific subtest if it emerges as a significant strength or weakness and (b) comparing the child's performance on Picture Naming (expressive vocabulary) versus Receptive Vocabulary. Interpretation of the GLC or even its computation may be unnecessary.

WPPSI-III Battery for Ages 4-0 to 7-3

For older children, we recommend that examiners routinely administer the supplemental Symbol Search subtest, regardless of the reason for the evaluation. The core battery includes only one of the two subtests that contribute to the PSQ, so the only way to compute this global measure of processing speed is to administer the supplemental Symbol Search subtest in addition to the core Coding task. The extra 3 minutes of administration time is well worth it. The median administration time, including Symbol Search, was about 45 minutes for the normative group (Wechsler, 2002, Table 2.1)

The WPPSI-III battery for children ages 4-0 to 7-3 includes four other supplemental subtests in addition to Symbol Search — Comprehension, Picture Completion, Similarities, and Object Assembly — all of which are steeped in Wechsler tradition and have been included in most Wechsler tests since their inception. Taken together, Similarities and Object Assembly required an average of about 16 minutes to give for the standardization sample, but comparable data are not provided for Comprehension or Picture Completion (Wechsler, 2002, Table 2.1). We have found that Comprehension takes about 7–10 minutes to administer and Picture Completion takes about 4–7 minutes. Thus, an extra half hour of so of administration time is needed if the two Verbal and the two Performance supplemental subtests are administered, bringing the overall testing time to about 75 minutes. That length is unwieldy for many children in the 4- to 7-year age range, so administration of any or all of these subtests should not be automatic and needs to be personalized to the individual child.

The core battery provides limited measurement of verbal reasoning (just Word Reasoning), an ability that is measured by *both* Similarities and Comprehension. Of these two Verbal supplemental subtests, Similarities is easier and quicker to administer and score, making it the clear-cut favorite. Unless a child has attentional or related behavioral problems, we suggest routinely administering Similarities to bolster the measurement of verbal reasoning.

We do not make that kind of recommendation for the supplemental Performance subtests. Picture Completion is easy to administer and score, but its items usually elicit verbal responses, making it unclear whether it measures verbal or nonverbal ability for a given child; that ambiguity is considerable for children within the 4- to 7-year age range whose language skill development is in rapid transition. Object Assembly is clearly a nonverbal task, but it tends to be long to administer and is the least stable WPPSI-III subtest — not just for ages 4-0 to 7-3, but for children below age 4 as well (The Psychological Corporation, 2002, Table 4.4). Although Picture Completion and Object Assembly are good measures of simultaneous processing (Gv from the CHC system), that ability is covered fairly well in the core battery by Block Design and Matrix Reasoning. Appendix C (WPPSI-III shared abilities tables) shows how often each of these four supplemental subtests taps abilities shared with the core subtests. Because the data obtained from any intelligence test provides a limited snapshot of a child's functioning at any given point in time, adequately supporting hypotheses derived from subtest scores is more readily done with more rather than fewer subtests.

Generally, if time permits, rapport is good, and the child does not display notable attentional problems, then the examiner should plan to administer Symbol Search and Similarities, along with the core battery, to a child between 4 and 7 years old. When these nine subtests are completed, reassess the situation to decide whether to test further. Did the child demonstrate an unusually good or poor ability to express ideas in words? Did he or she evidence either well-developed or poorly developed social interaction skills? What about common sense? In all of these and related instances, consider administering Comprehension to provide more insight into verbal expression, social understanding, and common sense.

Likewise, one of the core Performance subtests, Picture Concepts, has a strong verbal component and may have functioned as a verbal task for some children — especially those who reasoned aloud for most items. Indeed, for ages 4 and 6, Picture Concepts did not behave as a Performance subtest in the factor analyses of data for all children. Think about administering Object Assembly to gain better understanding of a child's nonverbal ability whenever there is reason to suspect that Picture Concepts was primarily tapping the child's verbal skills.

This type of individualized tailoring of a test to a child's needs or abilities is illustrative of the kinds of problem solving that the examiner should do to decide whether to administer supplemental subtests. Whereas the comprehensive 12-subtest battery (core plus all supplements) will provide an adequate breadth of data to comfortably support or refute hypotheses regarding a child's strengths and weaknesses — with additional support from background information, behavioral observations, and so forth — realistically, many children between the of ages 4 and 7 years cannot handle 75 minutes or more of testing. In addition, the referral questions for the assessment of some children do not require a detailed analysis of their strengths and weaknesses, so the administration of Comprehension, Picture Completion, Object Assembly, or even Similarities is unnecessary. Also, if you only need to gather a global estimate of a child's intellectual functioning or you are administering the test for screening purposes, then the core battery and Symbol Search are certainly adequate.

Although we recommend that you consider administering some or all of the supplemental subtests when warranted, we feel differently about administration of the two optional WPPSI-III subtests for ages 4 to 7 — Receptive Vocabulary and Picture Naming. In our opinion, examiners should not routinely administer the two GLC subtests to children ages 4 and above because the additional 10 or so minutes of testing time (Wechsler, 2002, Table 2.1) does not usually justify the amount of new information provided. The core battery already includes the Vocabulary subtest, which has items at the easy end that require expressive vocabulary — no different from Picture Naming. The inclusion of measures of word knowledge on both the V-IQ and GLC makes these two global scores conceptually similar and hard to distinguish in terms of what they actually measure.

If children ages 4 or above are referred for language-related problems or have global cognitive delays, then administer the optional Receptive Vocabulary and Picture Naming subtests to provide extra information about their specific receptive and expressive language skills. In most other circumstances, administration of both GLC subtests is not advised. Receptive Vocabulary, however, is sometimes a good addition to the battery because it is the best measure of receptive language in the WPPSI-III. Administer this subtest

≡Rapid Reference 6.1

Median Number of Minutes to Complete Core Subtests and Additional Time Needed to Complete Supplemental and Optional Subtests for Children Ages 4-0 to 7-3

41 minutes	+	3 minutes	+	9 minutes	+	16 minutes	=	69 minutes
↑		↑		↑		↑		↑
7 core subtests		Symbol Search		Receptive Vocabulary & Picture Naming		Similarities & Object Assembly		Total for 7 core plus 5 supplemental and optional subtests
		↑		↑				
		Needed to calculate PSQ		Needed to calculate GLC				

Note. Data are based on the 50th percentile of the standardization sample, listed in Table 2.1 in the *WPPSI-III Administration and Scoring Manual* (Wechsler, 2002, p.17). The Manual did not specifically list the additional time needed to administer the other two supplemental subtests, Comprehension and Picture Completion, so these subtests are excluded from this Rapid Reference.

whenever a child seems to demonstrate expressive language difficulties during the evaluation, even if such problems are not part of the reason for referral. For such children, neither the V-IQ nor the two supplemental Verbal subtests will likely provide any insight into possible hidden strengths in receptive language.

As a means of providing an overview of some of the information presented in this section, two Rapid References are provided. Rapid Reference 6.1, based on data provided for the standardization sample, shows the precise median time to administer the core battery plus the additional time required to administer the optional GLC subtests and selected supplemental subtests. Rapid Reference 6.2 lists when we recommend administering the supplemental or optional subtests to children ages 4-0 to 7-3.

LANGUAGE DEVELOPMENT AND LANGUAGE DISORDERS

The chief presenting complaint of children brought in for an evaluation of developmental or behavioral problems in the preschool years is delayed speech or language skills (Field, 1987), with about 3–10% of preschool children estimated to have some form of developmental speech or language disorder (Ottem, 1999). However, assessing young children with potential deficits in language, speech, or communication is complex, in part because the range of normal development of language skills is quite large (Warner & Nelson, 2000).

The expectations for typical language development through age 7 are too numerous to list in this chapter — thus, here we review some general expectations and refer interested readers to some excellent, thorough resources on language development (Brown, 1973; Lahey, 1988; Tomasello & Bates, 2001; Warner & Nelson, 2000). Children develop a word knowledge base remarkably quickly. Between ages 18 months and 6 years, children add about five root words per day, eventually comprehending about 14,000 words by the time they are 6 (Crais, 1990). During preschool years, children's words become clearer and easier to understand. By age 7, most children produce all of the speech sounds of their language clearly and are able to blend them smoothly to produce intelligible words and sentences (Warner & Nelson, 2000). As soon as children form 3-word utterances (usually between ages 2 and 3), they rapidly acquire the rules of grammar (Chomsky, 1968; Pinker, 1994). Preschoolers are also able to vary their language to fit specific contexts,

Rapid Reference 6.2

Recommendations for When to Administer the Core, Supplemental, and Optional WPPSI-III Subtests to Children Ages 4-0 to 7-3

Situation	7 Core Subtests	Symbol Search	Supplemental Subtests			Optional Subtests	
			Comprehension and Similarities[a]	Picture Completion and Object Assembly[b]		Receptive Vocabulary	Picture Naming
Screening purposes	YES	YES	NO	NO		NO	NO
Only a global estimate of IQ needed	YES	YES	NO	NO		NO	NO
Time is limited	YES	YES	NO	NO		NO	NO
Child has limited attention skills	YES	YES	NO	NO		NO	NO
Language-related referral question	YES	YES	YES	NO		YES	YES
Child has estimated above-average IQ	YES	YES	YES	NO		NO	NO
Child has estimated below-average IQ	YES	YES	YES	NO		YES	YES

Situation	7 Core Subtests	Symbol Search	Supplemental Subtests		Optional Subtests	
			Comprehension and Similarities[a]	Picture Completion and Object Assembly[b]	Receptive Vocabulary	Picture Naming
Thorough analysis of subtest strengths and weaknesses is desired	YES	YES	YES	YES	YES	YES
Verbal reasoning ability is questionable	YES	YES	YES	NO	NO	NO
Nonverbal abilities need further assessment	YES	YES	NO	YES	NO	NO

[a]We suggest routinely administering Similarities to bolster the measurement of verbal reasoning. However, because Comprehension is longer to administer and more difficult to score, use Comprehension mainly when further assessment of verbal expression, social understanding, and common sense is desired.

[b]We suggest administering Object Assembly if there is reason to suspect that Picture Concepts is primarily tapping a child's verbal skills. Do not administer Picture Completion in this situation because although it is a performance subtest, it elicits verbal responses.

such as effectively getting attention and using persuasion and justification (Ervin-Tripp & Gordon, 1986). By the early elementary years, children "tell stories, follow multiple-step directions, and participate in conversations. . . They enjoy jokes, [but have difficulty retelling them]. . . because they have not yet mastered dual word meanings and other metalinguistic skills necessary for appreciating the subtleties of linguistic humor" (Warner & Nelson, 2000, p. 158).

Commonly Used Terms in Language Assessment and Research

Typical language development describes the condition in which a child's language is developing at an expected pace. *Late talker* describes toddlers who are slow at producing first words (expected at 12 to 18 months); are still producing few words (fewer than 50) and limited word combinations by 24 months; and show no other signs of developmental delays, such as cognitive, emotional, or sensory problems. *Specific language impairment–expressive* (SLI-E) and *slow expressive language development* (SELD) describe young children with age-appropriate cognitive and receptive language skills whose late-talker symptoms persist or who are especially impaired. *Language disorder, nonspecific language impairment, speech-language impairment,* and *communication disorder* describe children or adults with atypical language development, regardless of whether they have co-occurring special needs (Warner & Nelson, 2000).

When Is Language Development Abnormal?

Although the range of normal language development is quite large, there are points at which children's language development is considered outside the range of normal. Typically, children who score significantly low on standardized language testing (i.e., below measures of their nonverbal intellectual capacity) and who are perceived as having a problem, are diagnosed as language impaired (e.g., *DSM-IV-TR* diagnostic criteria; American Psychiatric Association, 2000). Researchers and clinicians use a variety of labels for preschoolers with atypical language development, with operational definitions for diagnosing speech or language impairment, which differ according to local and state policies.

Operational definitions of language impairment that compare standard scores on measures of language ability to standard scores from IQ tests (a comparison otherwise known as mental-age referencing or cognitive referencing) may underidentify children who need and can benefit from speech-language intervention (Warner & Nelson, 2000). Because depressed language skills may also depress scores on typical IQ tests, some language-impaired children do not exhibit large differences when IQs (even those based on nonverbal tasks) are compared to scores on language tests and therefore fail to be identified by a simplistic psychometric comparison.

Krassowski and Plante (1997) suggest that the IQs for children with specific language impairment are more properly interpreted as reflecting current abilities rather than potential for language learning. They derived their conclusions from their research findings, which showed that children with language impairment made significant shifts in WPPSI, WISC-R and WISC-III IQs over time (average test-retest interval was 3 years). Changes of 15 points or more were present in 16% of children for the FS-IQ, 27% for the V-IQ, and 17% for the P-IQ. Results indicated that the change in IQs for individual children occurred in both directions. Because of IQ variability over time for language-impaired children, Krassowski and Plante (1997) concluded that cognitive referencing is of questionable use in making diagnostic determinations for this population and that IQs "may better serve in the identification of cognitive strength and weaknesses than for decision making for service eligibility" (p. 6). However, these authors failed to take into account changes in the IQs of normal children who are retested, due to practice effects and variability of the different tests (i.e., WPPSI vs. WISC-R vs. WISC-III), so their conclusions may not be correct.

An alternative to using IQs to predict language abilities (i.e., cognitive referencing) is to compare children's level of language development to the language development of same-aged peers (chronological-age referencing). However, chronological-age referencing can lead to overidentification of children as language *impaired* when they in fact have language *differences* (Warner & Nelson, 2000). If only chronological-age referencing is used in diagnosis, children with low cognitive abilities who have commensurate language abilities may be identified as language impaired because they are compared to children at their chronological age level who have higher language scores. Local or state policy dictates whether cognitive referencing or chronological-age referencing is needed to demonstrate eligibility for intervention services. However, it is up to individual examiners to select and interpret cognitive and language assessment tools that provide the most accurate picture of a child's development.

Implications of Normal and Abnormal Language on the WPPSI-III

The Psychological Corporation (2002) stated that the WPPSI-III GLC was designed primarily as a measure of general language for children ages 2-6 to 3-11, but it may also be "useful as a less verbally demanding measure of language ability for older children suspected of having language delays" (p. 137). The general language that is tapped by the GLC includes simple one-word expression and receptive understanding of words in isolation (with no verbal expression). Thus, as we mentioned previously, examiners should consider administering the two optional GLC subtests when language-related concerns are embedded in the referral questions, but they need not do so routinely.

Even our suggestion to administer the GLC subtests to children with known or suspected language impairments requires validation. Thus, we examined WPPSI-III data for 27 children with Mixed Receptive-Expressive Language Disorder and 23 children with Expressive Language Disorder (The Psychological Corporation, 2002). (Rapid Reference 6.3 provides information about the diagnostic criteria for each of these language disorders.) Both samples ranged in age from 4-0 to 6-11 and had mean ages of 5.4 years; IQs for the Mixed group were in the Low Average range (82–87), with the Expressive group scoring in the Average range (91–95). Rapid Reference 6.4 lists the mean IQs for both samples. The fact that both language-impaired samples earned their highest mean score on GLC, a direct measure of receptive and expressive vocabulary, is provocative. However, small sample sizes and small intrascale mean differences for the two samples make this ironic

≡Rapid Reference 6.3

Diagnostic Features of Mixed Receptive-Expressive Language Disorder and Expressive Language Disorder

Diagnostic Feature	Mixed Receptive-Expressive Language Disorder	Expressive Language Disorder
Impairment in *expressive language* development demonstrated by scores on standardized measures of expressive language that are substantially lower than those on *nonverbal intellectual capacity.*	YES	YES
Impairment in *expressive language* development demonstrated by scores on standardized measures of expressive language that are substantially lower than those on *receptive vocabulary.*	YES	NO
Impairment in *receptive language* development demonstrated by scores on standardized measures of receptive language that are substantially lower than those on *nonverbal intellectual capacity.*	YES	NO
Example difficulties in *expression* may include limited vocabulary, errors in tense, difficulty recalling words, limited varieties of grammatical structures, difficulty producing complex sentences, difficulty expressing ideas.	YES	YES
Example difficulties in *receptive language* may include difficulty understanding words, sentences, or specific types of words.	YES	NO
In the developmental type (i.e., not due to neurological insult) children often begin speaking late and progress more slowly through the various stages of language development.	YES	YES

Note. Based on *DSM-IV-TR* criteria for each of the language disorders.

≡Rapid Reference 6.4

Mean WPPSI-III Global Standard Scores of Children with Language-Related Disorders

Mean WPPSI-III Standard Score

Scale	Expressive Language Disorder (N = 23)	Mixed Receptive-Expressive Language Disorder (N = 27)	Standard-Score Difference
Verbal	90.6	83.1	+7.5
Performance	92.9	85.2	+7.7
Processing Speed	94.1	82.7	+11.4
Full Scale	90.1	81.9	+8.2
General Language	94.7	86.7	+8.0

Note. Mean WPPSI-III standard scores are from WPPSI-III Technical and Interpretive Manual (Tables 5.22, 5.23, and 5.24).

result fodder for future research — nothing more. If these results are replicated, the usefulness of the scale as a screening tool for language disorders would be brought into question.

Rapid Reference 6.5 lists the highest and lowest subtest scores for the mixed and expressive groups. Again, small sample sizes limit interpretation, but there are a few interesting results. Predictably, both samples tended to score highest on nonverbal tasks, especially measures of simultaneous or holistic processing, such as Object Assembly, and lowest on measures of verbal reasoning. The good performance by the *Expressive* group but not the Mixed group on *Receptive* Vocabulary is consistent with their respective diagnoses. The relatively low score by the Mixed group on Coding is also a consistent finding because that WPPSI-III subtest — in addition to measuring processing speed — is heavily dependent on good receptive language for the examinee to understand the lengthy oral directions.

Why would samples of children with language impairment earn their highest mean WPPSI-III composite score on the GLC? The GLC's simple

≡Rapid Reference 6.5

Children With Language-Related Disorders: Their Highest and Lowest Mean WPPSI-III Subtest Scaled Scores

Expressive Language Disorder (FS-IQ = 90.1) (N = 23)		Mixed Receptive-Expressive Language Disorder (FS-IQ = 81.9) (N = 27)	
Highest	**Mean Scaled Score**	**Highest**	**Mean Scaled Score**
Picture Completion	9.9	Object Assembly	10.3
Object Assembly	9.7	Block Design	8.0
Receptive Vocabulary	9.4	Matrix Reasoning	8.0
Lowest		**Lowest**	
Comprehension	7.9	Coding	6.9
Word Reasoning	7.8	Comprehension	6.6
Similarities	7.7	Word Reasoning	6.4

Note. Mean scaled scores are from WPPSI-III Technical and Interpretive Manual (Tables 5.22, 5.23, and 5.24).

response style (pointing to a picture or saying a single word) may not reveal impairments in more complex language functions (such as those involving syntax, grammar, or verbal reasoning). With no visual stimuli, the Information subtest requires more extensive processing of language (in both the receptive and expressive arenas) than do the GLC subtests. Word Reasoning and Vocabulary also demand more extensive processing of language than do GLC subtests, with the former subtest providing a good measure of both verbal reasoning and verbal conceptualization. The supplemental Verbal subtests, Similarities and Comprehension, add further to the measurement of verbal reasoning and conceptualization as well as expressive and receptive language skill. Rapid References 6.6 and 6.7 list the language and nonlanguage abilities that we believe the Verbal subtests measure.

≡Rapid Reference 6.6

Abilities Tapped by WPPSI-III Verbal Subtests for Children Ages 2-6 to 3-11

Ability	Verbal Subtests		
	I	RV	PN
Input			
Auditory perception of complex verbal stimuli	I		
Simple verbal directions	I (1–6)	RV	PN
Visual motor channel	I (1–6)	RV	
Visual perception of complete meaningful stimuli	I (1–6)	RV	PN
Visual perception of meaningful stimuli	I (1–6)	RV	PN
Integration-Storage			
Acquired knowledge (Bannatyne)	I	RV	PN
Cognition (Guilford)		RV	
Crystallized ability (CHC)	I	RV	PN
Evaluation (Guilford)		RV	PN
Figural cognition (Guilford)			PN
Figural evaluation (Guilford)		RV	PN
Fund of information	I	RV	
General ability	I		
Language development		RV	PN
Lexical knowledge		RV	PN
Long-term memory	I	RV	PN
Memory (Guilford)	I		PN
Semantic content (Guilford)	I	RV	PN
Verbal comprehension	I	RV	
Verbal concept formation		RV	PN
Visual processing (CHC)			
Word knowledge		RV	PN
Output			
Simple vocal expression	I		PN
Visual-motor coordination	I (1–6)		

Note. I = Information; RV = Receptive Vocabulary; PN = Picture Naming; I (1–6)= First six Information items only.

≡Rapid Reference 6.7

Abilities Tapped by WPPSI-III Verbal Subtests for Children Ages 4-0 to 7-3

Ability	Core Subtests			Supple-mental Subtests		GLC Subtests	
	I	V	WR	C	S	RV	PN
Input							
Auditory-vocal channel	I	V	WR	C	S		
Auditory perception of complex verbal stimuli	I		WR	C			
Auditory perception of simple verbal stimuli		V		C	S		
Simple verbal directions	I (1–6)					RV	PN
Understanding long questions	I		WR	C			
Understanding words		V			S	RV	
Visual motor channel	I (1–6)					RV	
Visual perception of complete meaningful stimuli	I (1–6)	V (1–5)				RV	PN
Visual perception of meaningful stimuli	I (1–6)	V (1–5)				RV	PN
Integration-Storage							
Achievement	I	V		C	S		
Acquired knowledge (Bannatyne)	I	V	WR			RV	PN
Cognition (Guilford)		V	WR	C	S	RV	
Concept formation		V			S		
Convergent production (Guilford)			WR			RV	
Crystallized ability (CHC)	I	V	WR	C	S	RV	PN
Culture-loaded knowledge	I			C			
Decentration			WR				
Evaluation (Guilford)				C		RV	PN

(continued)

Ability	Core Subtests			Supple-mental Subtests		GLC Subtests	
	I	V	WR	C	S	RV	PN
Figural cognition (Guilford)							PN
Figural evaluation (Guilford)						RV	PN
Fluid ability (CHC)			WR		S		
Fund of information	I	V	WR			RV	
General ability	I	V		C	S		
General information (CHC)	I			C			
Handing abstract verbal concepts		V	WR		S		
Induction			WR				
Language development		V	WR	C	S	RV	PN
Learning ability		V	WR			RV	
Lexical knowledge		V	WR		S	RV	PN
Long-term memory	I	V	WR			RV	PN
Reasoning			WR	C	S		
Semantic cognition (Guilford)		V	WR	C	S	RV	
Semantic content (Guilford)	I	V	WR	C	S	RV	PN
Simultaneous processing			WR				
Synthesis (whole-part)			WR				
Verbal comprehension	I	V	WR	C	S	RV	
Verbal concept formation		V	WR		S	RV	PN
Verbal conceptualization (Bannatyne)		V	WR	C	S	RV	
Verbal reasoning			WR	C	S		
Word knowledge		V				RV	PN
Output							
Much verbal expression		V		C	S		
Simple motor response	I (1–6)					RV	
Simple vocal expression	I	V (1–5)	WR				PN
Visual-motor coordination	I (1–6)						

Note. I = Information; V = Vocabulary; WR = Word Reasoning; C = Comprehension; S = Similarities; RV = Receptive Vocabulary; PN = Picture Naming; I (1–6) = First 6 Information items only; V (1–5) = First 5 Vocabulary items only.

Intuitively, an IQ pattern of P > V is expected for children with language disorders, but the samples tested on the WPPSI-III (The Psychological Corporation, 2002) showed very little variability between scales (only about 2–3 points; see Rapid Reference 6.4). Indeed, consistent patterns of performance have not been found for children with language impairment on other tests of cognitive ability. The technical manual for the SB5 (Roid, 2003, Table 4.14) reports standard scores for 108 individuals with speech and language delays or disorders (age range 2 to 19 years; median age = 5) and the difference between their mean nonverbal IQ (87.2) and mean verbal IQ (84.9) was in the right direction but trivial. Similarly, Vig and Jedrysek (1996) administered the SB4 to 52 preschool children with a primary diagnosis of language impairment and 25 children with a secondary diagnosis of language impairment. Binet-4 Verbal Reasoning Area scores were higher than (or not significantly different from) Abstract/Visual Reasoning Area scores for 65% of the children with primary language impairment and for 80% of the children with secondary language impairment (Vig & Jedrysek, 1996). In general, Binet-4 Verbal Reasoning Area scores have been shown to relate moderately to language development for children with impaired language development. In a different study of preschool children with language impairment, Binet-4 Verbal Reasoning accounted for 31–50 % of the variance in language development, as measured by three separate language tests (Tedeschi, 1995).

On the McCarthy Scales (McCarthy, 1972), a sample of 25 children with speech and language disorders showed deficits on tasks requiring verbal expression, categorical thinking, and short-term auditory memory (Morgan, Dawson, & Kerby, 1992). This sample did not, however, perform significantly differently from children without disabilities on McCarthy's Motor scale and Perceptual-Performance scale. In a related finding, a sample of preschoolers identified as language impaired scored substantially higher on the K-ABC (Kaufman & Kaufman, 1983) Mental Processing Composite (mean MPC = 79.2) than on the General Cognitive Index yielded by the McCarthy Scales (mean GCI = 64.8; Ricciardi, Voelker, Carter, & Shore, 1991). This result is opposite to the well-known Flynn effect (Flynn, 1987) that posits lower mean scores on tests with more recent norms (the K-ABC was standardized about a decade after the McCarthy Scales), but it is consistent with an examination of test content. The MPC minimizes language requirements and achievement-related tasks, but McCarthy's GCI emphasizes language competencies and acquired information.

The studies reported here are a sampling of the literature, but they illustrate the general finding of inconsistency from study to study and from instrument to instrument regarding verbal-nonverbal discrepancies in children with language disorders.

Some researchers have looked beyond the traditional verbal-performance dichotomy to find patterns of performance that may help identify children with language impairments. Ottem (1999), for example, examined WPPSI profiles obtained by using Bannatyne's classification scheme and by recategorizing the subtests by level of structural complexity. Ottem asked of each WPPSI subtest: "What is the minimum number of categories needed by the examiner to decide that the problem has been correctly solved by the subject?" (p. 320). He concluded that six subtests were structurally simple: Information, Similarities, Vocabulary, Comprehension, Picture Completion, and Mazes; three were structurally moderate: Arithmetic, Block Design, and Animal House; and two were structurally complex: Sentences and Geometric Design. Because language-impaired children are limited in the amount of information that they can process at once (as we noted in our discussion of processing speed and working memory), Ottem (1999) hypothesized that these children would perform worse on structurally complex than on structurally simple tasks. His hypothesis was confirmed, as he found a statistically significant simple > moderate > complex pattern separately for WPPSI Verbal subtests and Performance subtests for the group of children with language impairment. That pattern discriminated the language-impaired children from a group of children with normally developing language skills, but all comparisons between the two samples must be tempered with caution because Ottem failed to control for IQ (the control sample significantly outscored the sample of children with language impairment on all three WPPSI IQs, including a 6-point superiority in P-IQ) Ottem also predicted a spatial > conceptual > sequential Bannatyne pattern for children with language impairment, but his results showed spatial = conceptual > sequential pattern (for the control sample, all Bannatyne categories were approximately equal).

We found that Ottem's (1999) method of classifying WPPSI subtests by level of complexity was itself complex. Nonetheless, examiners with experience and expertise in language assessment may find his approach a valuable supplement to the methods that we have provided for interpreting WPPSI-III subtest profiles; if so, they should apply Ottem's methodology to the subtests that are new to the WPPSI-III. Although simply using a pattern such as simple > moderate > complex or conceptual = spatial > sequential is not adequate to differentially diagnose a child, uncovering such a pattern in a child's WPPSI-III scores may provide clues to his or her language skills and warrant further investigation.

Children's Knowledge of Basic Linguistic Concepts

We have discussed the importance of evaluating how a child's expressive and receptive language skills may affect performance on the Verbal and General Language scales of the WPPSI-III. A related consideration in administration and interpretation of the WPPSI-III is the extent to which a child's knowledge of basic concepts affects his or her ability to understand and follow directions during the test administration. In a wide variety of situations, basic concepts are used to order, make comparisons, classify, conserve, and solve problems (Boehm, 1976). Knowledge of basic concepts (i.e., relational terms such as top-bottom, same-different, in front of-behind, near-far, and right-left) develops gradually and is not an all-or-none process (Boehm, 2000).

Kaufman (1978) reported on the importance of basic concepts in following directions on standardized tests (such as the McCarthy Scales, Binet L-M, and WPPSI). The Psychological Corporation (2002) recognized that the "relatively difficult basic concepts in the WPPSI-R instructions may have adversely affected a child's understanding of task requirements" (p. 12). Therefore, in the WPPSI-III, instructions were modified to omit more difficult basic concepts (The Psychological Corporation, 2002). However, despite these changes in the third edition, as we noted in chapter 5, basic concepts that are difficult for some preschoolers remain in the WPPSI-III. We review those basic concepts here to help examiners determine which ones may affect an individual child's WPPSI-III assessment (Don't Forget box, page 206). Certainly, if a child does not understand the verbal directions to a nonverbal task and performs relatively poorly on that task, the low score is more likely to reflect a verbal deficit and does not provide measurement of the nonverbal skills in question.

DON'T FORGET

Difficult Basic Relational Concepts Used in the WPPSI-III

Subtest	Basic Concept Used	Example
Block Design (p. 57, p. 65)	Top Same Up Down	"Only the *tops* of the blocks need to be the *same*." "The white part should point *up*, like mine, and the red part should point *down*."
Information (p. 77)	Before After	"What goes on a letter *before* you mail it?" "What day comes *after* Sunday?"
Symbol Search (p 114)	Same	"This shape here is the *same* as this shape here." "None of these shapes are the *same*."
Coding (p. 125)	Up Down Same In order Skip	"This star up here has one line going *up* and *down*." "Do these the *same* way. Start here, go *in order*, and don't *skip* any."

Note. Page numbers listed after the subtests refer to the pages in the *WPPSI-III Administration and Scoring Manual* (Wechsler, 2002) that contain examples of the basic concepts.

Multicultural Differences Masquerading as Language Impairment

Cultural and linguistic bias must be considered in interpretation of scores on tests that involve receptive or expressive language. Examiners need to be careful not to misinterpret low verbal scores or misdiagnose a language-related disorder if a child's language difficulties are a direct result of cultural or linguistic differences. Limited proficiency in English (when it is not a child's native or only language) is *never* a sufficient reason to diagnose language impairment. If an appropriate assessment determines that a child has age-appropriate skills in his or her home language, such a finding indicates that language-learning skills are not compromised (Barona & Santos de Barona,

2000). Therefore, before making diagnostic decisions, assess language skills in a child's native language as well as in English (Dodd, Nelson, & Splint, 1995; Hernandez, 1994). A language disorder may be present if assessments reveal that bilingual children have limited proficiency in English *and* their native language (Barrera, 1995).

Identifying language problems in bilingual children is complex. The continuity and richness of a child's language environment continually affect language development (Barona & Santos de Barona, 2000). Second languages are acquired at varying rates and are affected by the age of the child, the strength of the native language, language aptitude, and motivation to learn the language (Prince & Lawrence, 1993). Because the language-learning process is more complex for children who develop bilingually, these children may lag 4–5 months behind children who develop monolingually (Hamayan & Damico, 1991). In addition, children who hear two languages simultaneously from birth develop language skills differently from those who learn a second language after the first has been established. Barona and Santos de Barona (2000) explain further:

> A child learning two languages simultaneously will proceed linguistically in a developmental pattern similar to monolingual speakers, although there may be a slower rate of vocabulary development. A child who establishes skills in one language and then proceeds to learn a second language will progress through four distinct developmental stages that include a nonverbal period in which the child begins to crack the code of the second language. (p. 289)

An instrument such as the WPPSI-III, which was not standardized on a bilingual population, has limitations in assessing children who are not monolingual English speakers. To appropriately interpret scores on the WPPSI-III, be aware of how social, linguistic, and cultural differences can affect children's scores. Consider data from a sample of 44 children with limited English proficiency (84% Hispanic and 16% Asian) tested with the WPPSI-III (The Psychological Corporation, 2002; Table 5.25). The average IQs of this sample of children indicate that nonverbal tasks were least affected by English knowledge: mean P-IQ = 95 and mean PSQ = 100. In contrast, the Verbal tasks were strikingly affected by the children's limited English; they obtained a mean V-IQ of 80 and mean GLC of 79. The children's lowest scaled scores were on Picture Naming (5.8) and Word Reasoning (6.2), whereas their highest were on Coding (10.4) and Symbol Search (9.8).

Research has indicated that minorities are substantially overrepresented in special education programs (Padilla, 2001). To promote fair assessment, examiners need to carefully select the most appropriate tests when evaluating the cognitive and language skills of bilingual children; those who are not dominant in one language over another should be evaluated in both English and their home language by clinicians skilled in the child's native language as well as in English to ensure that the child's abilities are adequately sampled (Barona & Barona de Santos, 1987). Supplemental cognitive assessment may be warranted if concerns about language skills persist. Consider administering instruments with nonverbal scales such as the KABC-II (Kaufman & Kaufman, in press), the Leiter International Performance Scale — Revised (Roid & Miller, 1987), or the Universal Nonverbal Intelligence Test (UNIT; Bracken & McCallum, 1998).

PROCESSING SPEED

Flanagan et al. (2000) state that "processing speed is the ability to fluently and automatically perform cognitive tasks, especially when under pressure to maintain focused attention and concentration" (p. 44). According to information-processing models of cognitive functioning, "the speed of processing is critical because it determines in part how rapidly limited resources can be reallocated to other cognitive tasks" (Kail, 2000, p. 152).

Because processing speed has been identified as an important domain of cognitive functioning and research has shown its relationship to intelligence, The Psychological Corporation (2002) decided specifically to measure it in the WPPSI-III, just as they had previously decided for the WISC-III and WAIS-III. Factor-analytic studies of cognitive ability (Carroll, 1993, 1997; Horn & Noll, 1997) led major theorists to include processing speed or Gs as an important domain in their theories.

Recent studies have shown that measures of processing speed in infants predict future scores on measure of intelligence. For example, Kail (2000) discussed evidence that suggests a role for processing speed in the development of intelligence, and some findings suggest that children's deficits in processing speed and working memory following radiation treatment for leukemia may underlie declines in IQ (Schatz, Kramer, Ablin, & Matthay, 2000).

Dougherty and Haith (1997) found that speed of information processing is stable from infancy to childhood and that infants' processing speed predicted childhood IQ at age 4. Also, processing speed is a developmental phenomenon, increasing from ages 22 to 37 months (Zelazo, Kearsley, & Stack, 1995) and from ages 4 to 6 years (Miller & Vernon, 1996, 1997). For their sample of 4- to 6-year-olds, Miller and Vernon (1996) also found that (a) reaction time and memory each correlated with intelligence and (b) memory predicted general intelligence but reaction time did not add any significant variance over and above the contribution of memory. They suggested that the inability of reaction time to predict intelligence may be due to the fact that "speed is not encouraged or demanded until later childhood. . . Perhaps it is because of the lack of demand for speed in young children that the relationship between processing speed and intelligence is weaker in this sample than previously demonstrated in adult samples" (Miller & Vernon, 1996, p. 188).

The interesting developmental and predictive research results involving young children's processing speed supports the measurement of processing speed on the WPPSI-III, just as Miller and Vernon's findings support the publisher's decision to reduce the emphasis on problem-solving speed by eliminating time bonuses on Block Design and Object Assembly.

Processing Speed and Language

Children with specific language impairment are slower than their peers on a variety of linguistic and nonlinguistic tasks (Edwards & Lahey, 1996; Johnston & Ellis Weismer, 1983; Lahey, Edwards, & Munson, 2001; M. Reynolds & Fucci, 1998; Sininger, Klatzky, & Kirchner, 1989; Stark & Montgomery, 1995). Lahey et al. (2001) note that

since both processing speed and speed and accuracy are influenced by the knowledge base accessed, one might expect slower processing speeds on language tasks for children with language disorders, particularly when the tasks involve real-time processing. However, the finding that slower processing speed occurs across a wide variety of tasks, including nonlinguistic tasks, suggests that slow processing among children with specific language impairment may not simply be a consequence of language knowledge that is less developed than that of peers. (p. 1355)

The relationship between processing speed and language is important because speed may directly affect a child's ability to learn, comprehend, and produce language (Lahey et al., 2001; Leonard, 1998). For example, children who are slow to process the initial part of rapid verbal input may lose part of what follows. When producing language, slow processors may take more time to find words or construct sentences, which may directly affect their ability to communicate (Leonard, 1998). Reading has also been linked to speed. For example, speed in processing language in kindergarten can help predict reading proficiency in second grade (Troia & Roth, 1996; Wolf, Bally, & Morris, 1986; Wolf & Goodglass, 1986).

Mean scores of children with specific language impairments have been shown to be significantly slower than are those of normally developing peers (Edwards & Lahey, 1996; Lahey & Edwards, 1996; Lahey et al., 2001), although a direct linear relationship between processing speed and severity of language impairment has not been found (Lahey et al., 2001). Future research needs to determine whether processing-speed deficits affect language learning and language use more when children are first learning language (e. g., ages 1–3) than at older ages because by ages 4 and above, children may have compensated for the deficits.

Because children with deficits in processing speed often have particular difficulty in tasks that require reasoning ability and working memory (Carpenter, Just, & Shell, 1990; Fry & Hale, 1996; Kail & Salthouse, 1994), acquiring new information such as language skills may be affected by speed. Fry and Hale (1996) found that age-related changes in processing speed mediated developmental increases in working memory. They also found that age-related increases in speed and working memory accounted for nearly half of the total age-related effect on fluid intelligence (in 7- to 19-year-olds). The authors theorized that "differences in speed have a direct effect on working memory capacity, and these individual differences in memory are a direct determinant of fluid intelligence" (Fry & Hale, 1996, p. 241). However, it is unclear how differences in processing speed initiate the cascading effect to working memory and higher cognitive functions.

Processing Speed and Language on WPPSI-III

Previous findings on the processing-speed deficits of language-disordered children, coupled with predictions from Fry and Hale's (1996) cascading theory, suggest that children with language disorders should display relative weaknesses in both their processing speed and fluid reasoning. To test these hypotheses, we reexamined the WPPSI-III data presented and discussed earlier (see Rapid Reference 6.4) on the two small samples of children with Mixed and Expressive language disorders. Neither group evidenced a relative weakness in either processing speed or fluid intelligence; their mean PSQs and P-IQs were quite similar to their mean standard scores on the other WPPSI-III scales. Nonetheless, it is noteworthy that the Expressive group consistently scored higher than did the Mixed group on the WPPSI-III composite scores with the largest difference emerging in processing speed (see Rapid Reference 6.4). This finding is consistent with previous research (Windsor & Hwang, 1999), suggesting the possibility that the weaker performance on processing speed tasks by children with Mixed Receptive-Expressive Language Disorder — relative to children with Expressive Language Disorder — is a driving force behind their globally lower performance on other cognitive tasks.

Data from Ottem (1999), which included 75 preschool children with language impairments who were tested on the WPPSI, revealed that the lowest performance was on Sentences and Arithmetic (both requiring verbal working memory) and the strongest performance was on Mazes (a timed task requiring fine-motor skill) and Animal House (a cousin to the Coding subtest). Because these four WPPSI subtests are not included in the current WPPSI-III, Ottem's findings do not have direct implications for WPPSI-III performance. However, Ottem's findings do seem to suggest a pattern of poor performance on working memory tasks and stronger performance on nonverbal tasks. In contrast to the previous findings on the processing-speed deficits of language-impaired children and predictions from Fry and Hale's (1996) cascading theory, the WPPSI speeded subtest, Block Design, was not among the worst for this language-impaired group. Furthermore, despite the fact that the two highest and two lowest WPPSI subtests in Ottem's (1999) study were eliminated from the WPPSI-III, his results are consistent with the findings reported in Rapid Reference 6.5. The expressive group and mixed group each displayed their best performance on nonverbal subtests and they tended to perform worst on the WPPSI-III subtests that seem to place the largest demands on verbal working memory by virtue of their lengthy verbal stimuli (Comprehension, Word Reasoning) or wordy directions (Coding).

Processing Speed and Memory

An additional study presented in the *WPPSI-III Technical and Interpretive Manual* (The Psychological Corporation, 2002) provides information about the relationship between processing speed and memory and between memory and reasoning. Forty children ages 5-0 to 7-3 were administered the Children's Memory Scale (CMS; Cohen, 1997) concurrently with the WPPSI-III. The mean WPPSI-III composite scores for this sample were all in the Average range (99–102). The WPPSI-III PSQ was most strongly correlated with the Recognition Delayed Memory scale of the CMS and the Attention/Concentration scale of the CMS, with correlations of .49 and .42, respectively (see Rapid Reference 6.8). A notable correlation of .37 was also found between Verbal Immediate Memory and the PSQ. Of the two Processing Speed subtests, Symbol Search seemed to drive the strength of the correlations because Symbol Search's correlations with the CMS scales were consistently higher than were those of Coding (see Rapid Reference 6.9).

≡ *Rapid Reference 6.8*

Highest and Lowest Correlations Between CMS Composites and PSQ

CMS Composites	PSQ
Highest	
Recognition Delayed	.49
Attention/Concentration	.42
Lowest	
Verbal Delayed	.13
Visual Delayed	.07

Note. Correlations are from Table 5.15 of the *WPPSI-III Technical and Interpretive Manual* (The Psychological Corporation, 2002, p. 102).

⟰ Rapid Reference 6.9

Correlations Between CMS Composites and Symbol Search and Coding on the WPPSI-III

CMS Composites	Symbol Search	Coding
Recognition Delayed	.51	.37
Attention/Concentration	.46	.31
General Memory	.43	.11
Learning	.41	.17
Verbal Immediate	.40	.25
Visual Immediate	.34	.09
Verbal Delayed	.32	.03
Visual Delayed	.27	-.08

Note. Correlations are from Table 5.15 of the WPPSI-III Technical and Administration Manual (The Psychological Corporation, 2002, p. 102).

Flanagan et al. (2000) indicate that the subtests constituting the CMS Attention/Concentration scale may involve working memory. Thus, the moderate correlation between the PSQ and the Attention/Concentration scale supports a relationship between working memory and processing speed in 5- to 7-year-old children. Measures of WPPSI-III fluid intelligence also correlated moderately with measures of working memory (CMS Attention/Concentration scale correlated .54 to .63 with Matrix Reasoning, Word Reasoning, and Picture Concepts; see Rapid Reference 6.10). Although these correlations do not represent causal relationships, theories that purport a dynamic connection among processing speed, memory, and reasoning (e.g., Fry & Hale, 1996; Kail, 2000) are given some support by these results.

CONCURRENT ASSESSMENT OF ABILITY AND ACHIEVEMENT (WPPSI-III AND WIAT-II)

Children in the WPPSI-III's age range (2-6 to 7-3) are sometimes evaluated to identify those who may have difficulty in learning as they enter school. In

≡Rapid Reference 6.10

Correlations Between Children's Memory Scale Composites and WPPSI-III Subtests That Are Believed to Measure Fluid Reasoning

CMS Composites	Matrix Reasoning	Word Reasoning	Picture Concepts	Average Correlation With Fluid Subtests
Attention/ Concentration	.55	.63	.54	0.57
Recognition Delayed	.43	.58	.43	0.48
Learning	.58	.44	.36	0.46
Verbal Immediate	.28	.55	.29	0.37
General Memory	.37	.41	.28	0.35
Visual Immediate	.47	.21	.31	0.33
Verbal Delayed	.20	.42	.15	0.26
Visual Delayed	.19	.02	.07	0.09

Note. Data are from Table 5.15 of the *WPPSI-III Technical and Administration Manual* (The Psychological Corporation, 2002, p. 102).

conducting psychological and educational screenings of children at an early age, clinicians assume that

1. "Early identification can accurately pinpoint the child's difficulties and a program can then be tailored to help ameliorate these difficulties;
2. If early detection is not undertaken, the child is likely to remain behind during most of his or her school years;
3. Preschool screening will, in some cases, lead to total or near total remediation of . . . problems prior to the beginning of first grade" (C. R. Reynolds, 1979, p. 277).

Evaluations of children's cognitive and academic functioning are often administered together as the primary means for determining eligibility for special education services, although the use of standardized tests and discrepancy scores is under fire both professionally and politically (Kaufman & Kaufman, 2001).

Although intelligence and academic achievement are moderately to strongly correlated, the correlation of intelligence scores in preschool years with later achievement in elementary schools is only about .50 (Shepard & Graue, 1993). (Note that when measures of IQ and achievement are administered *concurrently* to preschool children, much higher coefficients are often obtained. See, for example, the substantial correlations between WPPSI-III IQs and WIAT-II standard scores summarized in Rapid Reference 1.9.) For school-age children, those values are commonly in the .50s and .60s, with the highest values reaching .70 (Naglieri, 1999, 2001). Thus, "only about 25% to 50% of the variance in achievement test scores overlaps with IQ variance. If IQ can be said to account for about one-quarter to one-half of the variance in achievement test scores, that means that up to three-quarters of the variance in achievement scores is due to factors other than IQ, such as motivation, quality of teaching, parental involvement, perseverance, and plain old 'error'" (Kaufman & Kaufman, 2001, p. 444).

Some professionals strongly question the reliability of available methods for identifying preschool-age children as being at risk for learning disabilities. For example, Brown (1996) stated, "unfortunately, a reliable method for identifying children with learning disabilities at an early age (before first grade, and usually not until beginning second grade) does not yet exist" (p. 38). Research supports Brown's skepticism: For example, in a study of children tested prior to kindergarten on the McCarthy Scales, Funk, Sturner, and Green (1986) found a high false-positive rate when using preschool IQ to predict which children would have learning problems in kindergarten. Funk et al. also found that 50% of the children who were predicted to have academic problems based on prekindergarten McCarthy IQs actually were performing adequately in second grade.

Predicting School Achievement

Although controversy exists about the utility of IQ tests for predicting later achievement, comparing IQ and academic achievement continues to be important as long as the Individuals with Disability Education Act (IDEA) of 1997 (PL 105-17) remains the standard for action. (It is constantly on the firing line on the political scene.) The literature indicates that the most scientifically defensible procedure for comparing achievement to ability is to account for regression toward the mean and standard errors of differences between test scores on standardized instruments (Braden, 1987; Gridley & Roid, 1998; C. R. Reynolds, 1984). In the predicted-difference method, a regression equation calculates predicted achievement scores by taking into account the reliability of the ability and achievement scales as well as the correlations between them. To determine the predicted WIAT-II values based on WPPSI-III IQs and to calculate difference values required for statistical significance between the obtained and predicted WIAT-II scores, use the tables provided in Appendix C of the *WPPSI-III Technical and Interpretive Manual* (The Psychological Corporation, 2002, pp.170–179). The process of calculating differences between obtained WIAT-II scores and predicted WIAT-II scores requires four steps:

1. Determine which WPPSI-III IQ to use in ability-achievement comparisons.
2. Look up predicted WIAT-II scores in the appropriate table of the *WPPSI-III Technical and Interpretive Manual.*
3. Calculate the difference between predicted and obtained WIAT-II scores.
4. Determine whether the difference between predicted and obtained WIAT-II scores is significant (Appendix C.4 of the *WPPSI-III Technical and Interpretive Manual*).

1. Determine Which WPPSI-III IQ to Use in Ability-Achievement Comparisons

For each child, consider which IQ is the best estimate of cognitive potential. In many cases, the FS-IQ will be the best estimate: It is the most global representation of children's abilities, the best representation of *g*, and the most reliable scale on the WPPSI-III. However, when children have an abnormally large discrepancy between their V-IQ and P-IQ, the FS-IQ no longer is the best (or most meaningful) estimate of cognitive ability. A compelling reason may exist to use either the V-IQ or P-IQ over the FS-IQ. For example, children who have visual or motor problems are likely to have a P-IQ of questionable validity, so in such cases, use the V-IQ. In contrast, the V-IQ of children with moderate to severe receptive or expressive language disorders will be of questionable use in estimating general cognitive ability. In such cases, use the P-IQ, just as one would select P-IQ for children with limited english proficiency.

2. Look Up Predicted WIAT-II Scores in the Appropriate Table of the WPPSI-III Technical and Interpretive Manual

After you have determined which IQ is the most appropriate estimate of a child's level of cognitive functioning, select the pertinent predicted WIAT-II scores. In the *WPPSI-III Technical and Interpretive Manual*, Table C.1 predicts WIAT-II scores from WPPSI-III FS-IQ scores, Table C.2 predicts WIAT-II scores from WPPSI-III V-IQ scores, and Table C.3 predicts WIAT-II scores from WPPSI-III P-IQ scores. Thus, reference the appropriate table to determine what the child's WIAT-II performance should look like based on his or her cognitive ability. Rapid Reference 6.11 is a worksheet for recording predicted WIAT-II scores based on WPPSI-III IQs and obtained WIAT-II scores.

3. Calculate the Difference Between Predicted and Obtained WIAT-II Scores

Subtract each obtained WIAT-II score from the predicted WIAT-II value. Values for WIAT-II composites and subtests may need to be calculated, depending on which achievement subtests you administered. Again, you may use the worksheet we created for recording and calculating predicted-obtained WIAT-II discrepancies (see Rapid Reference 6.11).

4. Determine Whether the Difference Between Predicted and Obtained WIAT-II Scores Is Statistically Significant

The final step in the predicted-difference method requires you to compare the difference values obtained to the values required for statistical significance that are provided in Appendix C.4 of the *WPPSI-III Technical and Interpretive Manual.* The values needed for significance are listed for both the .01 and .05 levels and are listed according to whether the FS-IQ, V-IQ, or P-IQ was the basis for predicting the WIAT-II score. Be careful to reference the appropriate column of the table according to the IQ used. The worksheet in Rapid Reference 6.11 also lists the critical values necessary for significance. Rapid Reference 6.12 indicates the size of the difference needed for the discrepancy to be considered abnormally large (i.e., the predicted-obtained WIAT-II difference that occurs in 15% or less of the theoretical normal distribution).

≡Rapid Reference 6.11

Worksheet for Calculating Predicted-Obtained WIAT-II Discrepancies Based on WPPSI-III IQs

WIAT-II Subtest	Predicted WIAT-II Score	Obtained WIAT-II Score	Predicted-Obtained WIAT-II Difference	Value Needed For Significance		
				FS-IQ	V-IQ	P-IQ
Word Reading				4.13 5.44	4.46 5.87	44.02 5.29
Numerical Operations				12.22 16.8	12.05 15.86	12.32 16.22
Reading Comprehension				6.22 8.18	6.56 8.64	6.07 8.00
Spelling				7.64 10.05	7.62 10.03	7.52 9.90
Pseudoword Decoding				4.88 6.42	5.10 6.72	4.94 6.50
Math Reasoning				9.53 12.55	9.77 12.86	9.67 12.73
Written Expression				10.88 14.32	10.95 14.42	10.80 14.22
Listening Comprehension				13.76 18.11	14.11 18.58	13.68 18.01
Oral Expression				10.28 13.53	10.62 13.98	10.25 13.50
WIAT-II Composite						
Reading				4.47 5.88	4.92 6.48	4.32 5.69
Math				9.19 12.10	9.09 11.97	9.37 12.34
Written Language				7.86 10.35	8.18 10.77	7.65 10.08
Oral Language				9.46 12.45	10.01 13.18	9.37 12.34

	Predicted WIAT-II Score	Obtained WIAT-II Score	Predicted-Obtained WIAT-II Difference	Value Needed For Significance		
				FS-IQ	V-IQ	P-IQ
Total Achievement				5.75 7.57	6.55 8.62	5.74 7.56

Note. The first value listed in each row under "Value Needed For Significance" is the critical value at the .05 level of significance and the second value listed the critical value at the .01 level of significance. Values are from Table C.4 of the *WPPSI-III Technical and Interpretive Manual* (The Psychological Corporation, 2002, p. 176).

≡Rapid Reference 6.12

Differences That Are Considered Abnormally Large Between Predicted and Obtained WIAT-II Subtest and Composite Scores

WIAT-II Subtest	WPPSI-III IQ Used to Predict WIAT-II Scores		
	FS-IQ	V-IQ	P-IQ
Word Reading	13	13	14
Numerical Operations	12	14	13
Reading Comprehension	11	12	14
Spelling	13	14	15
Pseudoword Decoding	13	14	14
Math Reasoning	11	12	13
Written Expression	13	14	15
Listening Comprehension	13	12	14
Oral Expression	12	12	14
WIAT-II Composite			
Reading	12	12	14
Math	10	13	12
Written Language	12	12	14
Oral Language	11	11	14
Total Achievement	10	10	13

Note. Abnormally large predicted-obtained WIAT-II score differences are considered those that occurred in 15% or less of the theoretical normal distribution. Values are from tables C.5, C.6, and C7 of the *WPPSI-III Technical and Interpretive Manual* (The Psychological Corporation, 2002, pp. 177–179). In this table, values of 10 should be read as *10 or greater*, values of 11 should be read as *10 or greater*, and so forth.

Supplemental Means of Predicting Achievement

The aforementioned predicted-difference method is the most appropriate to use for predicting achievement based on IQs. As an informal *supplementary* approach to help you create hypotheses about a child's potential for academic achievement in specific areas, consider the data presented in Rapid Reference 1.11 and summarized in Rapid Reference 6.13. Both of these boxes list the three WPPSI-III subtests that correlated highest and the three that correlated lowest with each WIAT-II achievement composite (sometimes four subtests are listed because of equal correlations). To develop further hypotheses about areas of academic difficulties or strengths, use the best correlates of each WIAT-II cluster to predict good or poor school achievement for young children. If children score relatively low on all (or all but one) of the subtests that correlate strongest with a WIAT-II cluster, then you may hypothesize that a child might have difficulty in that particular academic domain. In contrast,

≡Rapid Reference 6.13

WPPSI-III Subtests to Consider for Informally Predicting Poor or Strong Academic Achievement

WPPSI-III Subtest	WIAT-II Composite				
	Reading	Math	Written Language	Oral Language	Total Achievement
Information	X	X		X	X
Receptive Vocabulary	X	X	X		
Similarities		X		X	X
Word Reasoning			X	X	X
Comprehension			X		
Picture Naming	X				X
Block Design		X			

Note. An X in a column indicates that the WPPSI-III subtest is one of the top three correlates of the given WIAT-II composite. Correlations between WIAT-II clusters and these WPPSI-III subtests ranged from .51 to .72. Data are from Rapid Reference 1.11 which, in turn, are from The Psychological Corporation (2002, Table 5.14).

if children score relatively poorly on all (or all but one) of the lowest correlates, then that academic area might prove troublesome for the child. If a
hypothesis of either potential academic difficulty or academic strength
emerges from this informal analysis, then we recommend administering an
achievement battery.

GIFTED CHILDREN

Definitions of giftedness range from a single intellectual dimension (Sparrow
& Gurland, 1998; Terman, 1925) to multiple abilities and intelligences
(Gardner, 1993; Guilford, 1967; Sternberg, 1982). In a chapter specifically
focusing on assessing giftedness in preschoolers, Morelock and Feldman
(1992) present the following definition:

> Gifted children are those showing sustained evidence of advanced capa-
> bility relative to their peers in general academic skills and/or in more
> specific domains (music, art, science, etc.) to the extent that they need
> differentiated educational programming. (p. 302)

Horowitz (1992) recognizes that "when potential giftedness is identified
during the early years, there may be a much greater possibility for the real-
ization of those gifts" (p. 89). Parents and teachers alike recognize the importance of assessing the intellectual domain for identifying and placing gifted
children (Sankar-DeLeeuw, 2002). Historically, a cutoff score on an intelligence test has identified gifted children (Sparrow & Gurland, 1998). Indeed,
psychologists typically conduct an intellectual assessment if a child is believed
to be intellectually gifted, even though this means of identification has recognizable problems such as cultural bias (Tyerman, 1986), ceiling effects
(Harrington, 1982; Kaplan, 1992; Kaufman, 1993), and an overemphasis on
speed (Kaufman, 1992; Sternberg, 1982). Various tests of cognitive ability
tap different types of information, so if the identification criteria for giftedness is based on a single test, the population of gifted students identified will
vary greatly depending on which test is used (Tyler-Wood & Carri, 1991).
Whenever IQ tests are used for gifted assessment, the key to making appropriate decisions about giftedness is to consider more than a simple cutoff
score (such as a FS-IQ above 125 or 130). Examiners need to consider
important issues such as the appropriateness of a particular test for a child of

a certain cultural background, the ceiling effects, the effect of speed on a child's score, and the scatter within a child's profile. In addition, wise clinicians should supplement the IQ measurement by assessing variables that are not measured by traditional intelligence tests such as creativity and *noncognitive* factors like motivation, personality, emotional intelligence, and thinking styles (e.g., see Kaufman & Kaufman, 2001; J. C. Kaufman, 2002a, 2002b, in press).

Given the common practice of using single or multiple IQs to identify gifted children, understanding the limitations of our assessment instruments for this purpose is crucial. One of the widely recognized problems with the WPPSI-R for the assessment of gifted children was its significant emphasis on the speed of a child's response (Kaufman, 1992; Sparrow & Gurland, 1998). However, as we noted in chapter 1 of this book, the importance of speed of responding was reduced in the WPPSI-III by eliminating the developmentally inappropriate bonus points for speedy performance on WPPSI-III Block Design and Object Assembly items. Although subtests designed specifically to measure processing speed (Coding and Symbol Search) were added to the WPPSI-III for ages 4-0 to 7-3 (replacing the highly speeded WPPSI-R subtest Animal Pegs), they do not contribute to the computation of V-IQ or P-IQ, and only Coding contributes to FS-IQ. Thus, the WPPSI-III is much less affected than its predecessor by noncognitive variables such as speed of response in the measurement of a child's cognitive ability. That change is a good thing because it prevents behavioral variables such as reflectivity and anxiety from unduly influencing a child's obtained IQs. At the same time, it underscores the importance of supplementing the WPPSI-III (or any IQ test) with noncognitive measures when evaluating giftedness. Such extra measures not only add to the breadth of the assessment, but the results of this supplemental testing might also assist examiners in understanding children's test score fluctuations when examiners believe that a child's scores may have been affected by his or her reflective style, coordination problems, motivation, or thinking style. In addition to noncognitive assessment, examiners might also administer supplementary tests that — for example — do not emphasize speed of responding or motor coordination to better understand a child's low scores on WPPSI-III Coding or Symbol Search.

Data are presented in the *WPPSI-III Technical and Interpretive Manual* (The Psychological Corporation, 2002) for a sample of 70 gifted children that ranged in age from 4-6 to 7-3 and had a mean age of 6.1 years. They were primarily a White sample (87%) and from highly educated families. Criteria for participation in the study included earning a score from a previous IQ test that was 2 standard deviations or more above the mean.

Given the inclusion criteria for the gifted sample of IQs ≥ 130 on a different cognitive measure, the overall mean WPPSI-III IQs of the gifted sample would be predicted to regress to the normative mean of 100, which they did, earning a mean FS-IQ of 126 (V-IQ = 126 and P-IQ = 123) (The Psychological Corporation, 2002).

These mean IQs are similar to the values for gifted children in previous studies of the WPPSI-R and WISC-III (Wechsler, 1989, 1991) and in recent studies with the WISC-IV (The Psychological Corporation, 2003, Table 5.22) and Binet-5 (Roid, 2003, Table 4.12). In contrast to to mean WPPSI-III IQs in the mid-120s, the mean PSQ was only 113, again similar to the results for gifted children on the WISC-III (1991) and WISC-IV (The Psychological Corporation, 2003). The 10-point higher P-IQ than PSQ for the gifted sample mirrors the findings observed when examining those children (ages 4+) in the WPPSI-III normative sample who earned IQs of 120 or above. As reported in Table B.2 of both WPPSI-III manuals, nearly 40% of the 120+ portion of the standardization sample had discrepancies of 10 points or more favoring P-IQ (38.8%) versus only 15.5% who scored 10 or more points higher on PSQ than P-IQ. Previous research has shown that children may respond slowly if they have a reflective problem-solving style or if they have a mild coordination problem, even if they are intellectually gifted (Kaufman & Lichtenberger, 2000).

Rapid Reference 6.14 shows the highest and lowest mean scaled scores earned by the gifted sample tested on the WPPSI-III. Whereas the lowest scores are predictably on PSQ subtests, the highest scores were on measures of acquired knowledge (Information), reasoning ability (Matrix Reasoning), or both (Similarities). Kitano's (1985) study of gifted preschoolers found high levels of accumulated knowledge, prelogical thinking, and an incorporation of academic activities in free play, consistent with the pattern of high WPPSI-III subtest scores for the gifted sample.

Performance of gifted preschoolers on other tests of cognitive ability have also consistently shown that verbal skills and reasoning are particularly strong. For example, Kleuver and Green (1990) found the following pattern of mean Binet-4 Area scores in a sample of 51 preschoolers: Verbal Reasoning (135), Quantitative Reasoning (132), Memory (127), and Abstract/Visual Reasoning (121).

≡Rapid Reference 6.14

Children Who Are Intellectually Gifted or Have Mental Retardation: Their Highest and Lowest Mean WPPSI-III Subtest Scaled Scores

Intellectually Gifted (FS-IQ = 126.2) (N = 70)		Mild Mental Retardation (FS-IQ = 62.1) (N = 40)		Moderate Mental Retardation (FS-IQ = 53.1) (N = 19)	
Highest	**Mean Scaled Score**	**Highest**	**Mean Scaled Score**	**Highest**	**Mean Scaled Score**
Information	15.0	Similarities	5.1	Similarities	4.2
Similarities	14.4	Receptive Vocabulary	4.9	Picture Concepts	3.5
Matrix Reasoning	14.4	Picture Concepts	4.8	Comprehension	3.3
Lowest		**Lowest**		**Lowest**	
Picture Completion	12.9	Block Design	4.0	Matrix Reasoning	2.7
Picture Concepts	12.9	Vocabulary	4.0	Picture Naming	2.7
Symbol Search	12.8	Comprehension	4.0	Vocabulary	2.5
Coding	12.2	Word Reasoning	3.9	Coding	2.4
		Picture Completion	3.9		

Note. Mean FS-IQs and scaled scores are from *WPPSI-III Technical and Interpretive Manual* (Tables 5.17, 5.18, and 5.19).

As in most gifted samples, level of acquired knowledge (as measured by the mean K-ABC Achievement score of 131 for Kleuver and Green's preschool sample) was in line with the mean Binet-4 composite score of 134.

In another Binet-4 study with gifted preschoolers, creativity as measured by Torrance's (1981) *Thinking Creatively in Action and Movement* did not correlate significantly with global intelligence (Fuchs-Beauchamp, Karnes, & Johnson, 1993). These data support the need to measure potentially gifted and talented children by supplementing the traditional IQ tests with measures of creativity.

The WPPSI-III is recommended for use in gifted assessment, but some aspects reveal a need for caution. Although the WPPSI-III IQs are much less affected by speed of responding than is the WPPSI-R, some Performance subtests have time limits and the speeded Coding subtest does contribute to FS-IQ. Also, be aware that gifted children who are reflective or motorically impaired may have depressed FS-IQs or P-IQs, necessitating noncognitive assessment and supplementary cognitive testing to truly understand their gifted potential As astute examiners, go beyond simple IQs and try to make sense of why a child scored as he or she did. Observation of behaviors during testing in combination with information from a child's background and supplemental assessment of noncognitive variables can provide important clues to interpreting a profile. Take into account these clues, being careful not to interpret a single IQ or even the highest of several IQs as *the* number that indicates giftedness.

MENTAL RETARDATION

The diagnosis of mental retardation considers both a child's intellectual functioning and adaptive behavior. To fall in the category of mental retardation, a child's IQ on tests that have a standard deviation of 15, such as the WPPSI-III, must be less than 70 (American Psychiatric Association, 2000). In addition to subaverage intellectual functioning, both the American Association on Mental Retardation (AAMR) and the *DSM-IV-TR* (American Psychiatric Association, 2000) guidelines require impairment in two or more of the following adaptive skill areas: communication, self-care, home living, social skills, community use, self-direction, health, safety, functional academics, leisure, and work. Thus, although we focus in this section on the intellectual component, as measured by standardized tests like the WPPSI-III, keep in mind that assessment of mental retardation must also examine adaptive functioning (e.g., the ability to meet the standards of personal behavior and independence expected for children of their chronological age).

The *WPPSI-III Technical and Interpretive Manual* (The Psychological Corporation, 2002) reports the results of a study of 40 children diagnosed with mild mental retardation and 19 diagnosed with moderate mental retardation. Both groups of children had a mean age of 6 and none of the children were institutionalized. As has commonly been found in mentally retarded populations, there was very little variability in the subjects' performance. The standard deviations of the composite scores ranged from 7.5 to 10 points, which is in contrast to the 15-point standard deviation typically found in the general population; however, such restriction of range is common for low-functioning samples. The small amount of variability was also notable from the mean V-IQ and P-IQ for each sample of children diagnosed with mental retardation (both mean IQs were 66 for the mild group and they were 58–59 for the moderate sample). Generally, equally depressed performance on the Verbal and Performance Scales is found for children diagnosed with mental retardation (Slate, 1995; Wechsler, 1991). Young children assessed with other tests of cognitive ability also typically reveal little variability between scales. For example, the Binet-4 Verbal Reasoning and Abstract/Visual Reasoning Area Scores are often equally depressed (Bower & Hayes, 1995), and on the new Binet-5, mean Verbal and Nonverbal IQs were virtually identical for a sample of 119 individuals with documented diagnoses of mental retardation (ages 3–25 years; no mean or median age reported; Roid, 2003, Table 4.12). In addition, discrepancies between language and performance in young children with mental retardation do not usually add prognostic information beyond that contained in the global measure of cognitive ability (Vig, Kaminer, & Jedrysek, 1987).

The patterns of high and low subtests were slightly different for the mild and moderate groups (see Rapid Reference 6.14, which summarizes data for the groups of children with mental retardation alongside the data for the gifted children). Both groups had Similarities and Picture Concepts among their three highest subtests, but their lowest subtests were almost completely different (only Vocabulary was a relative weakness for both samples).

As discussed earlier in this book, at the ages of overlap (6-0 to 7-3), the WPPSI-III is a better measure to use than is the WISC-IV to assess children suspected of mental retardation. Administer the WPPSI-III to children referred for suspected retardation because it provides a better floor than does the WISC-III for those who are functioning at very low levels of ability. On the WISC-III, Similarities, Block Design, and Picture Arrangement have inadequate bottoms for 6-year-olds (Spruill, 1998). For example, a raw score of 1 earns a 6-year-old child a WISC-III scaled score of 4 on Similarities, Information, Picture Arrangement, and Block Design. In contrast, WPPSI-III raw scores of 1 will earn a 6-year-old a scaled score of 4 on only one subtest, Similarities, and scaled scores of 3 on two subtests: Symbol Search and Comprehension.

No characteristic Wechsler profiles for children with mental retardation have been consistently reported (Spruill, 1998). The occasional slight trend for some groups of children with very low ability to perform better on the Performance than on the Verbal Scale is not something that can be used as a diagnostic characteristic of the population; indeed, that pattern did not characterize either WPPSI-III sample of children with mental retardation. A diagnosis of mental retardation should only be made based on the results of appropriate measures of both IQ and adaptive functioning. Then consider all of the test data within the context of relevant clinical data from a child's background (developmental, educational, medical) history and behavioral observations before making a differential diagnosis of mental retardation.

 TEST YOURSELF

....

1. **Shanequa earned a WPPSI-III V-IQ of 135 and a P-IQ of 129, but her PSQ is only 112. Her scores are consistent with those of most gifted children because**

   (a) all gifted children have a V-IQ > P-IQ.

   (b) all gifted children are reflective and careful in their processing, which leads to a V-IQ > PSQ and P-IQ > PSQ.

   (c) her V-IQ is greater than 2 standard deviations above the mean, and it is not uncommon for gifted children to have V-IQ or P-IQ > PSQ.

   (d) gifted children always score the highest on Information, Similarities, and Vocabulary, which leads to strong V-IQs.

   (continued)

2. **Jack has been diagnosed as having moderate mental retardation. This diagnosis means that most likely Jack was tested on measures of IQ and**

(a) visual perception.

(b) gross motor coordination.

(c) working memory.

(d) adaptive behavior.

3. **Because measures of intelligence and creativity are so highly correlated for gifted children, scores from each type of test may be considered interchangable.** True or False?

4. **Children with specific language impairment tend to have significantly lower scores on measures of processing speed than children without such impairments.** True or False?

5. **Julia was found to perform very poorly on Symbol Search and Coding, both of which require speed for success, but performed about 2 standard deviations above normal on other subtests. Given that she has been classified as _____, this finding is not surprising.**

(a) mentally retarded

(b) gifted

(c) hearing impaired

(d) emotionally disturbed

6. **Ngu is a 6-year-old diagnosed with mild mental retardedation. His pattern of performance is typical for a child functioning in the below-70 IQ range, so not surprisingly, his**

(a) V-IQ is abnormally lower than his P-IQ.

(b) V-IQ and P-IQ are similar in magnitude.

(c) subtest scatter is abnormally large.

(d) GLC is significantly lower than his V-IQ.

7. **Which of the following domains have theorists causally linked to processing speed?**

(a) crystallized and fluid intelligence

(b) spatial processing and spatial memory

(c) working memory and reasoning

(d) long-term memory and auditory memory

8. **Which two noncore WPPSI-III subtests do we recommend examiners routinely give to children ages 4 and above, so long as time permits, rapport is good, and the child does not display notable attentional problems?**

   (a) Symbol Search and Similarities

   (b) Comprehension and Object Assembly

   (c) Picture Naming and Receptive Vocabulary

   (d) Picture Completion and Object Assembly

9. **For children ages 4 or above, unless language-related problems or global cognitive delays are suspected, then we recommend that you do *not* administer the GLC subtests.** True or False?

10. **Max, a 6-year-old who was previously diagnosed with language impairment, earned his highest WPPSI-III standard score on the GLC. His high GLC**

   (a) is surprising since most children with language impairments show a pattern of extremely poor performance on GLC subtests.

   (b) may not reflect his language deficits as effectively as subtests that require higher-levels of language skill such as Word Reasoning, Similarities, and Vocabulary.

   (c) can only be explained by his strong guessing ability, since Receptive Vocabulary is a forced-choice test.

   (d) simply proves that his previous diagnosis was incorrect.

11. **Three-year-old Rosa has an abnormally large V-P IQ discrepancy in favor of her P-IQ (95), with the V-IQ (69) falling in the Extremely Low range of cognitive functioning. Given that Rosa is bilingual, you must**

   (a) assume that her scores do not reflect a language impairment unless language assessment in her home language reveals similar levels of linguistic impairment.

   (b) automatically consider her V-IQ to be invalid.

   (c) assume that her P-IQ is an accurate assessment of her overall ability.

   (d) take her GLC as the value that best represents her overall linguistic potential for English learning ability.

12. **Most research indicates that measures of intelligence in preschool are excellent predictors of academic performance through the third grade.** True or False?

Answers: 1.c; 2. d; 3. False; 4. True; 5. b; 6. b; 7. c; 8. a; 9. True; 10. b; 11. a; 12. False.

Seven

ILLUSTRATIVE CASE REPORTS

This chapter includes the case studies of two children who were referred for psychoeducational evaluations. The WPPSI-III profile of Ophelia T. was presented in chapter 4 to illustrate the interpretive steps. The culmination of that interpretive process is presented here in Ophelia's case report. The second case report describes the profile of Antonio, a 3-year-old boy with features of both autistic disorder and attention deficit disorder.

The goals of this chapter are to bring all other facets of this book together, to demonstrate how the WPPSI-III may be used as part of a comprehensive test battery, and to demonstrate the cross-validation of hypotheses with behavioral observations, background information, and supplemental test scores. The basic outline for each report includes the following: reason for referral, background information, appearance of the client and behavioral observations during the assessment, tests administered, test results and interpretation, summary, diagnostic impression, and recommendations. For the cases presented here, we present all of the test scores prior to the text of the report; however, in a report to be given to the client, we would include this information at the very end of the report in a section labeled Psychometric Summary.

CASE REPORT 1

Name: Ophelia T.
Age: 6 years, 1 month
Grade: First
Examiner: Elizabeth O. Lichtenberger, PhD

**Wechsler Preschool and Primary Scales of Intelligence–
Third Edition (WPPSI-III)**

Published by The Psychological Corporation, 2002

Composite	Standard Score	90% Confidence Interval	Percentile Rank	Qualitative Description
Verbal IQ (V-IQ)	116	110–120	86	High Average
Performance IQ (P-IQ)	119	112–124	90	High Average
Processing Speed Quotient (PSQ)	104	96–111	61	Average
Full Scale IQ (FS-IQ)	120	115–124	91	Superior
General Language Composite (GLC)	113	106–118	81	High Average

Verbal Subtests	Scaled Score	Percentile Rank	Performance Subtests	Scaled Score	Percentile Rank
Information	13	84	Block Design	12	75
Vocabulary	11	63	Matrix Reasoning	16 S	98
Word Reasoning	15 S	95	Picture Concepts	11	63
(Comprehension)	(9) W	(37)	(Picture Completion)	(11)	(63)
(Similarities)	(13)	(84)	(Object Assembly)	(11)	(63)

General Language Subtests			Processing Speed Subtests		
Receptive Vocabulary	15 S	95	Coding	12	75
Picture Naming	10	50	(Symbol Search)	(10)	(50)

Note. Supplemental subtests and scores are in parentheses; optional subtests are in italics.

Kaufman Test of Educational Achievement Brief Form–Normative Update

Published by American Guidance Service, 1997

Subtests and Composite	Standard Score	90% Confidence Interval	Percentile Rank	Qualitative Description
Mathematics	112	103–121	79	Above Average
Reading	115	107–123	84	Above Average
Spelling	118	109–127	88	Above Average
Battery Composite	114	108–120	82	Above Average

Developmental Test of Visual-Motor Integration (VMI-4)

Published by Modern Curriculum Press, 1997

	Standard Score	Percentile Rank
VMI-4	112	79

Referral and Background Information

Mr. and Mrs. T. would like to know Ophelia's cognitive strengths and weaknesses to better understand how to help her reach her full academic potential. Although Ophelia is an average to above-average student, her parents want to know what they can do to ensure she is doing "the best she can with her intellectual abilities." Her parents have noted that recently Ophelia seems to perseverate on schoolwork problems that are difficult for her and cannot be encouraged to move on. Her parents would like recommendations on how to guide her through her academic career in a manner that will cause the least frustration.

Ophelia is the older of two children in her family. Her younger sister, Sophia, is four years her junior. Ophelia's mother works full-time as a nurse and her father is a full-time software engineer.

According to her mother, Ophelia was born after an uncomplicated full-term pregnancy; she was delivered via C-section, weighing 8 pounds, 6 ounces. The C-section was normal and had no related complications. Mrs. T. indicated that Ophelia's early developmental milestones were met at a normal rate and recalled that Ophelia sat alone at 5 months, walked alone at 15 months, and said sentences at 24 months.

Ophelia's medical history is relatively unremarkable with no major injuries or serious illnesses. However, she had a tonsillectomy and adenoidectomy at age 3. Due to postsurgical trouble with fluid in her lungs, she was subsequently hospitalized for 24 hours. Other than mild colds and bouts of the flu, Ophelia's health has been good. Her hearing and vision are within normal limits, and there were no reported problems at her last complete physical at age 5 and one half.

Ophelia's educational history began when she entered day care at 18 months. Mrs. T. indicated that Ophelia experienced anxiety separating from

DON'T FORGET

Pertinent Information to Include in Identifying Information Section

- Name of child
- Date of birth
- Age
- Grade in school (if applicable)
- Date(s) of testing
- Date of report
- Examiner's name

DON'T FORGET

....

Pertinent Information to Include
in Reason for Referral Section of Report

Who referred the child
  1. List name and position of referral source.
  2. Indicate questions of referral source
Specific symptoms and concerns
  1. Summarize current behaviors and relevant past behaviors.
  2. List any separate concerns that parents (or guardian) or children have.

her mother, but the anxiety dissipated after she "got to know the teacher." Ophelia attended day care until she began preschool at the age of 4, and then she entered kindergarten just before her fifth birthday. Ophelia, who is now in first grade at the local public elementary school, was able to read, spell, and perform basic mathematical computations by the end of kindergarten. Her mother reported that Ophelia has "always loved school," and "she seems to excel in writing, reading comprehension, and art." Her school reports indicate that Ophelia is a good student, achieving at grade level or above grade level. Despite Ophelia's overall love for school, Mrs. T. stated that recently she has expressed frustration with math word problems.

Socially, Ophelia seems to be easygoing, according to Mrs. T. Ophelia is able to make friends easily and to interact comfortably with adults. The main emotional struggle that Mr. and Mrs. T. report having with Ophelia relates to her inflexibility. Mrs. T. described Ophelia as a child who cannot "let go of things that are upsetting to her. . . . She has a very difficult time moving past her disappointment." If something does not go Ophelia's way, then she tries endlessly to negotiate with her parents, which then causes her to get into trouble. Mr. and Mrs. T. have tried to remedy the problem with positive reinforcement for good behavior and negative reinforcement or punishment when Ophelia's endless attempts at negotiation (or whining) persist. She has responded especially well to the family's token reward system and time-outs.

According to her parents, Ophelia has numerous strengths. She is emotionally intuitive and makes friends easily. She uses her strong verbal communication skills well in social situations at home, at school, and with

DON'T FORGET

Pertinent Information to Include in Background Information

Present in paragraph form the information you have obtained from all sources, including referral source, client, family members, social worker, teachers, medical records, and so forth. State only pertinent information, not needless details.

• The following information may be included:
• Current family situation (parents, siblings, etc.) — no gossip
• Other symptoms
• Medical history (including emotional disorders)
• Developmental history
• Educational history
• Previous treatment (educational or psychological)
• New or recent developments, including stressors
• Review of collateral documents (past evaluations)

friends. Problem solving in real-life situations seems to come naturally for Ophelia. She is also artistic, good at organizing, and a good story writer.

Appearance and Behavioral Characteristics

Ophelia is a cute 6-year-old girl of average height and weight with short brown hair and blue eyes. During the evaluation, the examiner easily established and maintained rapport with Ophelia, who spoke freely about her day at school and expressed curiosity about the tasks that would be presented. Ophelia's highly verbal nature was evident throughout each of the tasks. Whether she was asked a question that required a verbal response or was given a problem that required a nonverbal response, she talked as she processed the problems at hand. In fact, Ophelia's talkative nature prolonged the length of the testing session beyond the range that is typical for a child her age.

On nonverbal tasks, such as copying block models and determining which pictures best go together, Ophelia used verbal mediation to work through the problems. For example, as she manipulated blocks to match a model, she said, "There's a triangle . . . It's like a house." As she examined pictures on another

DON'T FORGET

Pertinent Information to Include in Appearance and Behavioral Characteristics

- Talk about significant patterns or themes you see going on during testing.
- Sequence information in order of importance rather than in order of occurrence (don't just present a chronological list).
- Describe the behavioral referents to your hypotheses (specific examples).
- Describe what makes this client unique (paint a picture for the reader).

Suggested areas to review (note only significant behaviors):

Appearance
- Size — height and weight
- Facial characteristics
- Grooming and cleanliness
- Posture
- Clothing style
- Maturity — whether the person looks his or her age

Behavior
- Speech articulation, language patterns
- Activity level (foot wiggling, excessive talking, nail biting, tension, etc.)
- Attention span, distractibility
- Cooperativeness or resistance
- Interest in doing well
- How the individual goes about solving problems
  - Trial and error
  - Quickly or reflectively
  - By checking answers
- Reactions to failure or challenge
  - Does child continue to work until time is up?
  - Does child ask for direction or help?
  - Did failure reduce interest in the task or working on other tasks?
  - When frustrated, is the child aggressive or dependent?

(continued)

- Attitude toward self
  - Does child regard self with confidence, a superior attitude, or feelings of inadequacy?
  - How did child strive to get approval? Response to your praise of effort?

Validity of test results

- If the results are valid, state why. "On the basis of Juanita's above behaviors, the results of this assessment are considered a valid indication of her current level of cognitive and academic ability."
- If not, state why not. "Corey's excessive distractibility and inability to tolerate even minor frustration renders the results of this assessment as probable underestimates of his actual current level of cognitive and academic ability."

task (that requires a simple pointing response), she said, "This doesn't go with that because you can't cut with both, but these could go together because you can turn them both on. However, sometimes these globes can have lights in them so it could go too, but this one doesn't look like it lights up so I don't think that it belongs. So, I guess that just leaves these two that go together because they light up." Ophelia's highly verbal approach aided her in solving nonverbal problems on the WPPSI-III, but this same approach could handicap her when problems require quick solutions.

Indeed, Ophelia's concern about accuracy was stronger than her desire to work quickly. On two paper-and-pencil tasks that directed her to "work as fast as you can without making any mistakes," Ophelia clearly maintained her focus on making no mistakes as she methodically and carefully went through each item. She was aware of the timed nature of the tasks (she asked how much time she had used), but she continued to work slowly and carefully in response to each item.

Ophelia was concerned with the accuracy of her performance throughout the assessment; she repeatedly asked, "Is that right?" When she was uncertain about the correctness of verbal responses, she examined the examiner's facial expression for reassurance and then added more verbiage to her response in an apparent effort to ensure accuracy. Although the examiner cannot give feedback about the correctness of responses, Ophelia appeared comforted by the examiner's praise for her efforts.

Ophelia attended well and showed a strong ability to focus during the assessment. As items became more challenging, she maintained her concentration but more frequently responded, "I don't know" to questions. However, when prompted to "just try your best" after she gave an "I don't know" response, Ophelia refocused her energy and came up with responses to challenging problems. Considering the length of the evaluation, she attended well to the tasks at hand from beginning to end.

In light of Ophelia's level of attention, concentration, and efforts to do her best on each task, the results of this evaluation are considered a valid estimate of her current level of cognitive and academic functioning.

Tests Administered and Data Collected

Background History from Mrs. T.
Wechsler Preschool and Primary Scale of Intelligence–Third Edition (WPPSI-III)
Kaufman Test of Educational Achievement–Normative Update (K-TEA-NU), Brief Form
Developmental Test of Visual-Motor Integration (VMI)
Kinetic Family Drawing

Test Results and Interpretation

Ophelia was administered the Wechsler Preschool and Primary Scale of Intelligence–3rd edition (WPPSI-III), an individually administered test of a child's intellectual ability and cognitive strengths and weaknesses. The WPPSI-III comprises 14 subtests for children ages 4 to 7 years; these subtests measure verbal abilities and specific nonverbal abilities. On the WPPSI-III, Ophelia earned a Full Scale IQ of 120 (115–124 with 90% confidence) based on her performance on the seven core subtests. Her Full Scale IQ ranks her at the 91st percentile compared to other children her age and is considered in the High Average to Superior range of intellectual functioning. Ophelia's overall verbal and nonverbal abilities were not significantly different from one another: Her Verbal IQ of 116 (86th percentile) and Performance IQ of 119 (90th percentile) are both in the High Average range of intellectual functioning.

DON'T FORGET

Pertinent Information to Include in Test Results and Interpretation

- Paragraph form should be used.
- Put numbers in this section, including IQs and other global scores with confidence intervals and percentile ranks. When discussing performance on subtests, use percentile ranks (most people aren't familiar with the scaled score's mean of 10 and standard deviation of 3); do not include raw scores.
- Tie in behaviors with results to serve as logical explanations or reminders whenever it is appropriate.
- With more than one test, find similarities in performances and differences (discrepancies) and use these similiarities and differences to generate hypotheses.
- Support hypotheses with multiple sources of data, including observed behaviors.
- Don't contradict yourself.
- Be sure that you are describing the subtests, not just naming them. Remember, the reader has no idea what *Picture Concepts* means.
- Describe the underlying abilities that the task is tapping.
- Talk about the child's abilities, not what the test or subtest measures.
- You need to be straightforward in your writing, not too literary — no writing in metaphors.

Although the nearly equal IQs suggest that Ophelia processes verbal and nonverbal information about equally well, she appears to have more difficulty when she is required to process information rapidly. Ophelia scored in the Average range on the Processing Speed scale, earning a standard score of 104 (61st percentile). Two nonverbal tasks comprise this scale: one requiring Ophelia to copy symbols from a key and another requiring her to scan a row of symbols to determine whether a target symbol was present. On both tasks Ophelia was more concerned with the accuracy of her response than on working quickly to complete the task. She was methodical rather than impulsive in her approach to these tasks and most others during the assessment.

Ophelia's careful approach to nonverbal problems was also evident during an untimed drawing task, the Developmental Test of Visual Motor Integration (VMI), which was administered to assess her ability to copy a series of increasingly complex abstract figures (e.g., ranging from a vertical line to a diamond to overlapping concentric rings). She earned a VMI standard score of 112 (79th percentile), commensurate with her WPPSI-III Performance IQ of 119 (90th percentile), suggesting equal development on a variety of nonverbal tasks. Her approach to each VMI item included carefully examining the figure to be copied and then taking her time drawing to ensure success.

When Ophelia was not required to process information at a rapid rate, her strong abstract reasoning ability was evident. In fact, her WPPSI-III subtest scores indicate that she has significant relative strengths in abstract reasoning and novel problem solving. On an untimed nonverbal task that required her to examine an incomplete matrix and select the missing portion from four or five response options, Ophelia scored at the 98th percentile. During this task, Ophelia's careful, methodical style of processing benefited her greatly. Similarly, on a verbal task requiring Ophelia to identify the common concept that was described in a series of increasingly specific clues, she used her strong reasoning skills to carefully solve the problems (95th percentile).

Generally, Ophelia's verbal strengths helped her in both verbal and nonverbal realms. When possible, she tried to interject verbiage to solve nonverbal problems; as noted earlier, she thought aloud, so to speak, to solve problems and also used talking to ease her anxiety as the problems became more difficult.

Ophelia's style of verbally processing information during the cognitive portion of the assessment was also evident during assessment of her academic achievement. The Kaufman Test of Educational Achievement–Normative Update (K-TEA-NU, Brief Form) was administered to obtain an estimate of Ophelia's level of academic functioning. As on the WPPSI-III, she worked through the K-TEA-NU problems with much verbiage. She earned a K-TEA-NU Battery Composite standard score of 114 (108–120 with 90% confidence). Her overall score placed her academic functioning at the 82nd percentile, which is considered the High Average range. She performed equally well in Mathematics, Reading, and Spelling, earning standard scores of 112, 115, and 118, respectively. As she worked on K-TEA-NU Mathematics and Spelling problems she whispered to herself, continuing to use her verbal manner of processing most problems.

Ophelia used both phonetics and whole-word recognition during the spelling and reading tasks. Some of her errors in spelling demonstrate her use of phonetics. For example, she spelled *dinner* as *diner* and *little* as *littll*. In contrast, her use of whole-word recognition was evident when she incorrectly read *elephant* as *elementary*. As words during the reading task became more difficult, Ophelia chose to respond, "I don't know," rather than using her phonetic skills to sound them out or her recognition skills to guess at what they may be. Even with gentle encouragement from the examiner and positive reinforcement about her other attempts, Ophelia did not want to try them. Overall, Ophelia's combination phonetic and whole-word approach benefited her, as she scored at the 84th percentile for Reading and 88th percentile for Spelling.

In contrast to her "I don't know" responses to the last few items on the Reading task, Ophelia eagerly attempted all addition and subtraction problems on the K-TEA-NU Mathematics subtest (she has not yet been taught multiplication or division in her first-grade class). As when she showed her desire to know the correctness of her responses during the cognitive testing, Ophelia inquired repeatedly about whether she added or subtracted correctly. However, even with no feedback about her accuracy, Ophelia showed eagerness to try most mathematics problems. Ultimately, her score on the Mathematics subtest placed her in the Above Average range at the 79th percentile.

A comparison of Ophelia's cognitive skills and academic skills indicates that her overall Above Average level of academic achievement (standard score of 114) is commensurate with her overall Above Average to Superior level of intellectual functioning (Full Scale IQ of 120). She appeared equally motivated to work on cognitive tasks and more specific academic tasks and used a highly verbal approach to problem solving on most tasks. Thus, the results of both types of tests indicate that Ophelia uses her cognitive strengths to help her achieve academically.

Summary and Diagnostic Impressions

Ophelia T. is a 6-year-old girl who was assessed to determine her cognitive strengths and weaknesses in order to ascertain how she can best reach her full academic potential. Mr. and Mrs. T. provided information about Ophelia's background. She was the product of an uncomplicated pregnancy and

DON'T FORGET

Pertinent Information to Include in Summary and Diagnostic Impressions

- Summary information should already be stated earlier in the body of the report.
- Include summary of primary reasons for referral, key background information, and prominent clinical observations of behavior.
- Summarize most important interpretations of global scores and strengths and weaknesses.
- Provide a rationale for your diagnosis if one is made.

normal C-section delivery. Her physical and psychosocial development have been normal, and she has a relatively unremarkable medical history. Academically, Ophelia has achieved at grade level or above since she began kindergarten. She has no reported social or psychological difficulties. Although Mr. and Mrs. T. struggle with Ophelia's inflexibility, overall, Ophelia presents with no major behavioral problems.

One of the most notable aspects of Ophelia's behavior during the evaluation was her highly verbal nature. She used verbal mediation on nonverbal problems and responded with excess verbiage to verbal problems. Ophelia showed great concern about the accuracy of her performance and desired much feedback from the examiner. Her approach to most problems was methodical and careful rather than speedy. She was focused and attentive throughout the evaluation.

Ophelia's overall cognitive ability is best represented by her WPPSI-III Full Scale IQ of 120 (91st percentile; High Average to Superior range of intelligence). Her verbal and nonverbal abilities were equally well developed (Verbal IQ = 116 and Performance IQ = 119). However, when she was required to respond in a rapid manner, Ophelia's performance was significantly lower (Processing Speed Quotient = 104; 61st percentile; Average range).

Ophelia's careful, methodical mode of responding was beneficial on tests of abstract reasoning ability. She displayed significant relative strengths in novel problem solving and abstract reasoning, both verbally and nonverbally.

During the assessment of her academic skills, Ophelia's verbal problem-solving style was also evident. Her K-TEA-NU standard scores of 112 for Mathematics (79th percentile), 115 for Reading (84th percentile), and 118 for Spelling (88th percentile) reflected her achievement at school that is at grade level or above grade level. Ophelia's High Average academic skills are also commensurate with her High Average to Superior level of intellectual functioning. Thus, she seems to be working to the best of her cognitive abilities.

Recommendations

1. Because of her desire to process information carefully and methodically, Ophelia will likely excel on tasks that do not require her to work under time pressure. Thus, at home and at school, place the emphasis in evaluation on accuracy rather than speed.

2. Because Ophelia may feel pressured and have more difficulty if she is required to work rapidly, provide her with ample time to complete work so that she can accomplish tasks within the allotted time. If more time is not available, consider reducing the amount of work required so that Ophelia does not feel pressured and unduly frustrated by time constraints.

3. Some situations in Ophelia's life will require more rapid responses and she may not be able to use her careful mode of responding. In preparation for such situations, encourage her to spend less time evaluating her own work and simply give a response. Giving her opportunity to succeed when she is not overanalyzing a problem will help her take a chance when she is in a situation with limited time to respond.

4. Ophelia's style of verbally processing problems, both verbal and nonverbal, is generally helpful for her. Encourage her to continue to use self-talk and talking aloud when encountering *new, challenging* activities. However, in activities that are less challenging, she does not need encouragement to self-talk and may even benefit from less verbiage and less self-evaluation.

5. Ophelia is an intelligent little girl who seeks much reassurance and feedback about her performance. Balance giving her needed feedback with teaching her to evaluate her own performance. For example, when working on subtraction problems, teach her how to check her

CAUTION

Common Errors to Avoid in Report Writing

- Inappropriate detail
- Unnecessary jargon or technical terms
- Vague language
- Abstract statements
- Failure to support hypotheses with adequate data
- Gross generalizations from isolated information
- Value judgments
- Discussion of the test itself rather than the person's abilities
- Poor grammar
- Presentation of behaviors or test scores without interpreting them
- Failure to adequately address reasons for referral
- Failure to provide confidence intervals or otherwise denote that all obtained test scores include a band of error
- Premature presentation of test results (e.g., in the section on appearance and behavioral characteristics)

own work by adding. When reading, teach her how to use the context of a sentence to ensure that the word she is trying to read makes sense.

6. Ophelia's strength in novel problem solving will benefit her in many areas — academic and social. Encourage her to further develop this strength by using problem-solving strategies that are generalizable to a variety of situations. Include the following steps:

  a. Decide what the problem is and what the best outcome would be.
  b. Brainstorm possible solutions.
  c. Consider which solutions are feasible.
  d. Consider the positive and negative outcomes of each solution.
  e. Choose the solution that seems best.
  f. Try it.
  g. Ask whether it is working.
  h. Modify it or select a different solution if the strategy does not work.

7. Ophelia's tendency to endlessly negotiate with her parents is not surprising given her highly verbal nature. Verbalizing is how Ophelia most readily problem solves. In order to prevent such negotiation-related conflicts from escalating, encourage Ophelia to take another approach to solve the problem. One suggestion is to have Ophelia write out three different ways to solve the problem. Have Ophelia start the process of writing before she begins to verbally negotiate (i.e., break the typical cycle of responding). After she writes out the solutions, go through each of her proposed solutions with her. If none is acceptable (i.e., close enough to what the parents desire), help her write other alternatives. Writing will often slow the pace of a verbal argument and will help Ophelia logically reason through the problem.

CASE REPORT 2

Name: Antonio Y.
Age: 3 years, 3 months
Examiner: Martha C. Hillyard, PhD

**Wechsler Preschool and Primary Scales of Intelligence–
Third Edition (WPPSI-III)**

Published by The Psychological Corporation, 2002

Composite	Standard Score	95% Confidence Interval	Percentile Rank	Qualitative Description
Verbal IQ (V-IQ)	88	82–95	21	Low Average
Performance IQ (P-IQ)	93	85–102	32	Average
Full Scale IQ (FS-IQ)	89	83–96	23	Low Average
General Language Composite (GLC)	102	95–109	55	Average

Verbal Subtests	Scaled Score	Percentile Rank	Performance Subtests	Scaled Score	Percentile Rank
Receptive Vocabulary	10	50	Block Design	8	25
Information	6 W	9	Object Assembly	10	50
General Language Subtests					
Receptive Vocabulary	10	50			
(Picture Naming)	(11)	(63)			

Note. The supplemental subtest and scores are in parentheses. Receptive Vocabulary is listed twice because it contributes to both the Verbal IQ and the General Language Composite.

Developmental Test of Visual-Motor Integration (VMI)
Published by Modern Curriculum Press, 1997

	Standard Score	Percentile Rank
VMI	92	30

Vineland Adaptive Behavior Scales
Published by American Guidance Service, 1984

Domain	Standard Score	Adaptive Level	Age Equivalent
Communication Skills	68 ± 8	Low	1–7
Daily Living Skills	64 ± 8	Low	1–8
Socialization Skills	74 ± 10	Low	1–9
Motor Skills	70 ± 8	Low	2–3

Gilliam Autism Rating Scale (GARS)
Published by PRO-ED, 1995

Subtest or Quotient	Standard Score	Percentile Rank	Probability of Autism
Stereotyped Behaviors	8	25	Average
Communication	11	63	Average
Social Interaction	9	37	Average
Developmental	9	37	Average
Autism Quotient	95	37	Average

Note. The normative group for the GARS was a sample of persons with autism, so the standard scores and percentile ranks compare the subject to a group of subjects who are known to be autistic. Thus, a person who is not autistic will score lower than the normative group does, and a person with more autistic characteristics will score higher. An average probability of autism indicates that approximately 50% of the subjects with autism scored in this range.

Reason for Referral

Antonio Y. was referred for a psychological evaluation by his social worker at the Agency for the Developmentally Disabled. The current assessment was requested to determine Antonio's present level of functioning so that appropriate recommendations can be made regarding programming and agency eligibility.

Background Information

Antonio is the only child of Mr. and Mrs. Y. Mrs. Y. is a full-time homemaker and Mr. Y. is a manager of a retail establishment; they both provided information about Antonio's history.

Antonio was born prematurely at 35 weeks gestation after a normal vaginal delivery. Although he was small at birth, weighing only 5 pounds, 1 ounce, Antonio was able to breathe freely on his own and did not need medical attention at birth. Shortly after birth, he was diagnosed with scaphocephaly, which is the result of premature closure of the sagittal suture (border between the bones of the skull). This disorder caused his head to appear elongated from front to back and narrowed from side to side. Surgical treatment was required for his scaphocephaly, and he had reconstructive craniectomy at 10 months. No postsurgical complications were noted and his parents reported that his recovery and development seemed to go well until Antonio reached 18 months, when he showed some developmental regression and behavioral difficulties in his language, social, and attentional skills. Just before his second birthday, Antonio had a developmental evaluation that revealed symptoms of attention-deficit hyperactivity disorder (ADHD) and mild to moderate autistic disorder. At age 2 and one half, Antonio was evaluated at the communications clinic and was found to have a moderate-severe speech production deficit, a moderate-severe language production disorder, and a mild language comprehension delay. "Attention-related and behavioral difficulties suggestive of possible ADHD or autistic spectrum disorder" were also noted during his language evaluation.

Other than the medical and developmental issues mentioned, Antonio appears to be a healthy 3-year-old. He recently had a complete physical exam, which found his hearing and vision to be normal. He has had no major injuries or illnesses that required hospitalization other than his craniecomy at 9 months.

Because of Antonio's developmental delays, Mr. and Mrs. Y. have chosen not to place him in preschool until he is 4 years old. However, Antonio currently attends speech therapy twice a week and sees a developmental specialist once a week. In addition, Mrs. Y. works extensively with Antonio at home on his language, social, and attentional skills.

Tests Administered

Wechsler Preschool and Primary Scale of Intelligence–Third Edition (WPPSI-III)
Developmental Test of Visual-Motor Integration (VMI-4)
Vineland Adaptive Behavior Scales
Gilliam Autism Rating Scale (GARS)

Appearance and Behavioral Characteristics

Antonio is a handsome Caucasian 3-year-old boy with sandy hair and green eyes. He looked at the examiner immediately when she introduced herself to him and his parents in the waiting room. However, he did not immediately say anything upon introduction.

After he was in the testing room, Antonio seated himself in a small chair on command. Mrs. Y. remained in the room throughout the evaluation seated to Antonio's left and slightly behind him, while his father observed the testing through the one-way mirror in the adjacent room. Antonio was immediately interactive and responsive. Using short, choppy phrases, he initiated conversation with the examiner and with his mother, and he sometimes asked for help. He seemed to enjoy working with the materials and responded positively to praise. However, Antonio also had a great deal of difficulty maintaining any sort of attentional focus. Although he did not get up out of his chair, he constantly moved in his chair — turning to his mother or swiveling to look at the window. It was necessary to continually call his attention back to the task at hand. Antonio also was quite impulsive in his response style, often grabbing for the materials and having difficulty waiting a few seconds while the materials were laid out. Extraneous features of the materials also distracted him. For example, he liked the numbers on the back of the puzzle pieces and turned each piece over to read the number before working the puzzle.

Antonio was rigid in his approach to nonverbal problem-solving tasks. He rigidly played with the blocks in his own way before he would complete some block constructions, such as stacking the blocks and building a three-block pyramid. In addition to block tasks, his rigidity was also seen in the manner in which he approached puzzle tasks (i.e., insisting on looking at the numbers on each puzzle piece before commencing with the task).

When formal testing was completed, Antonio was allowed to play with the available toys while the adults talked. During this period, he initially became involved with button pushing on a computer-like toy. When his parents took this toy away, he then examined various toys and finally settled on repetitive play with a stretching tube. At points during the play period, Antonio became a little fussy and his parents calmed him by holding him and by giving him a snack. He did initiate interaction with his parents, particularly his mother, mostly to request things from her.

The current results are thought to be reliable and to give a reasonably valid picture of Antonio's present functioning. However, due to his young age, they cannot be regarded as predictive. Also, the attentional and behavioral issues may have lowered Antonio's scores to some extent.

Test Results and Interpretation

Antonio was administered the Wechsler Preschool and Primary Scale of Intelligence–Third Edition (WPPSI-III), an individually administered test of a child's intellectual ability and cognitive strengths and weaknesses. The WPPSI-III comprises five subtests for children under the age of 4 that measure verbal abilities and nonverbal abilities. On the WPPSI-III, he achieved a Verbal IQ of 88 (true score of 82–95; 21st percentile). However, a significant amount of variability exists between the two subtests that comprise his Verbal IQ (ranging from the 9th to the 50th percentile), rendering it meaningless as a representation of his overall level of verbal cognition. His Performance IQ of 93 (true score of 85–102; 32nd percentile) falls within the Low Average to Average range of intellectual functioning. A comparison between Antonio's Verbal and Performance IQs is not possible because his Verbal IQ is not a meaningful construct. Thus, his Full Scale IQ of 89 (true score of 83–96; 23rd percentile), like his Verbal IQ, does not provide a meaningful representation of his overall level of intellectual ability. An examination of his specific subtest strengths and weaknesses provides more insight into Antonio's cognitive abilities.

The variability in the subtests comprising Antonio's Verbal IQ reflects the complexity of his language difficulties. His vocabulary is well developed and at age level for both expressive vocabulary (63rd percentile for his ability to name pictures) and receptive vocabulary (50th percentile for his ability to identify pictures). Antonio earned a standard score of 102 (true score: 95–109; 55th percentile) on the WPPSI-III General Language Composite, a measure of basic receptive and expressive vocabulary skills. However, he remains quite limited in his use of language. He had more trouble on a test of general verbal knowledge, performing at the 9th percentile. He identified some pictures relating to simple object functions (e.g., eating, drinking), identified body parts, and — when he was asked how old he was — Antonio put up some fingers. However, for the most part, he simply echoed the last word or two when asked questions. Thus, his Average scores on tests of simple expressive and receptive vocabulary do not reflect his difficulties in communication and general verbal knowledge.

Antonio's language skills were further assessed by his parents' report on the Communication Domain of the Vineland Adaptive Behavior Scales. Antonio's standard score on the Communication Domain was 68 ± 7 (2nd percentile), which falls within the range of Mild Deficit. Throughout the assessment, Antonio's spontaneous language consisted of single words, stock phrases, and echoed phrases and words. However, it was not clear whether any of his utterances truly represented spontaneous word combinations. Antonio usually does use his stock phrases with communicative intent and most of his language did appear to be communicative, although he also preseveratively repeated phrases and words. He also followed simple commands in context.

In contrast to his verbal skills, Antonio's nonverbal skills appear more evenly developed. He exhibited no relative strengths or weaknesses in his abilities on the WPPSI-III Performance scale. Although he was rigid in his approach to nonverbal problem-solving tasks (insisting on playing with the blocks in his own way and perseverating on the numbers on the back of puzzles), he performed at a Low Average to Average range on tasks involving manipulating puzzles and blocks. He was able to copy flat designs with blocks of one color but nearly always became confused when attempting designs with 2 colors. Similarly, he became confused when puzzles became more complicated with an increased number of pieces.

On another test of nonverbal ability, separate from the WPPSI-III, Antonio also performed within the Low Average to Average range. Specifically, on the Developmental Test of Visual-Motor Integration (VMI-4), a paper-and-pencil figure copying test, Antonio earned a standard score of 92 (30th percentile). Antonio easily copied vertical and horizontal lines and a circle. He showed a right-hand preference but used an immature fist grip.

In contrast to his Low Average to Average nonverbal and fine-motor skills assessed on the WPPSI-III and VMI-4, Antonio's gross-motor development appears delayed. According to information supplied by his parents, he runs well, can jump with both feet off the ground, and climbs on high play equipment. However, he does not alternate feet on stairs or pedal a tricycle. On the

Motor Skills domain of the Vineland (including both fine- and gross-motor skills), Antonio's standard score was 70 ± 13 (2nd percentile).

On the Daily Living Skills domain of the Vineland, Antonio's standard score was 64 (1st percentile), indicating self-help skills in the Mild Deficit range. His parents reported that Antonio eats a very narrow range of foods (approximately 10 specific foods). He feeds himself using a spoon and fork, drinks from a cup, and drinks using a straw. Toilet training is reportedly proceeding very slowly. Antonio sometimes indicates when he needs his diaper changed, but he does not initiate toileting. He sometimes urinates if he is taken to the potty, but he is not yet dry at night. When dressing, Antonio is partially able to remove clothing but does not yet dress himself. He brushes his own teeth but screams when put in the bathtub. He does pick up his own toys.

Behaviorally, Antonio was fairly socially responsive, although he did show a number of characteristics similar to those observed in children with autistic spectrum disorders. He also has characteristics in his developmental history suggestive of an autistic spectrum disorder, including a regression at 18 months of age. Although he does so with difficulty, Antonio makes spontaneous eye contact much of the time and rarely gives the impression of looking through people. His parents reported that recently Antonio has begun to sometimes accept affection and give hugs and kisses. In situations with other children, he still tends to withdraw and does not imitate the other children. Mr. and Mrs. Y. reported that his rigidity is also improving, although he still becomes upset when routines are changed. His parents stated that he frequently walks on his toes, stares, and is rigid about food, but he has no specific self-stimulatory behaviors. As described previously, Antonio is also echolalic. He does not try to share interests or experiences with others (verbally or nonverbally), although he does try to communicate. He does not yet have make-believe play, and he tends to fixate on trains and airplanes. On the other hand, Antonio does imitate and his parents said that he wants to please (although he also has frequent tantrums). On the Gilliam Autism Rating Scale (GARS), Antonio scored within the range indicating probable autism.

In addition to the autistic-like characteristics, Antonio also shows poor self-regulatory skills for his age. He is easily distracted and has trouble maintaining a consistent attentional focus. Antonio also appears quite impulsive and hyperactive, has limited frustration tolerance, and is generally immature in his development of basic socialization skills. He hits others and squeezes them in a pressure-seeking type of response. On the Socialization Skills Domain of the Vineland, Antonio's standard score was 74 (4th percentile), indicating socialization skills in the Borderline range.

Diagnostic Impression

Antonio is a darling little boy with a complicated medical history and a history of developmental regression at age 18 months. Since then he has reportedly shown delays in social interaction and communication skills, with atypical features suggestive of autism. He also has had difficulty with self-regulation and tends to be impulsive, to have trouble focusing, and to have poor frustration tolerance. Cognitively, Antonio's abilities are within the Low Average to Average range on the WPPSI-III, with a significant relative weakness in his general factual knowledge. In addition, he shows Mild to Borderline delay in motor, socialization, and self-help skill development.

Antonio has already had some intervention, and his parents have been working very diligently to increase his interactive and communicative skills. It is therefore possible that Antonio's current functioning represents a positive response to these efforts to modify an underlying pattern of emerging atypical behaviors. In support of this idea, his parents reported recent improvements in eye contact, tolerance of changes, initiation of communication, and affectionate responses. However, even if this is the case, it should be noted that Antonio has never engaged in self-stimulatory behaviors and his autistic-like symptoms have apparently been fairly mild.

It is also still possible that Antonio's symptoms may resolve in the direction of an attention deficit disorder along with a receptive language disorder. He does continue to show many ADHD symptoms including impulsivity, hyperactivity, poor attentional controls, and generally poor self-regulation. Similar symptoms often resolve later in very different ways, so Antonio will need to be followed carefully over time to help clarify the diagnostic picture.

In planning Antonio's program in the future, however, keep in mind that there is no clear line between classical autism and pervasive developmental disorder, NOS; rather, they represent a continuum of behaviors and symptoms that can be regarded as autistic spectrum disorders. In addition, as progress is made in understanding these disorders, both the diagnostic criteria and the terminology used in diagnostic manuals tend to change, producing confusion for parents when different terms are used at different times. At present, parents also need to be aware that although the referring agency uses the *DSM-IV* diagnostic system, the public schools often use other, less demanding criteria to classify a child as autistic. Thus, a child who does not qualify for one agency's services may still qualify for services geared to children with autistic spectrum disorders through the public schools.

Recommendations

1. Antonio could benefit from a preschool program geared to his developmental needs. He is likely to do best in a structured program in a small group setting that provides ample individual attention and a well-thought-out, positive program for behavior management. Initial goals of his program should be to increase and improve his social interactive and communication skills. Antonio is ready for age-appropriate content if it is presented visually or through hands-on activities, but he will need adaptations to help him follow directions because of his reduced verbal understanding. Because Antonio's parents are eager to follow through at home, good home-school communication will be important so that they can follow these suggestions as effectively as possible.

2. Antonio continues to need speech and language therapy. One emphasis should be on helping him develop flexible word combinations and on improving his pragmatic speech. The guidelines detailed in the recent speech and language evaluation indicate his specific needs in this area in some detail.

3. Antonio needs further evaluation of his motor needs and could benefit from an occupational therapy (OT) evaluation with regard to possible sensory-integration issues and self-help skill development issues.

4. A consultation with a registered dietician is recommended to provide information about the consequences of Antonio's very limited diet and to determine ways that he may be encouraged to eat more well-rounded meals.

5. A parent support group is recommended for Mr. and Mrs. Y. so that they can meet parents whose children are facing similar challenges.

6. If Antonio's behavioral issues do not resolve in a satisfactory way as a result of the above interventions, an additional consultation with a behavior modification specialist might be considered.

7. The current and prior evaluations should be regarded as providing baseline data. Antonio will need to be followed carefully over time and reassessed in about 6 months to see how his problems are resolving and how he is developing.

Appendix A

WPPSI-III Interpretation Worksheet

STEP 1: INTERPRET THE FULL SCALE IQ

Scale	IQ	90% or 95% Confidence Interval (circle one)	Percentile Rank	Descriptive Category
Full Scale				
Performance				
Verbal				

⇩

STEP 2: IS THE VERBAL IQ VERSUS PERFORMANCE IQ DISCREPANCY SIGNIFICANT?

V-IQ	P-IQ	Difference	Age Group	Significant (p<.01)	Significant (p<.05)	Not Significant	Is there a significant difference?	
			2:6-3:5	15+	12-14	0-11	YES	NO
			3:6-4:5	14+	11-13	0-10		
			4:6-4:11	13+	10-12	0-9		
			5:0-5:5	12+	9-11	0-8		
			5:6-6:11	13+	10-12	0-9		
			7:0-7:3	12+	9-11	0-8		
			All Ages	14+	10-13	0-9		

⇩

Step 2 Decision Box		
If the answer to Step 2 is **NO**, there is not a significant difference between the V-IQ and P-IQ	⇨	First explain the meaning of the scales not being significantly different. Then **Skip to Step 4.**
If the answer to Step 2 is **YES**, there is a significant difference between the V-IQ and P-IQ	⇨	Continue on to **Step 3.**

STEP 3: IS THE V-IQ VERSUS P-IQ DISCREPANCY ABNORMALLY LARGE?

V-IQ vs. P-IQ discrepancy	Percentage of Normal Children Showing Discrepancy	Size of V-IQ vs. P-IQ discrepancy needed to be considered abnormally large	Is there an abnormally large V-IQ vs. P-IQ discrepancy? (at least 20 points)	
	Extreme 15%	20		
	Extreme 10%	23		
	Extreme 5%	28	YES	NO
	Extreme 2%	33		
	Extreme 1%	36		

⇩

Step 3 Decision Box		
If **ANY abnormal** V-P IQ differences are found ⇨	then interpret this **abnormally** large discrepancy, even if significant subtest scatter exists (Step 4) ⇨	Explain the abnormally large Verbal and Performance differences. Then **go to Step 5** (or to Step 4 if you want to examine subtest scatter)
If **NO normal** V-P IQ difference is found ⇨	then determine whether the noted significant differences between V-IQ vs. P-IQ are interpretable ⇨	Examine subtest scatter in **Step 4**, prior to making global interpretations

STEP 4: IS VERBAL VERSUS PERFORMANCE IQ DISCREPANCY INTERPRETABLE?

Ages 2-6 to 3-11

A.) Is there abnormal Verbal scatter for ages 2-6 to 3-11?

Information Scaled Score	Receptive Vocab. Scaled Score	Difference	Abnormal Scatter	Not Abnormal	Is there abnormal scatter?	
			4 or more	0-3	YES	NO

B.) Is there abnormal Performance scatter for ages 2-6 to 3-11?

Object Assembly Scaled Score	Block Design Scaled Score	Difference	Abnormal Scatter	Not Abnormal	Is there abnormal scatter?	
			6 or more	0-5	YES	NO

⇩

Ages 4-0 to 7-3

A.) Is there abnormal Verbal scatter for ages 4-0 to 7-3?

High Scaled Score of 3 V-IQ Subtests	Low Scaled Score of 3 V-IQ Subtests	High-Low Difference	Abnormal Scatter	Not Abnormal	Is there abnormal scatter?	
			5 or more	0-4	YES	NO

B.) Is there abnormal Performance scatter for ages 4-0 to 7-3?

High Scaled Score of 3 P-IQ Subtests	Low Scaled Score of 3 P-IQ Subtests	High-Low Difference	Abnormal Scatter	Not Abnormal	Is there abnormal scatter?	
			7 or more	0-6	YES	NO

⇩

Step 4 Decision Box			
If the answers to both Step 4 questions (A and B) are **NO**	⇨ then V-IQ **versus** P-IQ discrepancy is interpretable	⇨	Explain the meaningful difference between V-IQ & P-IQ. **Then go to Step 5.**
If the answers to either Step 4 question (A or B) are **YES**	⇨ then do **not** interpret the V-IQ **versus** P-IQ difference	⇨	Examine the strengths and weaknesses in **Step 5.**

⇩

Note: If there is a significant difference between the component parts of the Full Scale IQ (i.e., the Verbal IQ and the performance IQ or significant subtest scatter), the Full Scale IQ should not be interpreted as a meaningful representation of the individual's overall performance.

STEP 5: IS THE PERFORMANCE IQ VERSUS PROCESSING SPEED QUOTIENT DISCREPANCY INTERPRETABLE? (COMPLETE ONLY FOR CHILDREN AGES 4-0 TO 7-3)

A.) Is there abnormal scatter in the PSQ?

Coding Scaled Score	Symbol Search Scaled Score	Difference	Abnormal Scatter	Not Abnormal	Is there abnormal scatter?	
			4 or more	0-3	YES	NO

B.) Is the PIQ versus. PSQ discrepancy significant?

P-IQ	PSQ	Difference	Significant (p<.01)	Significant (p<.05)	Not Significant	Is there a significant difference?	
			17	13	0-12	YES	NO

Step 5 Decision Box		
If there is no abnormal scatter in either the PSQ or the PIQ ⇨	then PSQ **versus** P-IQ discrepancy is interpretable ⇨	Explain the meaningful difference between PSQ and P-IQ. **Then go to Step 6.**
If abnormal scatter exists in either the PSQ or PIQ ⇨	then do **not** interpret the PSQ **versus** P-IQ difference ⇨	Examine the strengths and weaknesses in **Step 6.**
If no abnormal scatter exists in PSQ ⇨	then the PSQ is a unitary construct ⇨	Interpret the PSQ. **Then go to Step 6.**

⇩

STEP 6: DETERMINE SIGNIFICANT STRENGTHS AND WEAKNESSES OF PROFILE

Sum of scaled scores of all subtests administered	Divided by	Number of subtests administered	equals	Overall mean	⇨	Rounded mean
	/		=		⇨	

Strengths And Weakness For Ages 2-6 to 3-11

Verbal Subtest	Scaled Score	Rounded Mean	Difference[b]	Size of Difference Needed for Significance	Strength or Weakness (S or W)	Percentile Rank (See Table 4.3)
Receptive Vocabulary				±3		
Information				±3		
Picture Naming				±3		
Performance Subtest						
Block Design				±4		
Object Assembly				±4		

Strengths And Weakness For Ages 4-0 to 7-3

Verbal Subtest	Scaled Score	Rounded Mean	Difference[a]	Size of Difference Needed for Significance	Strength or Weakness (S or W)	Percentile Rank[b]
Information				±3		
Vocabulary				±3		
Word Reasoning				±3		
Comprehension				±3		
Similarities				±3		
Receptive Vocabulary				±3		
Picture Naming				±3		
Performance Subtest						
Block Design				±4		
Matrix Reasoning				±4		
Picture Concepts				±4		
Symbol Search				±4		
Coding				±4		
Picture Completion				±4		
Object Assembly				±4		

[a]Difference = Subtest scaled score minus appropriate rounded mean. [b] See Table 4.3.

STEP 7: INTERPRET GENERAL LANGUAGE COMPOSITE

Ages 2-6 to 3-11

A.) Is Receptive Vocabulary or Picture Naming a significant relative strength or weakness?

Receptive Vocabulary	Picture Naming	Is either subtest a relative S or W?	
		YES	NO
S or W in Step 6?	S or W in Step 6?		

B.) Is the difference between Receptive Vocabulary and Picture Naming normal (i.e., not abnormally large)?

Receptive Vocabulary Scaled Score	Picture Naming Scaled Score	Difference	Abnormal Scatter	Normal Variability	Is there normal variability?	
					YES	NO
			4 or more	0-3		

Ages 4-0 to 7-3

A.) Is Receptive Vocabulary or Picture Naming a significant relative strength or weakness?

Receptive Vocabulary	Picture Naming	Is either subtest a relative S or W?	
		YES	NO
S or W in Step 6?	S or W in Step 6?		

B.) Is the difference between Receptive Vocabulary and Picture Naming normal (i.e., not abnormally large)?

Receptive Vocabulary Scaled Score	Picture Naming Scaled Score	Difference	Abnormal Scatter	Normal Variability	Is there normal variability?	
					YES	NO
			4 or more	0-3		

C.) Is GLC significantly different from V-IQ?

GLC	V-IQ	Difference	Significant (p<.05)	Not Significant	Is there a significant difference?	
					YES	NO
			11+	0-10		

⇩

Step 7 Decision Box	
For ages 2-6 to 3-11	↗ If A and B are YES, then interpret the GLC ↘ If A or B are NO, then don't interpret the GLC
For ages 4-0 to 7-3	↗ If A, B, and C are YES, then interpret the GLC ↘ If A, B, or C are NO, then don't interpret the GLC

STEP 8: GENERATING HYPOTHESES ABOUT STRENGTHS AND WEAKNESSES

Review information presented in chapter 4 that details how to reorganize subtest profiles to systematically generate hypotheses about strengths and weaknesses.

Appendix B

Abilities Shared by Two or More WPPSI-III Verbal and Performance Subtests for Children Ages 4-0 to 7-3

Ability	Verbal Subtests							Performance Subtests							Reliability[a]	
	I	V	WR	C	S	RV	PN	BD	MR	PCon	SS	Cd	PC	OA	r_{xx}	r_{12}
Input																
Auditory-vocal channel	I	V	WR	C	S										.97	.96
Auditory perception of complex verbal stimuli	I		WR	C				BD			SS	Cd			.96	.95
Auditory perception of simple verbal stimuli		V		C	S										.96	.94
Complex verbal directions								BD			SS	Cd			.92	.91

(continued)

Note. I = Information; V = Vocabulary; WR = Word Reasoning; C = Comprehension; S = Similarities; RV = Receptive Vocabulary; PN = Picture Naming; BD = Block Design; MR = Matrix Reasoning; PCon = Picture Concepts; SS = Symbol Search; Cd = Coding; PC = Picture Completion; OA = Object Assembly; I (1–6)= First six Information items only; V (1–5) = First five Vocabulary items only.

[a] r_{xx} = Split-Half reliability; r_{12}= Test-Retest Reliability.

Ability	Verbal Subtests							Performance Subtests							Reliability[a]	
	I	V	WR	C	S	RV	PN	BD	MR	PCon	SS	Cd	PC	OA	r_{xx}	r_{12}
Input (*continued*)																
Distinguishing essential from nonessential detail					S				MR	PCon	SS		PC		.96	.94
Simple verbal directions	I (1–6)					RV	PN			PCon			PC	OA	.96	.94
Encode information for processing											SS	Cd			.90	.91
Understanding long questions	I		WR	C											.95	.93
Understanding words		V			S	RV									.96	.94
Visual motor channel	I (1–6)					RV		BD	MR	PCon	SS	Cd	PC	OA	.97	.95
Visual perception of abstract stimuli								BD	MR		SS	Cd			.94	.92
Visual perception of complete meaningful stimuli	I (1–6)	V (1–5)				RV	PN			PCon			PC		.96	.93
Visual perception of meaningful stimuli	I (1–6)	V (1–5)				RV	PN			PCon			PC	OA	.96	.94

Integration-Storage

	I	V	WR	C	S	RV	PN	BD	MR	PCon	SS	Cd	PC	OA	r_{xx}[a]	r_{12}
Achievement	I	V		C	S										.97	.95
Acquired knowledge (Bannatyne)	I	V	WR			RV	PN								.97	.96
Broad visualization								BD	MR				PC	OA	.95	.91
Cognition (Guilford)		V	WR	C	S	RV		BD	MR	PCon			PC	OA	.98	.97
Concept formation		V			S			BD		PCon					.96	.93
Convergent production (Guilford)			WR			RV			MR	PCon	SS	Cd			.96	.95
Crystallized ability (CHC)	I	V	WR	C	S	RV	PN			PCon					.98	.97
Culture-loaded knowledge	I			C											.92	.89
Decentration			WR							PCon					.94	.86
Evaluation (Guilford)				C		RV	PN	BD	MR	PCon	SS	Cd	PC	OA	.97	.96
Figural cognition (Guilford)							PN	BD	MR	PCon			PC	OA	.96	.94

(continued)

Note. I = Information; V = Vocabulary; WR = Word Reasoning; C = Comprehension; S = Similarities; RV = Receptive Vocabulary; PN = Picture Naming; BD = Block Design; MR = Matrix Reasoning; PCon = Picture Concepts; SS = Symbol Search; Cd = Coding; PC = Picture Completion; OA = Object Assembly; I (1–6)= First six Information items only; V (1–5) = First five Vocabulary items only.

[a]r_{xx} = Split-Half reliability; r_{12}= Test-Retest Reliability.

Integration-Storage (continued)

Ability	Verbal Subtests							Performance Subtests							Reliability[a]	
	I	V	WR	C	S	RV	PN	BD	MR	PCon	SS	Cd	PC	OA	r_{xx}	r_{12}
Figural evaluation (Guilford)						RV	PN			PCon	SS	Cd	PC	OA	.97	.96
Fluid ability (CHC)			WR		S			BD	MR	PCon				OA	.97	.94
Fund of information	I	V	WR			RV				PCon					.96	.95
General ability	I	V		C	S			BD	MR	PCon					.97	.96
General information (CHC)	I			C									PC		.94	.92
Handling abstract verbal concepts		V	WR		S										.96	.95
Holistic (right-brain) processing									MR	PCon			PC	OA	.95	.91
Induction			WR						MR	PCon					.95	.90
Language development		V	WR	C	S	RV	PN			PCon					.98	.96
Learning ability		V	WR			RV			MR	PCon	SS	Cd			.97	.95
Lexical knowledge		V	WR			RV	PN								.97	.96
Logical abstractive (categorical) thinking					S					PCon					.95	.89

Integration-Storage (continued)

	I	V	WR	C	S	RV	PN	BD	MR	PCon	SS	Cd	PC	OA	r_{xx}	r_{12}
Long-term memory	I	V	WR			RV	PN								.97	.96
Memory (Guilford)	I						PN								.92	.92
Nonverbal reasoning									MR	PCon				OA	.94	.88
Perceptual organization								BD	MR	PCon	SS	Cd	PC	OA	.96	.95
Planning ability								BD			SS	Cd		OA	.93	.92
Reasoning			WR	C	S				MR	PCon				OA	.97	.94
Reproduction of models								BD				Cd			.89	.85
Semantic cognition (Guilford)		V	WR	C	S	RV									.97	.96
Semantic content (Guilford)	I	V	WR	C	S	RV	PN			PCon					.98	.97
Short-term visual memory											SS	Cd			.90	.91
Simultaneous processing			WR					BD	MR	PCon			PC	OA	.97	.94
Spatial (Bannatyne)								BD	MR				PC	OA	.95	.91

(continued)

Note. I = Information; V = Vocabulary; WR = Word Reasoning; C = Comprehension; S = Similarities; RV = Receptive Vocabulary; PN = Picture Naming; BD = Block Design; MR = Matrix Reasoning; PCon = Picture Concepts; SS = Symbol Search; Cd = Coding; PC = Picture Completion; OA = Object Assembly; I (1–6)= First six Information items only; V (1–5) = First five Vocabulary items only.

[a]r_{xx} = Split-Half reliability; r_{12} = Test-Retest Reliability.

Ability	Verbal Subtests							Performance Subtests							Reliability	
	I	V	WR	C	S	RV	PN	BD	MR	PCon	SS	Cd	PC	OA	r_{xx}	r_{12}
Integration-Storage *(continued)*																
Spatial relations (CHC)								BD						OA	.90	.83
Spatial visualization								BD	MR		SS				.93	.90
Speed of mental processing								BD			SS			OA	.92	.89
Synthesis (whole-part)			WR					BD	MR					OA	.95	.91
Trial-and-error learning								BD						OA	.90	.83
Verbal comprehension	I	V	WR	C	S	RV									.98	.96
Verbal concept formation		V	WR	C	S	RV	PN			PCon					.97	.96
Verbal conceptualization (Bannatyne)		V	WR	C	S	RV				PCon					.98	.96
Verbal reasoning			WR	C	S					PCon					.97	.94
Visual association									MR	PCon					.94	.85
Visual memory											SS	Cd	PC		.93	.93

Integration-Storage *(continued)*

Ability	Subtests	r_{xx}[a]	r_{12}
Visual processing (CHC)	PC OA	.95	.91
Word knowledge	V RV PN	.95	.94
Output			
Broad speediness (CHC)	SS Cd OA	.91	.91
Clerical speed and accuracy	SS Cd	.90	.91
Much verbal expression	V C S	.96	.94
Paper-and-pencil skill	SS Cd	.90	.91
Processing speed	SS Cd	.90	.91
Rate of test taking (CHC)	SS Cd	.90	.91
Simple motor response	I (1–6) MR PCon RV PC	.96	.92

(continued)

Note. I = Information; V = Vocabulary; WR = Word Reasoning; C = Comprehension; S = Similarities; RV = Receptive Vocabulary; PN = Picture Naming; BD = Block Design; MR = Matrix Reasoning; PCon = Picture Concepts; SS = Symbol Search; Cd = Coding; PC = Picture Completion; OA = Object Assembly; I (1–6) = First six Information items only; V (1–5) = First five Vocabulary items only.

[a] r_{xx} = Split-Half reliability; r_{12} = Test-Retest Reliability.

Ability	Verbal Subtests							Performance Subtests							Reliability	
	I	V	WR	C	S	RV	PN	BD	MR	PCon	SS	Cd	PC	OA	r_{xx}	r_{12}
Output *(continued)*																
Simple vocal expression	I	V (1–5)	WR				PN			PCon			PC		.97	.95
Visual organization (without essential motor activity)									MR	PCon			PC		.95	.90
Visual-motor coordination	I (1–6)							BD			SS	Cd		OA	.93	.92
Influences Affecting Scores																
Ability to respond when uncertain			WR						MR	PCon			PC	OA	.96	.93
Alertness to environment	I												PC		.92	.90
Anxiety											SS	Cd			.90	.91
Attention span			WR								SS	Cd			.93	.92
Cognitive style (field dependence)								BD	MR				PC	OA	.95	.91
Concentration										PCon	SS	Cd	PC		.94	.93

Influences Affecting Scores *(continued)*

Influence	I	V	WR	C	S	RV	PN	BD	MR	PCon	SS	Cd	PC	OA	r_{xx}	r_{12}
Cultural opportunities	I	V	WR	C	S	RV	PN								.97	.96
Distractibility											SS	Cd			.90	.91
Flexibility			WR	C	S			BD	MR	PCon				OA	.97	.95
Foreign language background	I	V	WR			RV									.96	.95
Intellectual curiosity and striving	I	V	WR			RV	PN								.97	.96
Interests	I	V	WR		S	RV									.97	.96
Negativism				C	S				MR	PCon			PC		.97	.94
Obsessive concern with detail and accuracy											SS	Cd			.90	.91
Outside reading	I	V	WR		S	RV									.97	.96

(continued)

Note. I = Information; V = Vocabulary; WR = Word Reasoning; C = Comprehension; S = Similarities; RV = Receptive Vocabulary; PN = Picture Naming; BD = Block Design; MR = Matrix Reasoning; PCon = Picture Concepts; SS = Symbol Search; Cd = Coding; PC = Picture Completion; OA = Object Assembly; I (1–6)= First six Information items only; V (1–5) = First five Vocabulary items only.

$^{a}r_{xx}$= Split-Half reliability; r_{12}= Test-Retest Reliability.

Ability	Verbal Subtests							Performance Subtests							Reliability[a]	
	I	V	WR	C	S	RV	PN	BD	MR	PCon	SS	Cd	PC	OA	r_{xx}	r_{12}
Influences Affecting Scores (continued)																
Overly concrete thinking				C	S				MR	PCon					.96	.93
Persistence									MR	PCon	SS	Cd		OA	.95	.93
Richness of early environment	I	V	WR			RV	PN								.97	.96
School learning	I	V	WR			RV	PN								.97	.96
Visual perceptual problems						RV	PN	BD	MR	PCon	SS	Cd		OA	.97	.95
Work under time pressure								BD			SS	Cd	PC	OA	.95	.93

Note. I = Information; V = Vocabulary; WR = Word Reasoning; C = Comprehension; S = Similarities; RV = Receptive Vocabulary; PN = Picture Naming; BD = Block Design; MR = Matrix Reasoning; PCon = Picture Concepts; SS = Symbol Search; Cd = Coding; PC = Picture Completion; OA = Object Assembly; I (1–6)= First six Information items only; V (1–5) = First five Vocabulary items only.

[a] r_{xx} = Split-Half reliability; r_{12}= Test-Retest Reliability.

Appendix C

Abilities Shared by Two or More WPPSI-III Verbal and Performance Subtests for Children Ages 2-6 to 3-11

Ability	Verbal Subtests			Performance Subtests		Reliability[a]	
	I	RV	PN	BD	OA	r_{xx}	r_{12}
Input							
Auditory perception of complex verbal stimuli	I			BD		.92	.90
Simple verbal directions	I (1–6)	RV	PN		OA	.95	.91
Visual motor channel	I (1–6)	RV		BD	OA	.93	.88
Visual perception of complete meaningful stimuli	I (1–6)	RV	PN			.94	.92
Visual Perception of meaningful stimuli	I (1–6)	RV	PN		OA	.95	.91
Integration-Storage							
Acquired knowledge (Bannatyne)	I	RV	PN			.96	.95
Broad visualization				BD	OA	.90	.84
Cognition (Guilford)		RV		BD	OA	.93	.88
Crystallized ability (CHC)	I	RV	PN			.96	.95

(continued)

Note. I = Information; RV = Receptive Vocabulary; PN = Picture Naming; BD = Block Design; OA = Object Assembly; I (1–6) = First six Information items only.

[a] r_{xx} = Split-Half reliability; r_{12} = Test-Retest Reliability

Ability	Verbal Subtests			Performance Subtests		Reliability[a]	
	I	RV	PN	BD	OA	r_{xx}	r_{12}
Input (*continued*)							
Evaluation (Guilford)		RV	PN	BD	OA	.95	.92
Figural cognition (Guilford)			PN	BD	OA	.93	.90
Figural evaluation (Guilford)		RV	PN	BD	OA	.95	.92
Fluid ability (CHC)				BD	OA	.90	.84
Fund of information	I	RV				.95	.91
General ability	I			BD		.92	.90
Language development		RV	PN			.94	.92
Lexical knowledge		RV	PN			.94	.92
Long-term memory	I	RV	PN			.96	.95
Memory (Guilford)	I		PN			.95	.95
Perceptual organization				BD	OA	.90	.84
Planning ability				BD	OA	.90	.84
Semantic content (Guilford)	I	RV	PN			.96	.95
Simultaneous processing				BD	OA	.90	.84
Spatial (Bannatyne)				BD	OA	.90	.84
Spatial relations (CHC)				BD	OA	.90	.84

Input (continued)

	I	RV	PN	BD	OA	r_{xx}	r_{12}
Speed of mental processing				BD	OA	.90	.84
Synthesis (whole-part)				BD	OA	.90	.84
Trial-and-error learning				BD	OA	.90	.84
Verbal comprehension	I	RV				.95	.91
Verbal concept formation		RV	PN			.94	.92
Visual processing (CHC)				BD	OA	.90	.84
Word knowledge		RV	PN			.94	.92

Output

	I	RV	PN	BD	OA	r_{xx}	r_{12}
Simple vocal expression	I		PN			.95	.95
Visual-motor coordination	I (1–6)			BD	OA	.90	.84

Influences Affecting Scores

	I	RV	PN	BD	OA	r_{xx}	r_{12}
Cognitive style (field dependence)				BD	OA	.90	.84
Cultural opportunities	I	RV	PN			.96	.95
Flexibility				BD	OA	.90	.84
Foreign language background	I	RV				.95	.91

(continued)

Note. I = Information; RV = Receptive Vocabulary; PN = Picture Naming; BD = Block Design; OA = Object Assembly; I (1–6)= First six Information items only.
[a] r_{xx} = Split-Half reliability; r_{12} = Test-Retest Reliability

Influences Affecting Scores (*continued*)

Ability	Verbal Subtests			Performance Subtests		Reliability[a]	
	I	RV	PN	BD	OA	r_{xx}	r_{12}
Influences Affecting Scores (*continued*)							
Intellectual curiosity and striving	I	RV	PN			.96	.95
Interests	I	RV				.95	.91
Outside reading	I	RV				.95	.91
Richness of early environment	I	RV	PN			.96	.95
School learning	I	RV	PN			.96	.95
Visual perceptual problems		RV	PN	BD	OA	.95	.92
Work under time pressure				BD	OA	.90	.84

Note. I = Information; RV = Receptive Vocabulary; PN = Picture Naming; BD = Block Design; OA = Object Assembly; I (1–6)= First six Information items only.

[a]r_{xx} = Split-Half reliability; r_{12} = Test-Retest Reliability

References

American Psychiatric Association (2000). *Diagnostic and statistical manual of mental disorders* (4th ed., text rev.). Washington, DC: American Psychiatric Association.

Ammons, R. B., & Ammons, H. S. (1948). *The Full Range Vocabulary Test.* New Orleans, LA: Author.

Anastasi, A., & Urbina, S. (1997). *Psychological testing* (7th ed.). Upper Saddle River, NJ: Prentice Hall.

Bannatyne, A. (1974). Diagnosis: A note on recategorization of the WISC scaled scores. *Journal of Learning Disabilities, 7,* 272–274.

Barona, A., & Santos de Barona, M. (1987). A model for the assessment of limited English proficient students referred for special education services. In S. H. Fradd & W. J. Tikunoff (Eds.), *Bilingual education and bilingual special education: A guide for administrators* (pp. 183–210). Boston: College Hill Press.

Barona, A., & Santos de Barona, M. (2000). Assessing multicultural preschool children. In B. Bracken (Ed.), *The psychoeducational assessment of preschool children* (3rd ed., pp. 282–297). Needham Heights, MA: Allyn & Bacon.

Barrera, I. (1995). *To refer or not to refer: Untangling the web of diversity, "deficit," and disability.* New York State Association for Bilingual Education Journal, 10, 54–66.

Bayley, N. (1933). *The California First Year Mental Scale.* Berkeley: University of California Press.

Bayley, N. (1993). *Manual for the Bayley Scales of Infant Development* (2nd ed.). San Antonio, TX: The Psychological Corporation.

Binet, A., & Simon, T. (1905). Méthodes nouvelles pour le diagnostic du niveau intellectuel des anormaux [New methods for diagnosing the level of intelligence of abnormal persons]. *L'Année Psycholgique, 11,* 191–244.

Boehm, A. E. (2000). In B. Bracken (Ed.), *The psychoeducational assessment of preschool children* (3rd ed., pp. 186–203). Needham Heights, MA: Allyn & Bacon.

Boehm, A. E. (1976). *Boehem resource guide for basic concept teaching.* New York: The Psychological Corporation.

Bower, A., & Hayes, A. (1995). Relations of scores on the Stanford-Binet Fourth Edition and Form L-M. Concurrent validation study with children who have mental retardation. *American Journal on Mental Retardation, 99*(5), 555–563.

Bracken, B. (1992). Review of the Wechsler Preschool and Primary Scale of Intelligence–Revised. In J. J. Kramer & J. C. Conoley (Eds.), *The eleventh mental measurements yearbook* (pp. 1027–1029). Lincoln, NE: Buros Institute of Mental Measurements.

Bracken, B. A., & McCallum, R. S. (1998). *Universal Nonverbal Intelligence Test examiner's manual.* Itasca, IL: Riverside.

Braden, J. P. (1987). A comparison of regression and standard score discrepancy methods for learning disabilities identification: Effect on racial representation. *Journal of School Psychology, 25,* 23–29.

Brown, F. R. (1996). Neurodevelopmental evaluation (the physician's diagnostic role in learning disabilities). In F. R. Brown, E. H. Aylward, & B. K. Keogh (Eds.), *Diagnosis and management of learning disabilities* (3rd ed., pp. 37–59). San Diego, CA: Singular Publishing Group.

Brown, R. A. (1973). *A first language: The early stages.* Cambridge, MA: Harvard University Press.

Carptenter, P. A., Just, M. A., & Shell, P. (1990). What one intelligence test measures: A theoretical account of the processing in Raven Progressive Matrices Test. *Psychological Review, 97,* 404–431.

Carroll, J. B. (1993). *Human cognitive abilities: A survey of factor-analytic abilities.* Cambridge, England: Cambridge University Press.

Carroll, J. B. (1997). The three-stratum theory of cognitive abilities. In D. P. Flanagan, J. L. Genshaft, & P. L. Harrison (Eds.), *Contemporary intellectual assessment: Theories, tests, and issues* (pp. 122–130). New York: Guilford.

Cattell, P. (1940). *The measurement of intelligence of infants and young children.* New York: The Psychological Corporation.

Cattell, R. B. (1941). Some theoretical issues in adult intelligence testing. *Psychological Bulletin, 38,* 592.

Cattell, R. B. (1963). Theory of fluid and crystallized intelligence: A critical experiment. *Journal of Educational Psychology, 54,* 1–22.

Cattell, R. B., & Horn, J. L. (1978). A check on the theory of fluid and crystallized intelligence with description of new subtest designs. *Journal of Educational Measurement, 15,* 139–164.

Chomsky, N. (1968). *Language and mind.* New York: Harcourt, Brace, & World.

Cohen, M. (1997). *Children's Memory Scale.* San Antonio, TX: The Psychological Corporation.

Crais, E. R. (1990). World knowledge to word knowledge. World knowledge and language: Development and disorders. *Topics in Language Disorders, 10*(3), 45–62.

Daniel, M. H. (1997). Intelligence testing: Status and trends. *American Psychologist, 52,* 1038–1045.

Delugach, R. R. (1991). Review of Wechsler Preschool and Primary Scale of Intelligence–Revised (WPPSI-R). *Journal of Psychoeducational Assessment, 9,* 280–290.

Dodd, J. M., Nelson, J. R., & Spint, W. (1995). Prereferral activities: One way to avoid biased testing procedures and possible inappropriate special education placement for American Indian students. *The Journal of Educational Issues for Language Minority Students, 15.* Retrieved July 8, 1997, from http://ncbe .gwu.edu/jei/ms/vol15/prereferra.html.

Donders, J. (1996). Cluster subtypes in the WISC-III standardization sample: Analysis of factor index scores. *Psychological Assessment, 8*(3), 71–78.

Dougherty, T. M., & Haith, M. M. (1997). Infant expectations and reaction time as predictors of childhood speed of processing and IQ. *Developmental Psychology, 33*(1), 146–155.

Edwards, J., & Lahey, M. (1996). Auditory lexical decisions in children with specific language impairment. *Journal of Speech and Hearing Research, 39,* 1263–1273.

Elliott, C. D. (1990). *Differential Ability Scales (DAS) administration and scoring manual.* San Antonio, TX: The Psychological Corporation.

Ervin-Tripp, S., & Gordon, D. (1986). The development of requests. In R. L. Schiefelbusch (Ed.), *Language competence: Assessment and intervention* (pp. 61–95). Austin, TX: PRO-ED.

Fillmore, E. A. (1936). Iowa tests for young children. *University of Iowa Studies in Child Welfare, 22,* 4.

Flanagan, D. P., & Alfonso, V. C. (2000). Essentially, Essential for WAIS-III users. *Comtemporary Psychology: APA Review of Books, 45,* 528–533.

Flanagan, D. P., Genshaft, J. L., & Harrison, P. L. (Eds.). (1997). *Contemporary intellectual assessment: Theories, tests, and issues.* New York: Guilford.

Flanagan, D. P., McGrew, K. S., & Ortiz, S. O. (2000). *The Wechsler intelligence scales and Gf-Gc theory.* Boston, MA: Allyn & Bacon.

Flynn, J. R. (1987). Massive IQ gains in 14 nations: What IQ tests really measure. *Psychological Bulletin, 101,* 171–191.

Fry, A. F., & Hale, S. (1996). Processing speed, working memory, and fluid intelligence: Evidence for a developmental cascade. *Psychological Science, 7*(4), 237–241.

Fuchs-Beauchamp, K. D., Karnes, M. B., & Johnson, L. J. (1993). Creativity and intelligence. *Gifted Child Quarterly, 37*(3), 113–117.

Funk, S. G., Sturner, R. A., & Green, J. A. (1986). Preschool prediction of early school performance: Relationship of McCarthy Scales of Children's Abilities prior to school entry to achievement in kindergarten, first, and second grades. *Journal of School Psychology, 24,* 181–194.

Gardner, H. (1993). *Multiple intelligences: Theory in practice.* New York: Basic Books.

Gesell, A. (1925). *The mental growth of the preschool child: A psychological outline of normal development from birth to the sixth year.* New York: Macmillan.

Gilliland, A. R. (1948). The measurement of the mentality of infants. *Child Development, 19,* 155–158.

Giordano, F. G., Schwiebert, V. L., & Brotherton, W. D. (1997). School counselors' perceptions of the usefulness of standardized tests, frequency of their use, and assessment training needs. *School Counselor, 44,* 198–205.

Glutting, J. J., & McDermott, P. A. (1989). Using "teaching items" on ability tests: A nice idea, but does it work? *Educational and Psychological Measurement, 49,* 257–268.

Glutting, J. J., McDermott, P. A., Prifitera, A., McGrath, E. A. (1994). Core profile types for the WISC-III and WIAT: Their development and application in identifying multivariate IQ-achievement discrepancies. *School Psychology Review, 23,* 619–639.

Glutting, J. J., Robins, P. M., DeLancy, E. (1997). Discriminant validity of test observations for children with attention deficit/hyperactivity. *Journal of School Psychology, 35,* 391–401.

Goodenough, F. L. (1926). *Measurement of intelligence by drawings.* Chicago: World Book.

Goodenough, F. L. (1949). *Mental testing.* New York: Rinehart.

Goodenough, F. L., Maurer, K. M., & Van Wagenen, M. J. (1940). *Minnesota Preschool Scales: Manual of instructions.* Minneapolis, MN: Educational Testing Bureau.

Gridley, B. E., & Roid, G. H. (1988). The use of the WISC-III with achievement tests. In A. Prifitera & D. Saklofske (Eds.), *WISC-III clinical use and interpretation: Scientist-practitioner perspectives* (pp. 249–288). San Diego, CA: Academic Press.

Guilford, J. P. (1967). *The nature of human intelligence.* New York: McGraw-Hill.

Gyurke, J. S. (1991). The assessment of preschool children with the Wechsler Preschool and Primary Scale of Intelligence–Revised. In B. A. Bracken (Ed.), *The psychoeducational assessment of preschool children* (pp. 86–106). Boston, MA: Allyn & Bacon.

Gyurke, J. S., Prifiteria, A., & Sharp, S. A. (1991). Frequency of Verbal and Performance IQ discrepancies on the WPPSI-R at various levels of ability. *Journal of Psychoeducational Assessment, 9,* 230–239.

Hamayan, E. V., & Damico, J. S. (Eds.). (1991). *Limiting bias in the assessment of bilingual students.* Austin, TX: PRO-ED.

Harrington, R. G. (1982). Caution: Standardized testing may be hazardous to the educational programs of intellectually gifted children. *Education, 103,* 112–117.

Hernandez, R. D. (1994). Reducing bias in the assessment of culturally and linguistically diverse populations. *The Journal of Educational Issues of Language Minority Students, 14,* 269–300.

Horn, J. L. (1989). Cognitive diversity: A framework of learning. In P. L. Ackerman, R. J. Sternberg, & R. Glaser (Eds.), *Learning and individual differences* (pp. 61–116). New York: Freeman.

Horn, J. L. (1991). Measurement of intellectual capabilities: A review of theory. In K. S. McGrew, J. K. Werder, & R. W. Woodcock (Eds.), *Woodcock-Johnson*

Technical manual: A reference on theory and current research (pp. 197–246). Allen, TX: DLM Teaching Resources.

Horn, J. L., & Cattell, R. B. (1966). Refinement and test of theory of fluid and crystallized intelligence. *Journal of Educational Psychology, 57,* 253–270.

Horn, J. L., & Cattell, R. B. (1967). Age differences in fluid and crystallized intelligence. *Acta Psychologica, 26,* 107–129.

Horn, J. L., & Hofer, S. M. (1992). Major abilities and development in the adult period. In R. J. Sternberg & C. A. Berg (Eds.), *Intellectual development* (pp. 44–99). Boston, MA: Cambridge University Press.

Horn, J. L., & Noll, J. (1997). Human cognitive capabilities: Gf-Gc theory. In D. P. Flanagan, J. L. Genshaft, & P. L. Harrison (Eds.), *Contemporary intellectual assessment: Theories, tests, and issues* (pp. 53–91). New York: Guilford.

Horowitz, F. D. (1992). A developmental view on the early identification of the gifted. In P. S. Klein & A. J. Tannenbaum (Eds.), *To be young and gifted* (pp. 73–93). Norwood, NJ: Ablex.

Jensen, A. R. (1998). *The g factor: The science of mental ability.* Westport, CT: Praeger.

Johnston, J., & Ellis Weismer, S. (1983). Mental rotation abilities in language disordered children. *Journal of Speech and Hearing Research, 26,* 397–403.

Kail, R. (2000). Speed of information processing: developmental change and links to intelligence. *Journal of School Psychology, 38*(1), 51–61.

Kail, R., & Salthouse, T. A. (1994). Processing speed as a mental capacity. *Acta Psychologica, 86,* 199–225.

Kamphaus, R. W. (1993). Clinical assessment of children's intelligence. Boston, MA: Allyn & Bacon.

Kaplan, C. (1992). Ceiling effects in assessing high-IQ children with the WPPSI-R. *Journal of Clinical Child Psychology, 21,* 403–406.

Kaufman, A. S. (1978). The importance of basic concepts in individual assessment of preschool children. *Journal of School Psychology, 16,* 207–211.

Kaufman, A. S. (1983). Intelligence: Old concepts-new perspectives. In G. W. Hynd (Ed.), *The school psychologist: An introduction* (pp. 95–117). Syracuse, NY: Syracuse University Press.

Kaufman, A. S. (1990a). *Assessing adolescent and adult intelligence.* Boston, MA: Allyn & Bacon.

Kaufman, A. S. (1990b). You can't judge a test by its colors. *Journal of School Psychology*, 28, 387–394.

Kaufman, A. S. (1992). Evaluation of the WISC-III and WPPSI-R for gifted children. *Roeper Review, 14,* 154–158.

Kaufman, A. S. (1993). King WISC the third assumes the throne. *Journal of School Psychology, 31,* 345–354.

Kaufman, A. S. (1994a). A reply to Macmann and Barnett: Lessons from the blind men and the elephant. *School Psychology Quarterly, 9,* 199–207.

Kaufman, A. S. (1994b). *Intelligent testing with the WISC-III.* New York: Wiley.

Kaufman, A. S. (2000). Tests of intelligence. In R.J. Sternberg (Ed.), *Handbook of intelligence* (pp. 445–476). New York: Cambridge University Press.

Kaufman, A. S., & Horn, L. J. (1996). Age changes on test of fluid and crystallized ability for women and men on the Kaufman Adolescent and Adult Intelligence Test (KAIT) at ages 17–94 years. *Archives of Clinical Neuropsychology, 11,* 97–121.

Kaufman, A. S., & Kaufman, J. C. (2001). Emotional intelligence as an aspect of general intelligence: What would David Wechsler say? *Emotion, 1*(3), 258–264.

Kaufman, A. S., & Kaufman, N. L. (1977). *Clinical evaluation of young children with the McCarthy Scales.* New York: Grune & Stratton.

Kaufman, A. S., & Kaufman, N. L. (1983). *Kaufman Assessment Battery for Children (K-ABC) administration and scoring manual.* Circle Pines, MN: American Guidance Service.

Kaufman, A. S. & Kaufman, N. L. (2001). Assessment of specific learning disabilities in the new millennium: issues, conflicts, and controversies. In A. S. Kaufman & N. L. Kaufman (Eds.), *Specific learning disabilities and difficulties in children and adolescents: Psychological assessment and evaluation* (pp. 433–461). Cambridge, England: Cambridge University Press.

Kaufman, A. S., & Kaufman, N. L. (in press). *Kaufman Assessment Battery for Children — Second Edition (K-ABC-II).* Circle Pines, MN: American Guidance Service.

Kaufman, A. S., & Lichtenberger, E. O. (1998). Intellectual assessment. In A. S. Bellack & M. Hersen (Series Eds.) & C. R. Reynolds (Vol. Ed.), *Comprehensive clinical psychology: Vol. 4. Assessment* (pp. 203–238). Oxford, England: Elsevier Science.

Kaufman, A. S., & Lichtenberger, E. O. (1999). *Essentials of WAIS-III assessment.* New York: Wiley.

Kaufman, A. S., & Lichtenberger, E. O. (2000). *Essentials of WISC-III and WPPSI-R assessment.* New York: Wiley.

Kaufman, A. S., & Lichtenberger, E. O. (2002). *Assessing adolescent and adult intelligence* (2nd ed.). Boston, MA: Allyn & Bacon.

Kaufman, J. C. (2002a). Narrative and paradigmatic thinking styles in creative writing and journalism students. *Journal of Creative Behavior, 36*(3), 201–220.

Kaufman, J. C. (Ed.). (2002b). Creativity in the schools [Special issue]. *Research in the Schools, 9*(2).

Kaufman, J. C. (in press). Four ways that non-cognitive assessment can help in the classroom. *Journal of Classroom Interaction.*

Kelley, M. F., & Surbeck, E. (1991). History of preschool assessment. In B. A. Bracken (Ed.), *The psychoeducational assessment of preschool children* (2nd ed., pp. 1–17). Boston: Allyn & Bacon.

Kitano, M. (1985). Ethnography of a preschool for the gifted: What gifted young children actually do. *Gifted Children Quarterly, 29,* 67–71.

Kluever, R. C., & Green K. E., (1990). Identification of gifted children: A comparison of the scores on Stanford-Binet–Fourth Edition and Form LM. *Roeper Review, 13*(1), 16–20.

Krassowski, E., & Plante, E. (1997). IQ variability in children with SLI: Implications for use of cognitive referencing in determining SLI. *Journal of Communication Disorders, 30*(1), 1–9.

Lahey, M. (1988). *Language disorders and language development.* New York: Macmillan.

Lahey, M., Edwards, J., & Munson, B. (2001). Is processing speed related to severity of language impairment? *Journal of Speech, Language, and Hearing Research, 44*(6), 1354–1361.

Layey, M., & Edwards, J. (1996). Why do children with specific language impairment name pictures more slowly than their peers. *Journal of Speech and Hearing Research, 39*(5), 1081–1098.

Leiter, R. G. (1948). *International Performance Scale.* Chicago: Stoelting Co.

Leonard, L. (1998). *Children with specific language impairment.* Cambridge, MA: MIT Press.

Lichtenberger, E.O., Broadbooks, D. Y., & Kaufman, A. S. (2000). *Essentials of cognitive assessment with the KAIT and other cognitive instruments.* New York: Wiley.

Lipsitz, J. D., Dworkin, R. H., & Erlenmeyer-Kimling, L. (1993). Wechsler Comprehension and Picture Arrangement subtests and social adjustment. *Psychological Assessment, 5,* 430–473.

Matarazzo, J. D. (1972). *Wechsler's measurement and appraisal of adult intelligence* (5th ed.). New York: Oxford.

McCarthy, D. (1972). *The McCarthy Scales of Children's Abilities.* San Antonio, TX: The Psychological Corporation.

McDermott, P. A., Fantuzzo, J. W., & Glutting, J. J. (1990). Just say no to subtest analysis: A critique on Wechsler theory and practice. *Journal of Psychoeducational Assessment, 8,* 290–302.

McGrew, K.S., & Flanagan, D. P. (1998). *The intelligence test desk reference (ITDR): Gf-Gc cross-battery assessment.* Boston: Allyn & Bacon.

Meeker, M. N. (1969). *The structure of intellect.* Columbus, OH: Charles E. Merrill.

Miller, L. T., & Vernon, P. A. (1996). Intelligence, reaction time, and working memory in 4- to 6-year-old children. *Intelligence, 22,* 155–190.

Miller, L. T., & Vernon, P. A. (1997). Developmental changes in speed of information processing in young children. *Developmental Psychology, 33*(3), 549–554.

Morelock, M. J., & Feldman, D. H. (1992). The assessment of giftedness in young children. In E. V. Nuttall, I. Romero, & J. Kalesnk (Eds.), *Assessing and screening preschoolers: Psychological and educational dimensions* (pp. 301–309). Boston: Allyn & Bacon.

Morgan, R. L., Dawson, B., & Kirby, D. (1992). The performance of preschoolers with speech/language disorders on the McCarthy Scales of Children's Abilities. *Psychology in the Schools, 29,* 11–17.

Naglieri, J. A. (1999). *Essentials of CAS Assessment.* New York: Wiley.

Naglieri, J. A. (2001). Using the Cognitive Assessment System (CAS) with learning-disabled children. In A. S. Kaufman & N. L. Kaufman (Eds.), *Specific learning disabilities and difficulties in children and adolescents: Psychological assessment and evaluation* (pp.141–177). Cambridge, England: Cambridge University Press.

Neisser, U. (Ed.). (1998). *The rising curve: Long-term gains in IQ and related measures.* Washington, DC: American Psychological Association.

Ochoa, S. H., Powell, M. P., & Robles-Pina, R. (1996). School psychologists' assessment practices with bilingual and limited-English-proficient students. *Journal of Psychoeducational Assessment, 14,* 250–275.

Ottem, E. (1999). Interpreting the WPPSI subtests scores of language impaired children: A structural approach. *Scandinavian Journal of Psychology, 40,* 319–329.

Padilla, A. M. (2001). Issues in culturally appropriate assessment. In L. Suzuki, & Ponterotto, & P. J. Meller (Eds.), *Handbook of multicultural assessment: Clinical, psychological and educational applications* (2nd ed., pp. 5–27). San Francisco: Jossey-Bass.

Parker, F. (1981). *Ideas that shaped American schools.* Phi Delta Kappan, 62, 314–319.

Pinker, S. (1994). *The language instinct.* New York: William Morrow.

Prifitera, A. & Saklofske, D. (Eds.). (1998). *WISC-III clinical use and interpretation.* San Diego, CA: Academic Press.

The Psychological Corporation. (1991). *The WPPSI-R Writer.* San Antonio, TX: Author.

The Psychological Corporation. (1994). *Scoring assistant for the Wechsler scales (SAWS).* San Antonio, TX: Author.

The Psychological Corporation. (2001). *The Wechsler Individual Achievement Test* (2nd ed.). San Antonio, TX: Author.

The Psychological Corporation. (2002a). *WPPSI-III technical and interpretive manual.* San Antonio, TX: Author.

The Psychological Corporation. (2002b). *WPPSI™-III Scoring Assistant®.* San Antonio, TX: Author.

The Psychological Corporation. (2003). *WPPSI™-III Writer™.* San Antonio, TX: Author.

The Psychological Corporation. (2003). *WISC-IV technical and interpretive manual.* San Antonio, TX: The Psychological Corporation.

Reynolds, C. R. (1979). Should we screen preschools? *Contemporary Educational Psychology, 4*(2), 175–181.

Reynolds, C. R. (1984). Critical measurement issues in learning disabilities. *Journal of Special Education, 18,* 451–475.

Reynolds, M., & Fucci, D. (1998). Synthetic speech compression: A comparison of children with normal and impaired language skills. *Journal of Speech, Language, and Hearing Research, 41,* 458–466.

Ricciardi, P. W., Voelker, S., Carter, R. A., & Shore, D. L. (1991). K-ABC sequential-simultaneous processing and language-impaired preschoolers. *Developmental Neuropsychology, 7,* 523–535.

Roid, G. H. (2003). *Stanford-Binet Intelligence Scales, Fifth. edition, technical manual.* Itasca, IL: Riverside.

Roid, G., & Miller, L. (1987). *Leiter International Performance Scale–Revised.* Wood Dale, IL: Stoelting.

Sanker-DeLeeuw, N. (2002). Gifted preschoolers: Parent and teacher view on identification, early admission, and programming. *Roeper Review, 24*(3), 172–177.

Sattler, J. M. (2001). *Assessment of children: Cognitive applications* (4th ed.). San Diego, CA: Author.

Schaefer, B. A. (2002). Review of Kaufman and Lichtenberger's (2000) *Essentials of WISC-III and WPPSI-R assessment. Journal of Psychoeducational Assessment, 20,* 391–395.

Schatz. J. U., Kramer, J. H., Ablin, A., & Matthay, K. K., (2000). Processing speed, working memory, and IQ: A developmental model of cognitive deficits following cranial radiation therapy. *Neuropsychology, 14*(2), 189–200.

Shepard, L. A., & Graue, M. E. (1993). The morass of school readiness screening' Research on test use and validity. In B. Spodek (Ed.), *Handbook of research on the education of young children* (pp. 293–305). New York: Macmillan.

Silver, L. B. (Ed.). (1993). *Child and Adolescent Psychiatric Clinics of North America, 2,* 181–353.

Sininger, Y., Klatzky, R., & Kirchner, D. (1989). Memory scanning speed in language-disordered children. *Journal of Speech and Hearing Research, 32,* 289–297.

Slate, J. R., & Jones, C. H. (1995). Relationship of the WISC-III and WISC-R for students with specific learning disabilities and mental retardation. *Diagnostique, 21,* 9–17.

Sparrow, S. S., & Gurland, S. T. (1998). Assessment of gifted children with the WISC-III. In A. Prifitera & D. Saklofske (Eds.), *WISC-III clinical use and interpretation* (pp. 59–72). San Diego, CA: Academic Press.

Sparrow, S. S. (1991, August). WISC-R and WISC-III: Profiles of gifted boys. In A. Prifitera (Chair), *Clinical validity of the WISC-III.* Symposium conducted at the annual convention of the American Psychological Association, San Francisco, CA.

Spruill, J. (1998). Assessment of mental retardation with the WISC-III. In A. Prifitera & D. Saklofske (Eds.), *WISC-III clinical use and interpretation* (pp. 73–90). San Diego, CA: Academic Press.

Stark, R., & Montgomery, J. (1995). Sentence processing in language-imparied children under conditions of filtering and time compression. *Applied Psycholinguistics, 16,* 137–154.

Sternberg, R. J. (1982). Lies we live by: Misapplication of test in identifying the gifted. *Gifted Child Quarterly, 26,* 157–161.

Stott, L. H., & Ball, R. S. (1965). Infant and preschool mental tests: Review and evaluation. *Monographs of the Society for Research in Child Development, 30*(3, Whole No. 101).

Stutsman, R. (1931). *Mental measurement of preschool children.* New York: World Book.

Tedeschi, M. J. (1995). Stanford-Binet Fourth Edition and language development: Relationships for a group of referred/delayed preschoolers. *Dissertation Abstracts International; Section B; The Sciences and Engineering,* 56(5-B), 2907.

Tellegen, A., & Briggs, P. F. (1967). Old wine in new skins: Grouping Wechsler subtests into new scales. *Journal of Consulting Psychology, 31,* 499–506.

Terman, L. M. (1916). *The measurement of intelligence.* Boston: Houghton-Mifflin.

Terman, L. M. (1925). *Genetic studies of genius* (Vol. 1). Standford, CA: Standford University Press.

Terman, L. M., & Merrill, M. A. (1937). *Measuring intelligence.* Boston: Houghton-Mifflin.

Terman, L. M., & Merrill, M. A. (1960). *Stanford-Binet Intelligence Scale.* Boston: Houghton-Mifflin.

Thorndike, R. E., Hagecn, E. P., & Sattler, J. M. (1986). *Stanford-Binet Intelligence Scale: Fourth edition.* Chicago: Riverside.

Tiholov, T. T., Zawallich, A., & Janzen, H. L. (1996). Diagnosis based on the WISC-III processing speed factor. *Canadian Journal of School Psychology, 12,* 23–34.

Tomasello, M., & Bates, E. (Eds.). (2001). *Language development: The essential readings. Essential readings in developmental psychology.* Malden, MA: Blackwell.

Torrance, E. P. (1981). *Thinking creatively in action and movement (TCAM).* Bensenville, IL: Scholastic Testing Service.

Troia, G. A., & Roth, F. P. (1996). Word frequency and age effects in normally developing children's phonological processing. *Journal of Speech and Hearing Research, 39*(5). 1099–1098.

Truch, S. (1993). *The WISC-III companion: A guide to interpretation and educational intervention.* Austin: TX: PRO-ED.

Tyerman, M. J. (1986). Gifted children and their identification: Learning ability not intelligence. *Gifted Education International, 4,* 81–84.

Tyler-Wood, T., & Carri, L. (1991). Identification of gifted children: The effectiveness of various measures of cognitive ability. *Roeper Review, 14*(2), 63–64.

U.S. Department of Education. (2001). *Annual report to Congress on the implementation of the Individuals with Disabilities Education Act.* Washington, DC: Author.

Vig, S., & Jedrysek, E. (1996). Stanford-Binet Fourth Edition: Useful for young children with language impairment? *Psychology in the Schools, 33*(2), 124–131.

Vig, S., Kaminer, R. K., & Jedrysek, E. (1987). A later look at borderline and mentally retarded preschoolers. *Journal of Developmental and Behavioral Pediatrics, 8,* 12–17.

Warner, C., & Nelson, N. W. (2000). Assessment of communication, language, and speech. In B. Bracken (Ed.), *The psychoeducational assessment of preschool children* (3rd ed., pp. 145–185). Needham Heights, MA: Allyn & Bacon.

Wechsler, D. (1939). *Measurement of adult intelligence.* Baltimore, MD: Williams & Wilkins.

Wechsler, D. (1944). *The measurement of adult intelligence* (3rd ed.). Baltimore: Williams & Wilkins.

Wechsler, D. (1946). *The Wechsler-Bellevue Intelligence Scale, Form II.* New York: The Psychological Corporation.

Wechsler, D. (1949). *Manual for the Wechsler Intelligence Scale for Children.* New York: The Psychological Corporation.

Wechsler, D. (1955). *Manual for the Wechsler Adult Intelligence Scale (WAIS).* San Antonio, TX: The Psychological Corporation.

Wechsler, D. (1958). *Measurement and appraisal of adult intelligence (4th ed.).* Baltimore: Williams & Wilkens.

Wechsler, D. (1974). Manual for the Wechsler Preschool and Primary Scale of Intelligence (WPPSI). New York: The Psychological Corporation.

Wechsler, D. (1981). *Manual for the Wechsler Adult Intelligence Scale–Revised (WAIS-R).* San Antonio, TX: The Psychological Corporation.

Wechsler, D. (1989). *Manual for the Wechsler Preschool and Primary Scale of Intelligence–Revised (WPPSI-R).* San Antonio, TX: The Psychological Corporation.

Wechsler, D. (1991). *Manual for the Wechsler Intelligence Scale for Children–Third Edition (WISC-III).* San Antonio, TX: The Psychological Corporation.

Wechsler, D. (1997). *Wechsler Adult Intelligence Scale–Third Edition (WAIS-III) administration and scoring manual.* San Antonio, TX: The Psychological Corporation.

Wechsler, D. (2002). *WPPSI-III administration and scoring manual.* San Antonio, TX: The Psychological Corporation.

Wechsler, D. (2003). *WISC-IV administration and scoring manual.* San Antonio, TX: The Psychological Corporation.

Werner, H., & Kaplan, E. (1950). Development of word meaning through verbal context: an experimental study. *Journal of Psychology, 29,* 251–257.

Wilson, M. S., & Reschly, D. J. (1996). Assessment in school psychology training and practice. *School Psychology Review, 25,* 9–23.

Windsor, J., & Hwang, M. (1999). Testing the generalized slowing hypothesis in specific language impairment. *Journal of Speech, Language, & Hearing Research, 42*(5), 1205–1218.

Wolf, M., & Goodglass H. (1986). Dyslexia, dysnomia, and lexical retrieval: A longitudinal investigation. *Brain and Language, 28,* 154–168.

Wolf, M., Bally, H., & Morris, R. (1996). Automaticity, retrieval processes, and reading: A longitudinal study in average and impaired readers. *Child Development, 57,* 988–1000.

Woodcock, R. W. (1990). Theoretical foundations of the WJ-R measures of cognitive ability. *Journal of Psychoeducational Assessment, 8,* 231–258.

Woodrich, D. L., & Barry, C. T. (1991). A survey of school psychologists' practices for identifying mentally retarded students. *Psychology in the Schools, 28,* 165–171.

Zelazo, P. R., Kearsley, R. B., & Stack, D. M. (1995). Mental representations for visual sequences: Increased speed of central processing from 22 to 32 months. *Intelligence, 20,* 41–63.

Zimmerman, I. L., & Woo-Sam, J. M. (1973). *Clinical interpretation of the Wechsler Adult Intelligence Scale.* New York: Grune & Stratton.

Zimmerman, I. L., & Woo-Sam, J. M. (1990, April). *The interchangeability of major measures of intelligence.* Paper presented at Western Psychological Association Convention, Los Angeles, CA.

Zimmerman, I. L., & Woo-Sam, J. M. (1997). Review of the criterion-related validity of the WISC-III: The first five years. *Perceptual and Motor Skills, 85,* 531–546.

Annotated Bibliography

Flanagan, D. P., McGrew, K. S., & Ortiz, S. O. (2000). *The Wechsler intelligence scales and Gf-Gc theory: A contemporary approach to interpretation.* Needham Heights, MA: Allyn & Bacon.

This book provides a theory-driven approach to interpreting the Wechsler scales, including the WPPSI-R. The authors apply the CHC theory to cross-battery interpretation and focus on the Wechsler scales. They provide visual guides, summary pages, and worksheets to apply their interpretive approach.

Gyurke, J. S., Marmor, D. S., & Melrose, S. E. (2000). The assessment of preschool children with the Wechsler Preschool and Primary Scale of Intelligence–Revised. In B. A. Bracken (Ed.), *The psychoeducational assessment of preschool children* (3rd ed., pp. 57–75). Boston, MA: Allyn & Bacon.

This chapter provides a description of the WPPSI-R, including each of its individual subtests. Psychometric qualities of the test, including reliability and validity, are also evaluated. A brief section on interpretation of the WPPSI-R is presented. The remaining chapters in this book contain useful information pertaining to the assessment of preschool children in general. Other topics covered include assessment of adaptive behavior, communication, motor development, visual functioning, severe disabilities, emotional development, and multicultural issues.

Kaufman, A. S. (1994). *Intelligent testing with the WISC-III.* New York: Wiley.

This book on the WISC-III covers several topics relevant to the WPPSI-R as well as the WISC-III. Processing Speed is reviewed in depth through multiple possible explanations and interpretations. A theoretical understanding of scales and tasks (especially from Horn's theory) is presented along with many hypothesized explanations for Verbal > Performance and Performance > Verbal profiles. Numerous case reports illustrate how to combine and present complex test data and how to utilize the philosophy of intelligent testing.

Kaufman, A. S., & Lichtenberger, E. O. (1998). Intellectual assessment. In A. S. Bellack & M. Hersen (Series Eds.) & C. R. Reynolds (Vol. Ed.), *Comprehensive clinical psychology: Vol. 4. Assessment* (pp. 187–238). New York: Pergamon.

This chapter reviews several measures of intelligence with a focus on the Wechsler scales. It provides an overview of the WPPSI-R and WISC-III, their standardization properties, and the research available on the tests. A brief guide to analysis of WISC-III data is introduced. This chapter also discusses how clinicians may integrate various cognitive instruments with the Wechsler scales. to provide a more comprehensive picture of client functioning.

Lichtenberger, E. O., & Kaufman, A. S. (2000). *Essentials of WISC-III and WPPSI-R Assessment.* New York: Wiley.

This book is the predecessor to the current Essentials of WPPSI-III Assessment; it provides readers with succinct, straightforward methods for competent clinical interpretation and application of these popular Wechsler instruments. Parallel topics are covered for both tests: administration, scoring, interpretation, and clinical use. Practitioners are provided with information to help them better understand the continuum that binds the preschool and primary-age test (WPPSI-R) with the instrument designed for elementary and high school-age students (WISC-III).

McGrew, K. S., & Flanagan, D. P. (1998). *The intelligence test desk reference (ITDR): Gf-Gc cross-battery assessment.* Boston: Allyn & Bacon.

This book provides information about the fluid and crystallized (Gf-Gc) intelligence theory. It presents information on various tests of intelligence, including the WPPSI-R. The authors detail an approach that spells out how practitioners can conduct assessments that tap a broader range of abilities than any single cognitive test alone can. Suggestions are made that help practitioners combine Wechsler subtests with other batterys' subtests to measure abilities from the Gf-Gc theory.

The Psychological Corporation. (2002). *WPPSI-III technical and interpretive manual.* San Antonio, TX: The Psychological Corporation.

This manual comes as part of the WPPSI-III kit. It provides a basic description of the WPPSI-III scales and subtests. Revisions from the previous version of the WPPSI are reviewed in a subtest-by-subtest manner. The standardization procedures and process of norms development are detailed. Evidence of reliability and validity are provided in the text along with numerous related tables. A brief chapter on considerations for interpretation suggests some basic guidelines for WPPSI-III interpretation. Intercorrelation tables are provided in Appendix A, critical value and base rate tables for WPPSI-III discrepancy comparisons are provided in Appendix B, and WIAT-II — WPPSI-III Discrepancy score tables are provided in Appendix C.

Sattler, J. M. (2001). *Assessment of children: Cognitive applications.* San Diego, CA: Author.

The eleventh chapter of this text provides information on the WPPSI-R. Basic technical information such as reliability and validity is reviewed, as well as statistical information such as factor analyses and intercorrelations between subtests and scales. Values obtained on the WPPSI-R are compared to those obtained from the WPPSI.

A checklist is provided for examiners to use to ensure proper administration of each of the subtests. Very brief information is provided on interpreting the tests. Strengths and weaknesses of the test are reviewed. Supplementary tables are provided for calculating short form scores.

Truch, S. (1993). *The WISC-III companion: A guide to interpretation and educational intervention.* Austin: TX: PRO-ED.

This book attempts to help practitioners develop hypotheses concerning children's learning patterns on the basis of their WISC-III performance. Although this book is structured around WISC-III performance, useful information may be applied to the WPPSI-III. Those in the field of school psychology, clinical psychology, and counseling psychology were the intended audience for the book, according to the author. The book reviews practical educational applications of the WISC-III profile.

Wechsler, D. (2002). *WPPSI-III administrative and scoring manual.* San Antonio, TX: The Psychological Corporation.

This manual comes as part of the WPPSI-III kit. It provides a basic description of the WPPSI-III scales and subtests. Revisions from the previous version of the WPPSI are reviewed in a subtest-by-subtest manner. Important information about administration is detailed in the manual. For each WPPSI-III subtest, the starting, discontinue, and timing rules are articulated. Examiners are provided a basic script and detailed directions of how to administer each subtest in a standardized manner. Subtest norms and IQ conversion tables are provided in Appendix A. Critical value and base rate tables for WPPSI-III discrepancy comparisons are provided in Appendix B.

Index

Abilities:
    for each subtest, 100-128
    shared with other subtests,
        (tables), 266-273, 276-278
        guidelines for use,
        156-171
        tapped by verbal
        subtests, 200-202
Accepting/rejecting hypotheses, 161
Achievement, 19-21
    WPPSI-III and, 22, 213-221
ADHD, *see* Attention Deficit
    Hyperactivity Disorder (ADHD)
Administration:
    common pitfalls, 38, 61-63
    errors, *see* common pitfalls
    modifying standardized
        procedure, 24-26
    parental separation, 28, 30
    querying, 41-42
    rapport, 29-33
    recording responses, 38-39
        abbreviations for, 39
    repeating items, 42
    reverse sequence, 36
    rules of administration, 43-63
    special considerations, 35
        seven-year-olds, 35
        six-year-olds, 35
        special needs individuals,
        33-34

    starting/discontinuing
        subtests, 36-37
        subtest-by-subtest rules,
        43-63
    teaching the task, 43, 44,
        47, 48, 49, 50, 51, 55,
        56, 57, 59
    testing environment, 27-28
    testing materials, 28-29
    timing, 40-41
Age, 35, 186-191
    seven-year-olds, 35
    six-year-olds, 35
    two- to three-year-olds, 51,
        71, 73, 135-136, 150-154,
        155, 186-187
    four- to seven-year-olds, 51,
        73, 134-135, 151-154,
        182, 186-191
American Sign Language, 34
Attention Deficit Hyperactivity
    Disorder (ADHD), 140

Background information, 233-236,
    248-249
Bannatyne's categories, 99
Bannatyne's (1974) Model, 91, 99
Bayley Scales of Infant
    Development-II (BSID-II), 19
Behavioral observations,
    see individual subtests

Verbal-Performance IQ
discrepancy:
    abnormal Verbal and
        Performance scatter,
        133-134
    calculation of, 131
    interpretability, 134-136
    statistical significance,
        131-132
Iowa Test for Young Children, 2
Ipsative comparison, 146-147. *See
    also* Strengths and weaknesses;
    Weaknesses

K-ABC, *see* Kaufman Assessment
    Battery for Children
Kaufman Assessment Battery for
    Children (K-ABC), 185, 203
Kaufman-Lichtenberger approach,
    85-86
Kaufman Test of Educational
    Achievement-Brief Form:
    in the case of Ophelia T., 233

Language:
    abnormal development and,
        194-196
    basic linguistic concepts,
        205-206
    commonly used terms, 194
    developmental expectations,
        191, 194
    processing speed and, 209-210
        WPPSI-III and, 210-212

Language impairment, 191
    assessment of, 194-205
    clinical applications, 196-199,
        203-205, 206-208
    definition of, 194-195
    examples of, 197
    multicultural differences and,
        206-208
Learning disabilities, 137
Leiter International Performance
    Scale, 2

Matrix Reasoning subtest 52-53
    abilities shared with other
        subtests, 114-115
    administration of, 52-53
    behaviors to note, 54
    clinical considerations,
        115-116
    Coding subtest and, 144-146
    common pitfalls, 62
    g factor, 87-88
    influences affecting subtest
        scores, 115
    rules of administration, 52-53
    scoring keys, 78
    specificity, 88-89, 90
    Symbol Search subtest and,
        144-146
McCarthy Scales of Children's
    Abilities (MSCA), 3-4
Mental Retardation, 137
    adaptive functioning, 225
    clinical application, 225-227